THE ASIAN WALL STREET JOURNAL.
ASIA BUSINESS NEWS

GUIDE TO UNDERSTANDING MONEY & INVESTING IN ASIA

KENNETH M. MORRIS, ALAN M. SIEGEL
AND
BEVERLY LARSON

Published in the U.S. by Lightbulb Press, Inc.
10 Rockefeller Plaza, New York, NY 10020

Published in Hong Kong by Dow Jones Publishing Company (Asia) Inc.
G.P.O. Box 9825, Hong Kong

LIGHTBULB PRESS

Creative Director Dean Scharf
Design Dave Wilder
Editor Virginia B. Morris
Production Janice Edelman-Lee, Chris Hiebert, Sally Minker, Thomas F. Trojan, Kwee Wang
Illustration Krista K. Glasser, Barnes Tilney
Photography Danielle Berman, Andy Shen
Film Quad Right, Inc.

SPECIAL THANKS TO

DOW JONES & CO.

DOWJONES

William Adamopoulos, Urban Lehner, James McGregor, Marcus Brauchli, Suman Dubey, Bob Hagerty, Douglas Sease, Matt Roberts, Pui-Wing Tam, Robert Steiner, Jathon Sapsford, John A. Prestbo, Julia Lichtblau, Nicholas Elliott, Angelo Palmisano, Apu Sikri, Deborah Ciervo, Tom Herman, Alexandra Peers, Anita Raghavan, Dan Austin, Joan Wolf-Woolley, Lottie Lindberg and Elizabeth Yeh

ASIA BUSINESS NEWS

Christopher Graves, Patricia Bjaaland Welch and Georgette Tan

PICTURE CREDITS

American Bank Note Company, American Stock Exchange, Bureau of Engraving and Printing, Chase Manhattan Archives, Chicago Board of Trade, CUC International, Museum of the City of New York, National Association of Securities Dealers, New York Stock Exchange

Dow Jones & Company, Inc., 200 Liberty Street, New York, NY 10281 Tel. 212-416-2000
Lightbulb Press, Inc., 10 Rockefeller Plaza, Suite 720, New York, NY 10020 Tel. 212-218-7969
FIRESIDE and colophon are registered trademarks of Simon & Schuster Inc.
10 9 8 7 6 5 4 3 2 1
ISBN: 0-684-84650-0
Library of Congress Cataloging-in-Publication Data is available.

In no region are so many people so fast emerging as investors than in the Asian-Pacific area. In Japan, housewives join investment clubs with money they save in boxes given to them by door-to-door securities salesmen. In China, hundreds of millions of people own government bonds and tens of millions more are starting to dabble in stocks. In India, big mutual-fund companies have salesmen plying their ever-more sophisticated products to people across the dry Punjab, in the steamy villages of Tamil Nadu and up in the foothills of the Himalayas.

At the same time, investors in the U.S. are increasingly investing in the Asian-Pacific markets directly or through mutual funds, which brings into sharper focus the global nature of financial markets. To meet this burgeoning interest, we are pleased to provide this handy primer to money and investing in the area. Building on the highly popular Wall Street Journal Guide to Understanding Money & Investing, *this new edition incorporates updated information and new text and graphics focusing specifically on the Asian-Pacific region.*

Through straightforward language and colorful graphics, we go behind the scenes to show how the markets work, how money gains and loses value, the meaning of financial trends and indicators, and other things essential to making investments and measuring their performance.

Kenneth Morris
Alan Siegel
Beverly Larson

THE ASIAN WALL STREET JOURNAL.

ASIA BUSINESS NEWS

GUIDE TO UNDERSTANDING MONEY & INVESTING

MONEY

STOCKS

BONDS

MUTUAL FUNDS

FUTURES & OPTIONS

The History of Money

Most money doesn't have any value of its own. It's worth what it can buy at any given time.

The history of money began with people trading the things they had for the things they wanted. If they wanted an ax, they found someone who had one and was willing to exchange it for something of theirs. The system works the same way today, with one important variation: we use **money** in exchange for the items we want. The sellers can keep the money until they're ready to buy the things they want.

IN THE BEGINNING WAS BARTER

Our earliest ancestors were self-sufficient, providing their own food, clothing and shelter from their surroundings. There was rarely anything extra—and nothing much to trade it for.

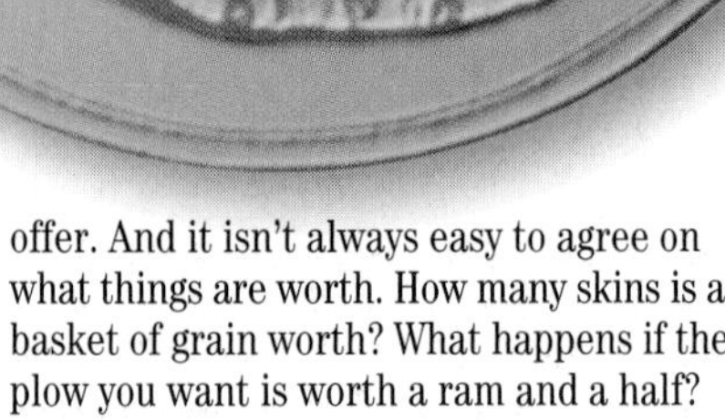

But as communities formed, hunting and gathering became more efficient; occasionally there were surpluses of one commodity or another. A people with extra animal skins but not enough grain could exchange its surplus with another people who had plenty of food but no skins. **Barter** was born and became commonplace.

As societies grew more complex, barter flourished. But it takes time and energy to find someone with exactly what you want who's also willing to take what you have to offer. And it isn't always easy to agree on what things are worth. How many skins is a basket of grain worth? What happens if the plow you want is worth a ram and a half?

STONE MONEY
Large stone wheels, some nearly ten feet in diameter, served as money on Yap Island in the South Pacific until the early 20th century. The bigger the fei, or stone, was, the more it was worth. Of course, the money didn't always change hands when it was spent. If it was too heavy to move, it simply stayed where it was, and the ownership changed.

MONEY FILLS THE BILL

As trade flourished, money came into use. The biggest advantage of using money was that buying and selling no longer had to happen at the same time. Sellers could keep what they'd earned, and use it to pay a different seller when—and where—they were ready to buy. In other words, money provided purchasing power.

For money to fill the bill, buyers and sellers had to agree on an acceptable form of payment, not only between themselves, but in the wider circle where the seller might wish to use the money. In other words, the money had to have value, and the people using it had to believe that its value would be recognized by others.

Many different items have been considered money over the years. In fact, the term currency, another word for money, means anything that's used as a form of payment. In the ancient world, for example, cowrie shells from the Maldive Islands were one of the basic forms of

A DOUBLE SYSTEM

In 9th century China, people used salt to pay for small purchases and silk to pay for larger ones. By the 13th century, they used salt and gold. That's called bi-level valuation.

currency. So was salt. In fact, the root of the word salary, which refers to money you're paid for the work you perform, is *sal*, or salt.

A METAL STANDARD

As early as 2500 B.C. precious metals—gold, silver and copper—were used as money in Egypt and Asia Minor and stamped metal was used in China around 2000 B.C. By 700 B.C. the kingdom of Lydia was minting coins made of electrum, an alloy of gold and silver. The coins were valuable, durable and portable.

In addition, using coins permitted payments by **tale**, or counting out the right amount, rather than weighing it. That simplified the exchange process even more. For a long time, the relative value of currencies was measured against precious metals, usually gold or silver. That's where terms such as **pound sterling** and **gold standard** originated. In modern times, though, national economies have moved away from basing their currency on metal reserves.

MONEY BY FIAT

When money was made of gold or silver—or could be exchanged for one of them—it was **commodity** or **fiduciary currency**. But money that has no intrinsic value and can't be redeemed for precious metal is **fiat currency**. Most currency circulating today is fiat money, created and authorized by various governments as their official currency.

FORMS OF PAYMENT

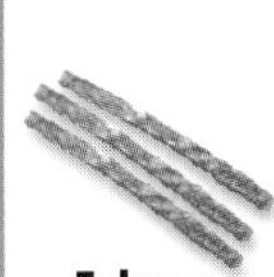

Tobacco
Solomon Islands

Salt
China

Wampum
American Indian

Elephant Hair
Africa

Ivory (Whale Tooth)
Fiji

Brick Tea Money
Siberia

Gold Stater
Turkey

Copper Money
Alaskan Indian

Owl Coin
Athens

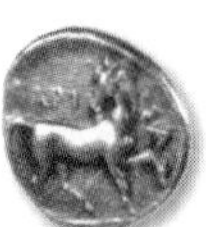

Drachma
Thessaly

Sestertius of Caesar Augustus
Rome

East Indian Money Tree
Malay Peninsula

Yen, or Round Money
Japan

Piece of Eight (8 Reals)
Spain

Paper Money

Bills come in different sizes, colors and denominations, but their real value is based on the economic strength of the country that issues them.

THE ORIGINS OF PAPER MONEY

Records indicate that paper money was used as early as 2500 B.C. by the Babylonians. In 1282, Kublai Khan issued paper notes made of mulberry bark bearing his seal and his treasurers' signatures. The **kuan**, issued in China by the Ming dynasty between 1368 and 1399, is the oldest surviving paper money. It measures 21.6 x 29.9 cm.

Sao, the first paper money in Vietnam, was issued in 1396, and printed in seven different denominations. In contrast, paper money was not circulated widely in Europe or the Americas until the 18th century when France popularized its use.

Paper money took some getting used to, though, and often fluctuated wildly in value. The U.S. system, now considered among the most stable, was chaotic until 1863, when the government regularized the currency and the banking system.

PAPER VALUE

Paper money is convenient. But the reason it's valuable is that people are willing to use it even though it can't be exchanged for **hard currency** (gold or silver coins, also known as **specie**). That's because they believe that other people assign the same value to it that they do and will accept it in payment for the goods and services they want to purchase. In fact, today when most people think of money, it's the paper currency they use in their everyday lives that they think of first.

Since each country has its own official currency, that's usually the money people use within its borders. But sometimes, especially if the government is unstable, another form of currency is worth more in day-to-day transactions such as buying food. In fact, governments under economic pressure sometimes issue a substitute currency called **scrip**, which people can use at the time and later redeem for official currency when stability returns.

DOLLARS AROUND THE WORLD

The word **dollar** comes from a silver coin called the Joachimsthaler, minted in 1518 in the valley (thal) of St. Joachim in Bohemia. The coin was widely circulated and called the **daalder** in Holland, the **daler** in Scandinavia and the **dollar** in England. Today, two dozen countries call their currency dollars.

Joachimstaler 1581

Australia **Hong Kong**

Antigua & Barbuda
Bahamas
Barbados
Belize
Bermuda
Brunei
Canada
Cayman Islands
Dominica
Fiji Islands
Grenada
Guyana
Jamaica
Liberia
Namibia
New Zealand
St. Kitts and Nevis
St. Lucia
St. Vincent
Singapore
Solomon Islands
Taiwan
Trinidad & Tobago
U.S.
Zimbabwe

In this book, dollar references are to U.S. currency unless otherwise specified.

THE UPS AND DOWNS OF PAPER MONEY

Paper money has had its ups and downs because its value changes with changing economic conditions in a particular country. When there's lots of paper money in circulation, prices go up and the currency buys less. That's known as inflation.

For example, because of the economic upheaval following World War I, in Germany in 1923, you needed 726,000,000 marks to buy what you'd been able to get for one mark in 1918.

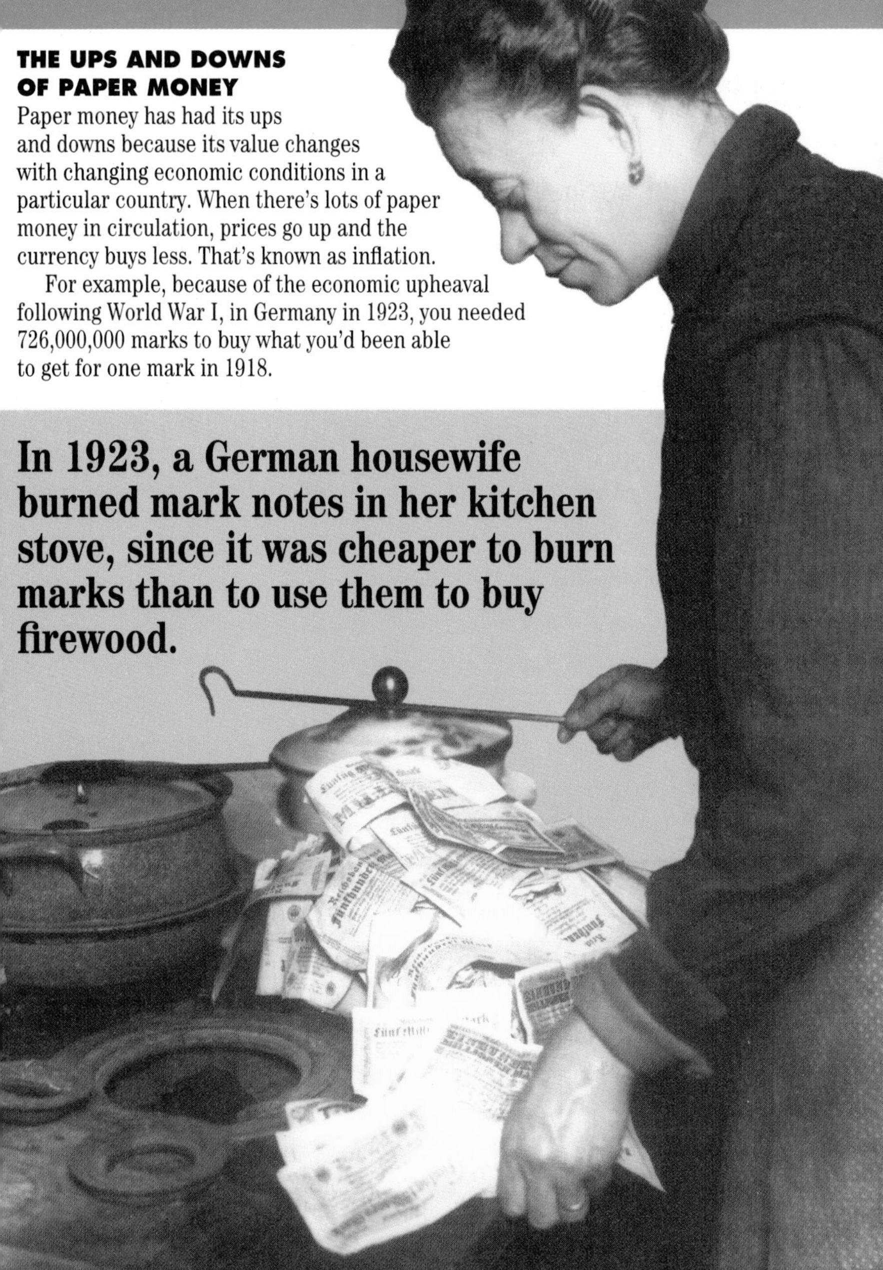

In 1923, a German housewife burned mark notes in her kitchen stove, since it was cheaper to burn marks than to use them to buy firewood.

PRINTING PAPER MONEY

Paper currency around the world is designed to prevent **counterfeiting**, or unauthorized printing, a problem governments have been fighting since the Ming Dynasty. Counterfeiting is a problem because it undermines money's value as a medium of exchange. If sellers suspect that money may be counterfeit, they won't take it as payment. They fear that if the phony bills are detected and confiscated, they'll lose money.

To increase security for U.S. currency, for example, the bills are printed using distinctive paper, special ink that appears to change colors when you look at it from different angles and embedded polymer threads. Australia introduced hard-to-copy plastic bank notes in 1993, a technique they're exporting to other countries.

A NEW LOOK

The U.S.'s recent redesign of the $100 bill, with its enlarged, off-center face of Benjamin Franklin, is a good example of changes intended to protect the integrity of paper currency in an era of extremely sophisticated new computer and photocopying techniques. Because the bill circulates widely around the world—there's an estimated $200 billion in that denomination outside the U.S.—the old bill will still be valid while the new one is being phased in.

The Money Cycle

Money is a permanent fixture of modern society, but the bills and coins we use have a limited life span.

When a government prints new bills and stamps new coins, it's not usually creating new money, but replacing the bills and coins that wear out from changing hands so often. Bills wear out in a year or two, but a coin can last for 20 to 40 years. That's why many countries have replaced small bills with more durable coins. But the move is seldom popular, as Hong Kong found when it replaced the HK$10 bill with a coin a few years ago. Singapore got a similar reaction when it replaced its S$1 bill with a coin.

DEMAND AND SUPPLY CHANGE
The number of coins and bills in circulation in a country keeps changing. Vending machine use, for example, has increased coin circulation in many places. Even when the machines take paper money, they often give coins in change. A more recent increase in bank demand for paper currency is the result of the growing use of automated teller machines (ATMs), which dispense a steady stream of bills.

The Money Cycle

Old money is taken out of circulation and replaced on a regular basis.

Japan's Ministry of Finance issues new bills and coins and ships them to the central bank.

The Bank of Japan burns old bills and sends worn coins back to the Ministry of Finance for melting and reminting.

MONEY ON A STRING
You're probably used to your coins weighing down your purse or pocket. But in ancient China and Japan, there was an easier way. Coins were minted with holes in the center (square ones in China and round ones in Japan) so they could be strung together on a string. And while that method of keeping track of money has disappeared, the holes remain in some denominations of yen.

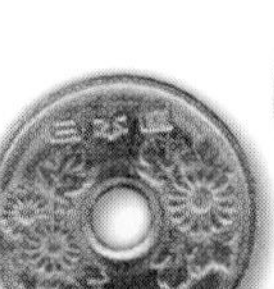

MAKING MONEY DISTINCTIVE

In many countries different denominations of paper money are printed in different colors and sometimes in different sizes. The Thai baht shown above are just one example. And while much of the world's currency depicts famous or powerful people, many bills are also engraved with scenes of natural beauty, animal life or artistic design.

The design variations have practical purposes. The differences in size and color can make it easier to distinguish between bills.

THE U.S. TWO-DOLLAR BILL

The U.S. Treasury from time to time issues $2 bills, but they've never been very popular in the U.S. When they were printed in 1976, they faced all kinds of hurdles—including no place for them in cash register drawers. And, a surprisingly large portion of the population is superstitious about using them.

The Bank of Japan sends the new money to banks across the country.

The banks distribute the money to their customers, including businesses and individuals.

The money circulates through the economy, changing hands many times as people buy things and get change back.

Businesses and individuals deposit their cash, including old bills, in their bank accounts.

Bank payments to **the central bank** are checked for worn bills and coins.

MONETARY SYSTEMS

In most countries, the monetary system has three levels: (1) a central bank that issues money, creates financial policy and influences the way the economy functions, (2) commercial banks that circulate money and (3) the people and institutions who use it to buy and sell.

When the system works effectively, the public has confidence in the banks and is willing to deposit money in them. The banks can then loan that money to other customers, increasing the amount of money in circulation and keeping the economy healthy.

Other Forms of Money

Money doesn't always change hands. It's often transferred from one account to another by written or electronic instructions.

Technology is revolutionizing the way we use money. One evidence of change is that the money we're most familiar with—bills and coins—represents only about 8% of the trillions of dollars that circulate in the U.S. economy. And while people in some countries, such as Japan, use cash more frequently than people in the U.S. do, the changing definition of money is a world-wide phenomenon.

One big difference between cash and all other forms of money—checks, electronic transfers and cards—is that cash is private, or anonymous. When you spend it, there's no record of who you are or what you bought. But other money is networked, and creates a spending trail.

THE NEW MONEY

Just as currency replaced barter and paper money replaced specie, electronic money in the form of **credit**, **debit** and **smart cards** is increasingly replacing cash—even for small items. Credit cards let you charge a purchase and pay for it later by agreement with a bank or other financial institution. Debit cards instantly subtract the amount of your purchase from your bank account and credit it to the seller's account. Smart cards are electronic purses filled with electronic cash that you can spend until it's gone.

HOW CHECKS MOVE MONEY

High-speed electronic equipment **reads** the sorting and payment instructions, called **MICR** (Magnetic Image Character Recognition) **Codes**, printed in magnetic ink along the bottom of the check. The money is then **debited** (subtracted) from the writer's account and **credited** (added) to the receiver's.

The check number is printed on the bottom of the check.

Your bank account number, beginning with the branch number, identifies the account that money will be taken from to pay the check.

Information written and stamped on the back of the check shows the account it was credited to, the bank where it was cashed or deposited and the payment stamp from your bank.

CREDIT IN CHINA

Revolving credit became available in China in 1996, when credit cards with finance charges, grace periods and credit limits were introduced. Before that, only debit cards were available. With these credit cards, holders can make purchases in any currency, but must pay their bills in dollars because the yuan isn't fully convertible.

USING CREDIT

In many countries, the majority of people use credit cards on a regular basis, while in others they're used infrequently if at all. Based on the number of people who pay their bill in full every month, it seems that many people use their cards as a convenient way to consolidate payment for purchases rather than as a source of credit. And cards provide the added advantage of giving the user a period of time to enjoy the use of a purchase before actually having to lay out the cash to pay for it. Sellers don't mind, though, because there's evidence that people spend more when they're using a card than they do when they're laying out the cash.

MONEY 'ROUND THE CLOCK

With a **PIN** (Personal Identification Number) or PIC (Personal Identification Code) and a bank ATM card linked to one or more of your accounts, you can withdraw or deposit money, find out how much you have in an account, pay bills or choose from a growing list of other services—without ever entering a bank.

Most banks are part of regional, national and even international systems that give you direct access to your accounts almost anywhere.

The card number is linked to your bank account, though it is not the same as your account number.

Details of your transactions are printed on the receipt the ATM provides. The **date and location of the ATM branch** may be important if you question certain transactions. Cameras often record the activity at an ATM, and can provide evidence in unresolved disputes.

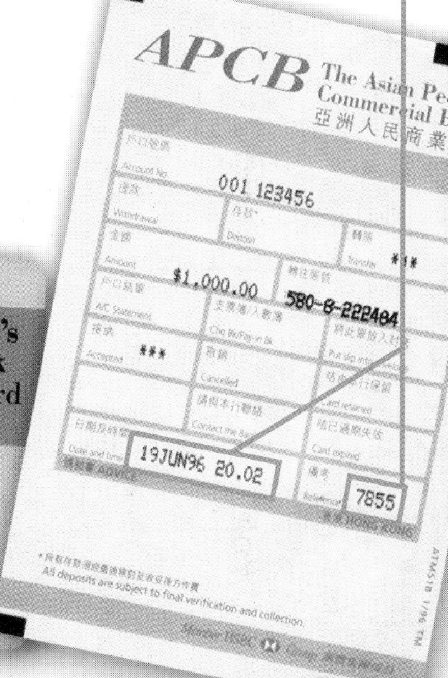

About 42% of the people living in Hong Kong have ATM cards, according to a recent survey.

MONEY 'ROUND THE WORLD

Credit cards are a modern substitute for paper currency. You can charge goods and services around the world and pay the bill in the currency you normally use. Each transaction is converted from the currency of the country where you used the card to the currency you're paying in—usually at favorable rates because the card companies do such a huge volume of business. The only catch is that the rate you pay is the rate in effect when the card company pays the seller—not the rate on the day you made the purchase. There's no way to predict whether you'll come out ahead or not. The card company may also make a modest profit on the exchange—but probably less than a local bureau of exchange.

SMART CARDS

A smart card, sometimes known as a chip card, looks like a credit card but it's embedded with a microprocessor loaded with its own verification codes and passwords that store more information than the electronic strip of current credit cards. When you've used up the amount of the card, you can either replace the card, or add value to it.

The money that a smart card represents is digital. It's transferred from your card to any terminal that accepts it without being seen or handled. You might insert the card, or simply wave it at a terminal for a transaction to take place.

Will smart cards be the new money? That depends on how widely accepted they become around the world, and how willing people will be to use them in place of money they can touch.

The Central Bank System

The aim of a central bank is to monitor its country's monetary system.

For financial systems to function effectively, they have to be governed. In most countries, that's the job of the central bank. Sometimes the bank is a government institution, with little independence. In other places, the bank has more freedom to set policy and influence the economy.

In some places there's one bank, and in others more than one. In the U.S., the Federal Reserve System has 12 separate banks around the nation, each with its own directors. The system is governed by a seven-member Federal Reserve Board, with headquarters in Washington, D.C.

How One Central Bank Works

The U.S.'s central bank is called the Federal Reserve, or the Fed.

The Fed plays many roles as part of its work in keeping the economy healthy. It is a regulator, banker, lender, auditor and guardian.

Its Federal Open Market Committee is probably the most closely watched monetary-policy maker in the world.

REGULATOR

By buying and selling government securities, the Fed tries to balance the money in circulation. When the economy is stable, the demand for goods and services is fairly constant, and so are prices. Achieving that stability supports the Fed's goals of keeping the economy healthy and maintaining the value of the dollar.

BANKER

The Fed maintains bank accounts for the U.S. Treasury and many government and quasigovernment agencies. It deposits and withdraws funds the way you do at your own bank, but in bigger volume: over 80 million Treasury checks are written every year.

The Fed is also the national clearing house for checks. It facilitates quick and accurate transfer of funds in more than 15 billion transactions a year.

LENDER

If a bank needs to borrow money, it can turn to a Federal Reserve bank. The interest the Fed charges banks is called the **discount rate**. Bankers don't like to borrow from the Fed, since it may suggest they have problems. And they can borrow more cheaply from other banks.

INTERNATIONAL BANKING

The central bank tries to regulate the value of its country's currency at home and in the international market. The bank issues currency and may trade gold or other currencies in exchange for its own. It also holds some form of money in reserve that it can use in making international transactions, generally gold or a currency that's widely used, such as the dollar or the yen. Many central banks still rely heavily on persuasion or even direct credit controls, limiting the amount banks can lend.

Recognizing that monetary systems are increasingly interrelated, central banks also cooperate with each other, formally and informally, to protect the stability of the world's currencies.

AUDITOR

The Fed monitors the business affairs and audits the records of all of the banks in its system. Its particular concerns are compliance with banking rules and the quality of loans.

When currency wears out or gets damaged, the Fed takes it out of circulation and authorizes its replacement. Then the Treasury has new bills printed and new coins minted.

GUARDIAN

Gold stored in the U.S. by foreign governments is held in the vault at the New York Federal Reserve Bank—some 10,000 tons of it. That's more gold in one place than anywhere else in the world, as far as anyone knows. Among its many tasks, the Fed administers the exchange of bullion between countries.

THE INTERNATIONAL MONETARY FUND

The International Monetary Fund (IMF) is a cooperative institution of 178 member nations working to maintain an orderly and stable system of international currency exchange, specifically payments and receipts between various countries. The member nations pool foreign exchange reserves through the IMF, and can draw against the reserves under certain circumstances to correct imbalances in their economies. IMF reserves are also used to reduce the debt of developing countries.

Although some would argue that the IMF has outlived its usefulness, others say it has a good record in encouraging countries to adopt policies that foster stable economies. And most agree it plays an important role in collecting and sharing economic data world-wide.

CENTRAL BANKS IN ASIA

Like their counterparts throughout the world, central banks in the Asian-Pacific region distribute currency, set monetary policy and monitor the financial workings of their countries.

They include:

- **Australia**: Reserve Bank of Australia
- **Bangladesh**: Bangladesh Bank
- **Burma**: Union Bank of Burma
- **Cambodia**: National Bank of Cambodia
- **China**: People's Bank of China
- **Fiji**: Reserve Bank of Fiji
- **Hong Kong**: The Monetary Authority of Hong Kong is the de facto central bank
- **India**: Reserve Bank of India
- **Indonesia**: Bank Indonesia
- **Japan**: Bank of Japan
- **Laos**: Banque d'Etat de la RDP Lao
- **Malaysia**: Bank Negara Malaysia
- **Maldives**: The Maldives Monetary Authority
- **Nepal**: Nepal Rastra Bank
- **New Zealand**: Reserve Bank of New Zealand
- **Papua New Guinea**: Bank of Papua New Guinea
- **Pakistan**: State Bank of Pakistan
- **Philippines**: Central Bank of the Philippines
- **Singapore**: The Monetary Authority of Singapore is the de facto central bank
- **Solomon Islands**: The Solomon Islands Monetary Authority
- **South Korea**: Bank of Korea
- **Sri Lanka**: Bank of Ceylon
- **Thailand**: Bank of Thailand
- **Vietnam**: State Bank of Vietnam

Controlling the Money Flow

The money that powers an economy is created essentially out of nothing by a central bank.

Keeping a modern economy running smoothly requires a pilot who'll keep it from stalling or overaccelerating.

Most countries try to control the amount of money in circulation. The process of injecting or withdrawing money reflects the monetary policy that the central bank adopts to regulate the economy.

Monetary policy doesn't have to be a fixed ideology. It often is a juggling act to keep enough money in the economy so that it flourishes without growing too fast.

Central banks take different approaches. In certain countries the bank may follow a fixed policy and change direction slowly. Or a bank may keep a tight rein on the money supply to encourage a currency's stability. In some cases, though, a bank may not be able to control the currency tightly enough to keep inflation in check. Or it might risk increasing the money supply, despite inflation, to help the economy shake off recession.

HOW IT WORKS

In the U.S., the Fed's Open Market Committee meets about every six weeks to evaluate how the economy is performing and whether to change direction.

Then it tells the Federal Reserve Bank of New York whether to speed up or slow down the creation of new money, and the bank acts regularly to implement those policy decisions.

Meanwhile, markets around the world watch for news of its decisions.

HOW FAST MONEY GOES

Money's velocity is the speed at which it changes hands. If a 1,000-yen note is used by 20 different people in a year, its velocity is 20. An increase in either the quantity of money in circulation or its velocity makes prices go up—though if both increase they can cancel each other's effect.

A MARKET FOR MONEY

A money market isn't a place. It's a country's system for handling wholesale transactions between banks. What they're trading is money and short-term loans, the resources participating banks need to provide to their retail customers. They're the individuals and institutions who write checks, make deposits and borrow money.

Money markets vary from country to country. But in most open economies, the system generally ensures a common price for money—the interest rate—because of competition among the suppliers and the seekers of funds.

FAST OR SLOW GROWTH

For all practical purposes, there isn't any limit on the amount of money a central bank can create. The $100 million in the example to the right is only a modest increase in the U.S. money supply. In a typical month, the Fed might pump as much as $4 billion or as little as $1 billion into the economy. The danger of increasing the money supply too much, however, is that inflation can intensify and eventually reduce the value of the currency. To slow down an economy where too much money is in circulation, the central bank sells government securities, taking in the cash that would otherwise be available for lending.

CHANGING THE DISCOUNT RATE

In its role as banker to banks, the central bank can also influence the amount of money in circulation by changing the **discount rate**, the interest rate it charges banks to borrow money. If the discount rate is high, banks are discouraged from borrowing. If the discount rate is low, banks borrow more freely and lend money to their clients more freely. But that approach doesn't work if the rate is already low. In economist John Maynard Keynes's words, it's like trying to push on a string.

REGULATION IS A TOUGH JOB

It isn't easy to regulate the money supply or control the rate of growth. That's because the economy doesn't always respond quickly or precisely when the central bank acts. In the U.S. for example, it takes about six months for significant policy changes to affect the economy directly. That lag helps explain why the economy seems to have a life of its own, growing too much in some years and not enough in others.

CREATING MONEY

To create money in the U.S., the New York Fed buys government securities from banks and brokerage houses. The money that pays for the securities hasn't existed before, but it has value, or worth, because the securities the bank buys with it are valuable.

More new money is created when the banks and brokerages lend the money they receive from selling the securities to their clients who spend it on goods and services. The simplified steps below illustrate how the process works.

1

The Fed writes a check for $100 million to buy the securities from a brokerage house. The brokerage house deposits the check in its own bank (A), increasing the bank's cash.

2

Bank A can lend its customers $90 million of that deposit after setting aside 10%. The Fed requires all banks to hold 10% of their deposits (in this example, $10 million) in reserve. A small company borrows $100,000 from Bank A to buy equipment. The sellers deposit the money in their bank (B).

3

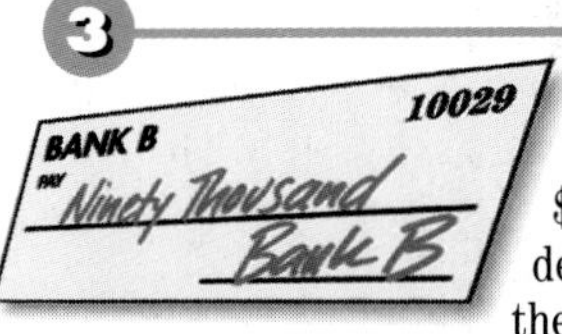

Now Bank B has $90,000 (the deposit minus the required reserve) to lend that it didn't have before. A business borrows $10,000 from Bank B to buy a computer system and the dealer deposits the money in Bank C.

4

Bank C can now loan $9,000.

This series of transactions has created $190,099,000 in just four steps. Through a repetition of the loan process involving a wide range of banks and their customers, the $100 million that the Fed initially added to the money supply could theoretically become almost $900 million in new money.

The Money Supply

There's no ideal money supply. The goal is to keep the economy running smoothly by keeping an eye on the money that people have to spend.

The money supply measures the amount of money that people have available to spend—including cash on hand and funds that can be **liquidated**, or turned into cash.

When a central bank is following an easy money policy—increasing the money supply at a rapid rate—the money supply and the economy tend to grow quickly, companies hire more workers and a feeling of prosperity sweeps over the country. But if the bank adopts a tight money policy—slowing the money supply to combat inflation—the economy bogs down, unemployment increases and gloom spreads.

In general, when an economy is strong, demand for its currency increases, and the amount of its money in circulation goes up. The number of dollars, for example, has grown regularly in the 1990s, reflecting demand both inside the U.S. and in other countries. However, dollars that are used abroad are not counted as part of the U.S. money supply.

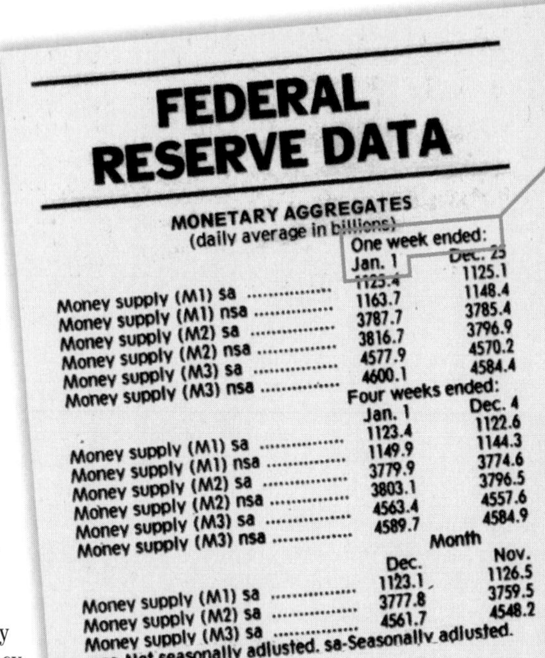

FEDERAL RESERVE DATA

MONETARY AGGREGATES
(daily average in billions)

	One week ended: Jan. 1	Dec. 25
Money supply (M1) sa	1125.4	1125.1
Money supply (M1) nsa	1163.7	1148.4
Money supply (M2) sa	3787.7	3785.4
Money supply (M2) nsa	3816.7	3796.9
Money supply (M3) sa	4577.9	4570.2
Money supply (M3) nsa	4600.1	4584.4
	Four weeks ended: Jan. 1	**Dec. 4**
Money supply (M1) sa	1123.4	1122.6
Money supply (M1) nsa	1149.9	1144.3
Money supply (M2) sa	3779.9	3774.6
Money supply (M2) nsa	3803.1	3796.5
Money supply (M3) sa	4563.4	4557.6
Money supply (M3) nsa	4589.7	4584.9
	Month: Dec.	**Nov.**
Money supply (M1) sa	1123.1	1126.5
Money supply (M2) sa	3777.8	3759.5
Money supply (M3) sa	4561.7	4548.2

nsa-Not seasonally adjusted. sa-Seasonally adjusted.

MEASURING THE MONEY SUPPLY

If you keep careful track of your personal money supply, you know, for instance, how much cash you have in your wallet and how much money is in your bank account. You also know how much salary is coming in and which investments, such as savings accounts, can be turned into cash quickly.

Similarly, economists and policy makers around the world keep careful track of the public money supply using measures called M0, M1, M2 and M3.

The Ms are **monetary aggregates**, or ways to group assets which people use in roughly the same way. M0 and M1, for instance, count **liquid assets**, such as cash. The object is to separate money that's being saved from money that's being spent, in order to predict impending changes in the economy.

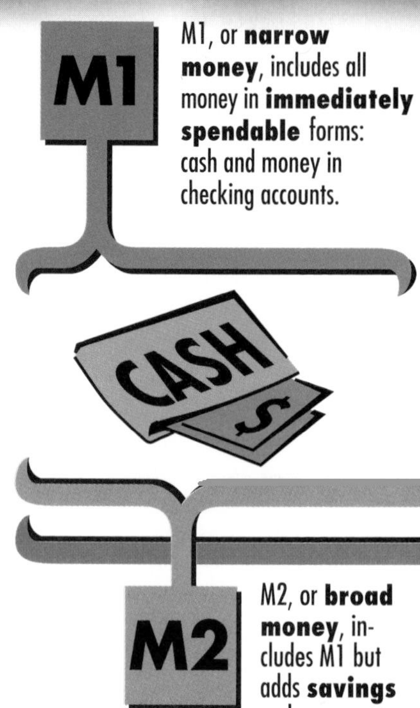

M1, or **narrow money**, includes all money in **immediately spendable** forms: cash and money in checking accounts.

M2, or **broad money**, includes M1 but adds **savings** and money in small **time deposits** (such as CDs). The latter can't be spent directly but can be converted easily to cash.

READING THE CHARTS

In the U.S., the Federal Reserve reports the financial details of the money supply every week. The average daily amounts—in billions of dollars—are provided for each component, M1, M2 and M3, in these charts. The M3 figure, the most inclusive, is always the largest.

The money supply is tracked across several different time periods to measure short-term changes as well as longer-term trends. The examples shown here, for instance, show figures for the weeks of Jan. 1 and July 22. The July numbers are compared with those of May and June, and January's with December and November.

FEDERAL RESERVE DATA

MONETARY AGGREGATES
(daily average in billions)

	One week ended:	
	Jul. 22	Jul. 15
Money supply (M1) sa	1100.8	1103.4
Money supply (M1) nsa	1100.6	1113.3
Money supply (M2) sa	3755.2	3748.5
Money supply (M2) nsa	3754.1	3770.3
Money supply (M3) sa	4740.5	4733.5
Money supply (M3) nsa	4736.6	4749.4
	Four weeks ended:	
	Jul.22	Jun. 24
Money supply (M1) sa	1109.2	1110.9
Money supply (M1) nsa	1113.4	1112.1
Money supply (M2) sa	3752.0	3749.3
Money supply (M2) nsa	3761.4	3753.3
Money supply (M3) sa	4733.9	4728.0
Money supply (M3) nsa	4736.0	4724.7
	Month	
	Jun	May
Money supply (M1) sa	1117.2	1117.6
Money supply (M2) sa	3748.7	3731.2
Money supply (M3) sa	4724.7	4705.8

nsa-Not seasonally adjusted. sa-Seasonally adjusted.

CHANGING YARDSTICK

In mid 1993, the U.S. Federal Reserve stopped using its long-standing yardstick for measuring the economy—growth in the M2 money supply. Because people in the U.S. increasingly keep their cash in mutual-fund money-market accounts, which aren't included in the M2, the Fed found that the numbers weren't reliable indicators of economic growth.

Instead of adjusting interest rates to control the money supply, the new method is to set short-term real interest rates (the current interest rates minus the rate of inflation) at a level that the U.S. central bank believes will produce growth without inflation.

In countries where more money is held in cash and deposit accounts, as it is in many Asian countries, the M2 may be a more accurate measure.

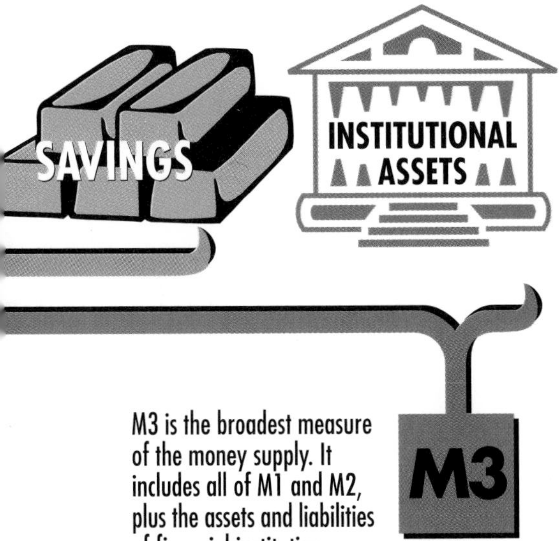

M3 is the broadest measure of the money supply. It includes all of M1 and M2, plus the assets and liabilities of financial institutions, including long-term deposits, which can't be easily converted into spendable forms.

Measuring Economic Health

Economists keep their fingers on the pulse of the economy at all times, determined to cure what ails it.

Intensive care is a 24-hour business. Doctors and nurses measure vital signs, record changes in temperature and physical functions, conduct test after test. That gives you an idea of how thousands of experts—and countless more interested amateurs—watch the economies of countries around the world.

The biggest differences? The vigil never stops—even when the economy seems healthy. And there's no consensus on how to cure what ails the patient when the vital signs are poor.

In the U.S., the factors that the government believes measure economic health are surveyed and reported regularly. Some of this information is shown below in chart form.

The Index of Leading Economic Indicators is released every month by the Conference Board, a provider of U.S. economic data. The numbers rarely surprise the experts, since the components are reported separately before the index is released. But the index does provide a simple way to keep an eye on the economy's health. Generally, three consecutive rises in the index are considered a sign that the economy is growing—and three drops, a sign of decline.

The list of 11 indicators that the Conference Board averages to produce the index is restructured from time to time to improve its forecasting performance. In the past, it has done a reliable job of signaling economic downturns eight to 18 months in advance, but it has also predicted recessions that didn't occur.

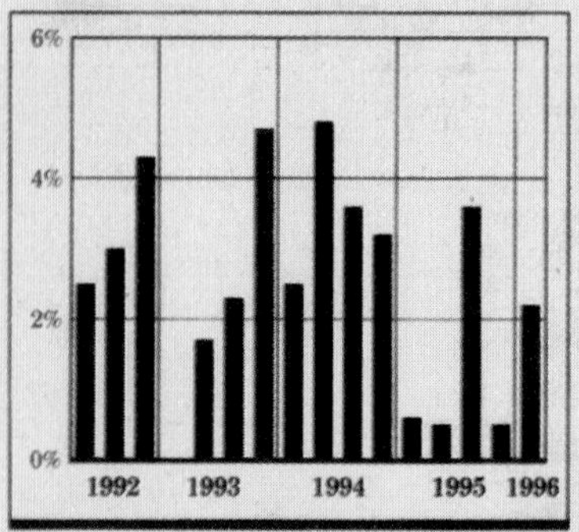

Gross Domestic Product
GDP is the value of the goods and services produced within the country's borders. It reflects the rate at which the economy is growing. This chart shows the quarterly pattern of growth from 1992 through mid-1996. GDP replaced gross national product as the U.S. Commerce Department's main measure of U.S. economic output. GNP is the total value of a nation's output of goods and services, including those produced abroad.

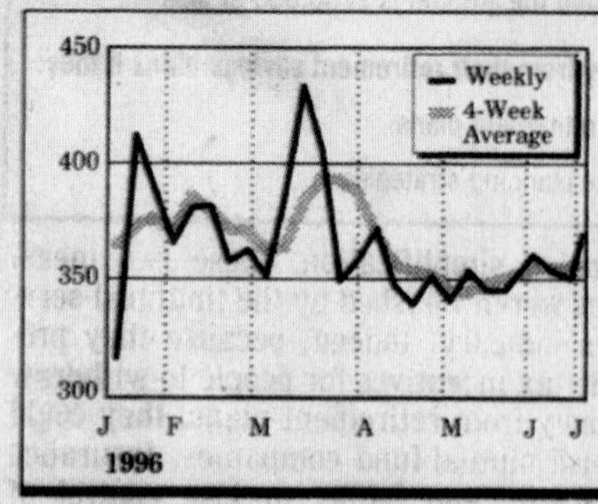

Unemployment Figures
New unemployment claims for state unemployment insurance give a sense of the number of people looking for work. A steady or falling number is a sign the economy may be growing. This chart suggests a fairly stable situation, despite a sudden surge in mid-March.

Leading Indicators

Index (1987 = 100)

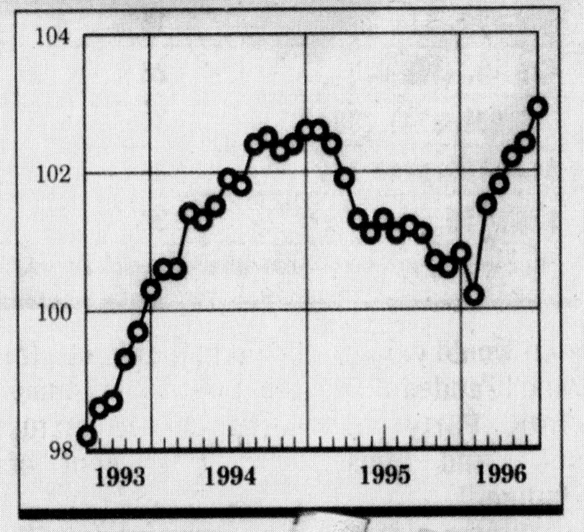

COMPOSITE of ke[illegible]icat[illegible]f future economic activity ro[illegible]Ju[illegible]102.9 of

CONSUMER PRICE INDEX

In many countries, the impact of economic changes on individual citizens is measured by a consumer price index. It measures what people are paying for goods and services in comparison with the past. It also often influences the central bank's policy decisions.

Housing Starts

Annual rate, in millions of dwelling units.

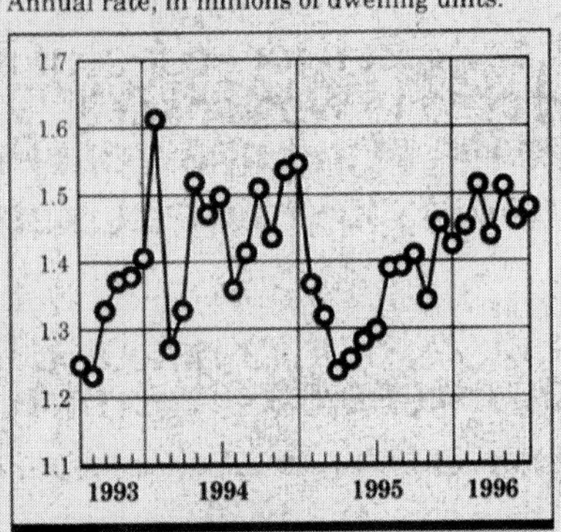

HOUSING STARTS in June rose to a seasonally adjusted rate of 1,480,000 units

New Factory Orders

In billions of dollars.

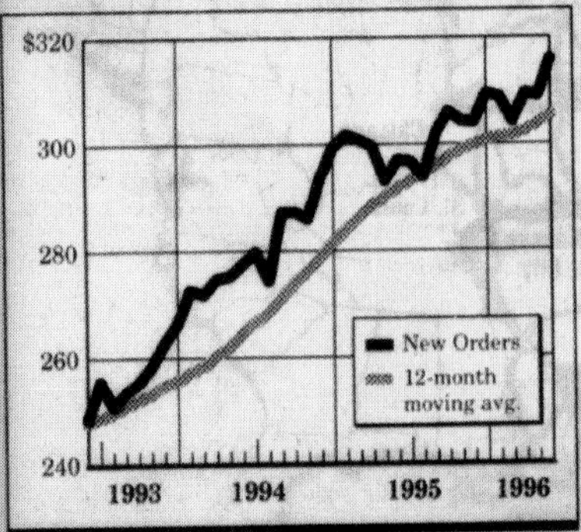

NEW ORDERS reported by manufacturers in May rose to a seasonally adjusted $315.90 billion from a revised $310.04 billion

Housing Starts

The number of building permits being issued is a measure of economic health. A growing economy generates increased demand for new housing. This chart shows a dramatic drop in early 1995 and a fairly steady growth into 1996.

New Factory Orders

The value of new orders is reported by manufacturers—shown here at nearly $320 billion in mid-1996. Steady increases signal that consumers are spending more freely and retail stores are restocking.

Tracking an Economy

A range of indicators provides information on the health of a nation's economy.

Governments track a range of economic indicators. Some reflect the economic experiences of individuals, including joblessness, the availability of new homes and consumer prices, while others focus on the behavior of businesses. People often respond slowly to reports of an economic recovery if they don't see an immediate, positive impact on their lives or businesses. The lack of confidence can slow the pace of recovery.

In Japan, the **tankan survey**, a quarterly poll of more than 10,000 companies, is the most closely watched indicator of economic sentiment. It's also considered a reliable short-term forecasting device for predicting the direction the economy is likely to take.

That's the case, at least in part, because when manufacturers and other business leaders feel confident about the current economic situation and their prospects, they tend to spend more to build their businesses. But if they're worried about a slowdown, they tend to spend less. That in turn slows growth and can weaken the economy still further.

Another indicator of Japan's industrial health is **capacity utilization**, or the degree to which production capabilities are used. Utilization figures for 1994 through early 1996, for instance, trail the 1990 benchmark level by between 12 and 18 points, providing evidence of a drag on domestic output.

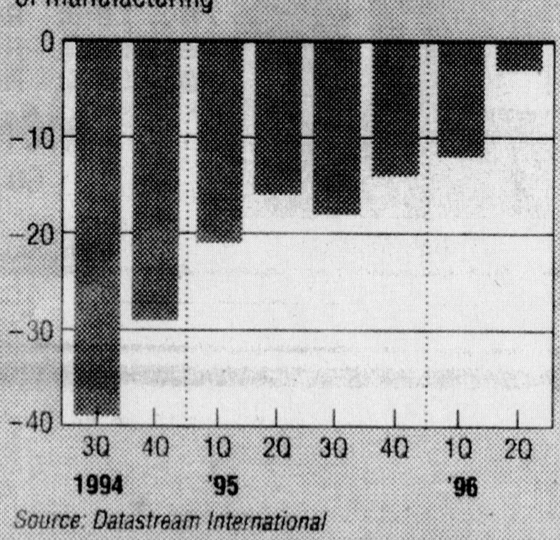

TAKING A CLOSER LOOK

Japan's central bank administers the tankan poll, which asks corporations a series of questions about projected inventory levels and plans for domestic and overseas investment, for instance.

The replies—"good," "neutral" and "bad"—are expressed as **diffusion indexes**, which are created by subtracting the percentage of negative responses from the percentage of positive ones. In this example, the mood among manufacturers shows signs of improvement, with the latest period ranking as the least negative in eight quarters.

MEASURING THE HEART BEATS

Many economic indicators are standard around the world. One that's used frequently is a country's **gross domestic product (GDP)**.

Related data, especially the differences between levels of imports and exports, or the trade balance, are also key measures of economic health. They're reflected in a country's **current account**, a broad measure of trade in goods and services and some financial transfers. When a country exports more than it imports, it has a surplus on the current account of its international balance of payments. In the reverse case, it has a deficit.

A chronic deficit is often seen as an indicator of potential problems. For instance, the availability of overseas money to fund a shortfall will influence a nation's economic prospects.

Given the role of trade, the economic health of a country's trading partners also affects its own economy. For example, export growth of developing Asian nations to Japan fell sharply in the early 1990s when the Japanese economy began floundering. But that trade picked up as the yen strengthened, making imported goods more affordable in Japan. These same nations are likely to benefit from economic growth in Japan, where the GDP jumped in early 1996.

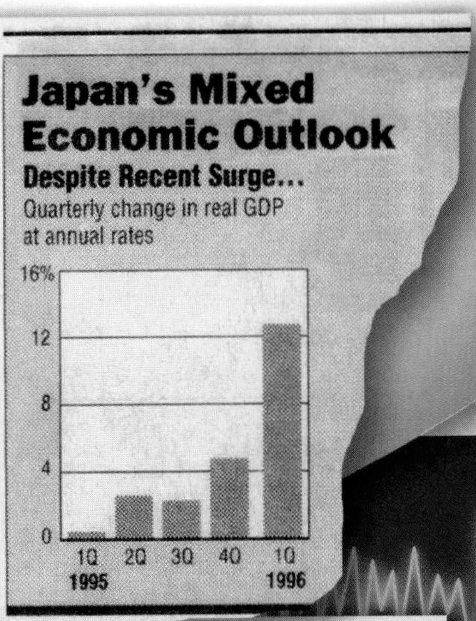

Japan's Mixed Economic Outlook

Despite Recent Surge...

Quarterly change in real GDP at annual rates

Real GDP growth (% increase)

	1995	1996F	1997F
Australia	3.2	2.9	3.4
China	10.2	9.4	9.6
Hong Kong	4.6	4.7	5.2
Indonesia	7.5	7.2	7.1
Japan	0.9	2.4	2.2
Malaysia	9.5	8.4	8.2
New Zealand	3.4	2.3	3.7
Singapore	8.9	8.0	7.4
South Korea	9.0	7.3	7.2
Taiwan	6.1	5.9	6.2
Thailand	8.7	8.2	7.9

Current-account balance (% of GDP)

	1994	1995	1996F	1997F
China	1.3	2.4	0.5	0.1
Indonesia	-1.6	-3.8	-3.8	-2.8
Malaysia	-5.9	-8.9	-8.0	-7.0
Philippines	-4.4	-2.8	-3.1	-3.2
Singapore	17.3	16.3	16.5	16.4
South Korea	-1.0	-1.9	-1.2	-0.8
Taiwan	2.6	2.8	2.8	2.6
Thailand	-5.9	-7.5	-7.6	-7.6

F=Forecast

MAKING COMPARISONS

The health of various nations' economies can be compared by looking at current and projected GDP growth and current-account balance figures. In the table for Asian-Pacific countries, Singapore and Thailand have similar rates of GDP growth. While Singapore has a positive current-account balance, Thailand is shown as having a widening deficit.

The Economic Cycle

Inflation and recession are recurring phases of a continuous economic cycle. Experts work hard to predict their timing and control their effects.

Inflation occurs when prices rise because there's too much money in circulation and not enough goods and services to spend it on. When prices go higher than people can—or will—pay, demand decreases and a downturn begins.

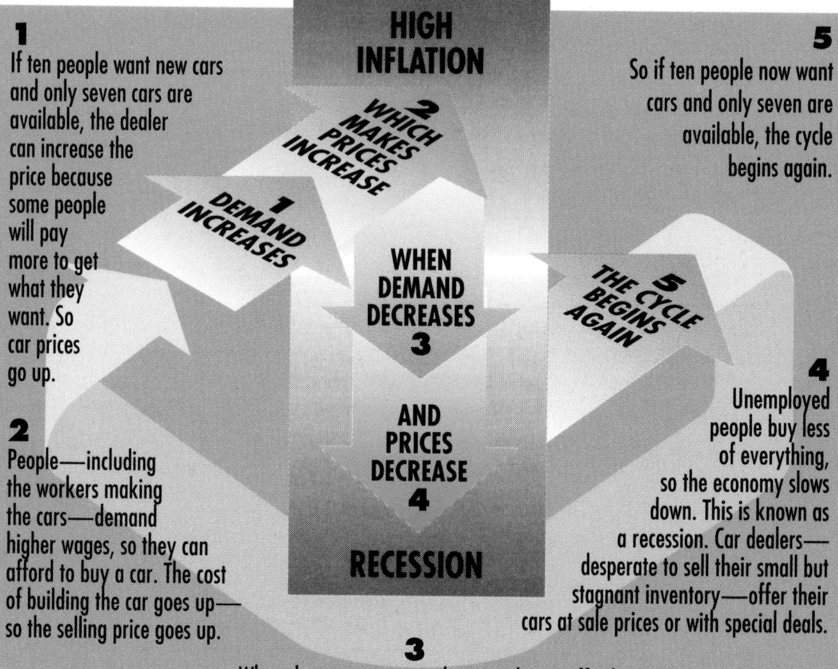

1
If ten people want new cars and only seven cars are available, the dealer can increase the price because some people will pay more to get what they want. So car prices go up.

2
People—including the workers making the cars—demand higher wages, so they can afford to buy a car. The cost of building the car goes up—so the selling price goes up.

3
When the car costs more than people can afford, they stop buying. Fewer cars are needed, and the factory lays off workers.

4
Unemployed people buy less of everything, so the economy slows down. This is known as a recession. Car dealers—desperate to sell their small but stagnant inventory—offer their cars at sale prices or with special deals.

5
So if ten people now want cars and only seven are available, the cycle begins again.

CONTROLLING THE CYCLE

Economic cycles usually aren't allowed to run unchecked, because the consequences could be a major worldwide **depression** such as the one that followed the U.S. stock market crash of 1929. In a depression, money is so tight that the economy virtually grinds to a halt, unemployment escalates, businesses collapse and the general mood is grim.

Instead, governments and central banks change their monetary policy to affect what's happening in the economy. In a recession, a central bank can create new money to make borrowing easier, lower interest rates, or take other measures to stimulate business. If the bank can't or doesn't make those adjustments, whether for political or policy reasons, it often prolongs the economic downturn.

Central bank decisions in industrialized countries affect more than just their own economies. That's because, increasingly, what happens in one country or region has a direct impact on the economic health of the rest of the world. A recession in Japan, for example, can create ripples in all of Asia, the U.S. and Europe.

WORKING TOGETHER

The Group of Seven leading industrialized nations meet regularly to assess the international economic situation, with finance ministers and central bankers coordinating their activities. The G-7 might decide, for example, that a stronger dollar and a weaker yen are desirable and agree that their central banks will act in concert to make it happen.

The G-7 nations are Japan, Britain, Germany, France, Italy, Canada and the U.S.

CONTROLLING INFLATION

Inflation is often the result of political pressures. A growing economy creates jobs and reduces unemployment. Politicians are almost always in favor of that, so they urge the central bank to adopt an easy money policy that stimulates the economy.

The most effective method for ending inflation is for the central bank to induce a recession, or downturn, in the economy. Two consecutive quarters in which the economy shrinks is considered a recession.

INFLATION DESTROYS VALUE

Most economists agree that inflation isn't good for the economy because, over time, it destroys value, including the value of money. If inflation is running at a 10% annual rate, for example, the book that cost about $10 in 1990 would cost almost $20 in 1997. For comparison's sake, if inflation averaged 5% a year, the same book wouldn't cost $20 until 2004.

The rule of 72 is a reliable guide to the impact of inflation. It works by dividing 72 by the annual inflation rate to find out the number of years it will take prices to double. For example, when inflation is at 10%, prices will double in 7 years (72 ÷ 10=7) and when it's 4% they will double in 18 years (72 ÷ 4=18).

BUT DEBTORS MAKE OUT LIKE BANDITS

Inflation isn't bad for everyone. Debtors love it. Say you borrow $100,000 today with the promise to repay it in seven years. If inflation runs at a 10% annual rate, the money you repay will really be worth only $50,000 in today's dollars.

Inflation also prompts investors to buy things they can resell at huge profits—such as art or real estate—rather than putting their money into companies that can create new products and jobs.

CONTROLLING RECESSIONS

To avert long-term slowdowns or the more serious problem of a depression, politicians and central bankers—once they observe that the economy is beginning to shrink—are likely to reverse their policies to stimulate more borrowing and economic growth. In time, the economy emerges from recession, begins growing, and the completed cycle begins anew.

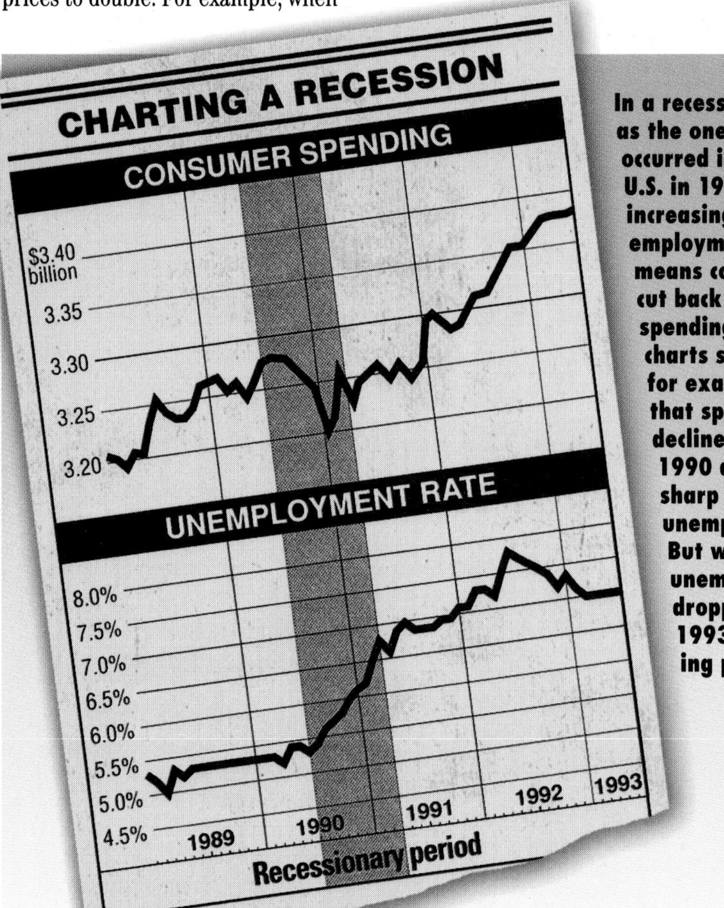

In a recession, such as the one that occurred in the U.S. in 1990–91, increasing unemployment means consumers cut back on spending. These charts show, for example, that spending declined in mid-1990 during a sharp rise in unemployment. But when unemployment dropped, in 1993, spending picked up.

The World of Money

Most currencies are **floated** against each other to measure their worth in the global marketplace.

A currency's **value**—what it's worth in relation to other currencies—depends on how attractive it is in the marketplace. If demand is high, its price will increase relative to other currencies.

SHIFTS IN VALUE

Wild or rapid changes in currency value usually indicate an economy in turmoil, including runaway inflation, defaults on loan agreements, serious balance-of-trade deficits, or economic policies the markets think won't work over the long term.

The political environment can also cause a currency to rise or fall in value. In threats of war, civil unrest or political instability, investors tend to flee to **safe haven** currencies, such as the U.S. dollar, the Swiss franc and sometimes the German mark. They move into so-called hard currencies, which they view as more stable. As a result, the value of the hard currencies increases.

CURRENCY CROSS RATES

	U.S.	A$	Pound	C$	RMB	FFr	DM	HK$	Rupee	Rph	Yen	
U.S.		1.260	0.661	1.372	8.288	5.209	1.539	7.736	35.020	2328.75	107.100	1.
Australia	0.794		0.524	1.089	6.577	4.134	1.221	6.138	[illegible]	[illegible]	84.984	1.
Britain	1.513	1.907		2.077	12.542	7.883	2.329	11.707	52.996	3524.10	162.074	2.2
Canada	0.729	0.918	0.482		6.039	3.796	1.121	5.637	25.519	1696.97	78.044	1.0
China	0.121	0.152	0.080	0.166		0.629	0.186	0.933	4.225	280.98	12.922	0.1
France	0.192	0.242	0.127	0.263	1.591		0.295	1.485	6.723	447.04	20.559	0.28
Germany	0.650	0.819	0.429	0.892	5.386	3.386		5.027	22.759	1513.45	69.604	0.95
Hong Kong	0.129	0.163	0.085	0.177	1.071	0.673	0.199		4.527	301.04	13.845	0.18
India	0.0286	0.0360	0.0189	0.0392	0.2367	0.1488	0.0439	0.2209		66.50	3.0583	0.041
Indonesia	0.0004	0.0005	0.0003	0.0006	0.0036	0.0022	0.0007	0.0033	0.0150		0.0460	0.0006
Japan	0.009	0.012	0.006	0.013	0.077	0.049	0.014	0.072	0.327	21.74		0.014
New Zealand	0.683	0.860	0.451	0.937	5.657	3.555	1.050	5.280	23.901	1589.37	73.096	
S. Korea	0.0013	0.0016	0.0008	0.0018	0.0106	0.0067	0.0020	0.0099	0.0449	2.987	0.1374	0.0019
Malaysia	0.401	0.505	0.265	0.550	3.321	2.087	0.617	3.100	14.033	933.18	42.917	0.587
Philippines	0.038	0.048	0.025	0.052	0.317	0.199	0.059	0.295	1.338	88.95	4.091	0.056
Singapore	0.710	0.894	0.469	0.974	5.881	3.697	1.092	5.489	24.851	1652.53	76.001	1.040
Switzerland	0.791	0.997	0.523	1.086	6.560	4.123	1.218	6.123	27.717	1843.09	84.765	1.160
Taiwan	0.037	0.046	0.024	0.050	0.303	0.191	0.056	0.283	1.282	85.26	3.921	0.054
Thailand	0.040	0.050	0.026	0.054	0.328	0.206	0.061	0.306	1.384	92.05	4.233	0.058

Calculated Cross Rates as of 5.30 p.m. Hong Kong time

DROPPING THE GOLD STANDARD

Between 1944 and 1971, major trading nations had a fixed, or official, rate of exchange tied to the U.S. dollar, redeemable in gold at $35 an ounce. Since 1971, when the U.S. abandoned the gold standard, currencies have floated against each other—influenced by supply and demand but also by various governments' efforts to manage their currency level.

Members of the European Union have been successful in creating a managed exchange-rate mechanism, which promotes rate stability.

ECONOMIC STRENGTH IS A FACTOR

The value of a given currency relative to others usually depends on a combination of economic trends, market mood and people's expectations for the future. For example, great demand for a nation's products

5/21/96

Ring	Peso	S$	SwFr	NT$	Baht
2.496	26.180	1.409	1.264	27.312	25.299
.980	20.774	1.118	1.003	21.672	20.075
776	39.618	2.133	1.912	41.331	38.285
818	19.077	1.027	0.921	19.902	18.435
301	3.159	0.170	0.152	3.295	3.052
79	5.026	0.271	0.243	5.243	4.857
22	[illegible]	0.916	0.821	17.750	16.442
23	3.384	[illegible]	0.163	3.531	3.270
13	0.7476	0.0402	[illegible]	0.7799	0.7224
1	0.0112	0.0006	0.0005	[illegible]	0.0109
3	0.244	0.013	0.012	0.255	0.236
	17.868	0.962	0.862	18.640	17.267
	0.0336	0.0018	0.0016	0.0350	0.0324
	10.491	0.565	0.506	10.945	10.138
		0.054	0.048	1.043	0.966
	18.578		0.897	19.381	17.953
	20.720	1.115		21.616	20.023
	0.959	0.052	0.046		0.926
	1.035	0.056	0.050	1.080	

Source: Dow Jones Telerate

creates demand for the currency needed to pay for those products.

Or, if there's a big demand for the stocks or bonds of a particular country, the value of that nation's currency can stay steady or rise as foreign investors bid for currency to make investments.

CURRENCY CROSS RATES

Currency cross rates, the late Hong Kong price of the basic units of 17 international currencies in relation to each other, are published daily in The Asian Wall Street Journal, as this example from May 21, 1996, demonstrates.

Some currencies float freely against each other, but some are **pegged**, or linked, to the value of another currency, often the dollar, or to a basket, or weighted average, of other currencies. The Thai baht, for instance, is pegged to a dollar-denominated basket of currencies.

In the chart, the U. S. appears first, followed by an alphabetical listing of Asian and European countries. To find the current exchange rate between two currencies, you find the place where two columns intersect. For example, the Australian dollar was valued at HK$6.138, while trading at a rate of one to 84.984 yen.

With its global perspective, the chart provides up-to-date exchange information for trading partners whose transactions aren't figured in dollars, which is increasingly the case in Asia. Since these exchange rates are based on wholesale trading, they usually differ from the rate you would get in a retail transaction, such as changing money at a bank.

LOSING ALTITUDE

A currency can lose value and drift downward in relation to other currencies, or it can be officially **devalued**. However, if a government decides to devalue its currency in response to economic problems, such as runaway inflation or a deficit, there can be a ripple effect world-wide, in part because the value of investments in that country also declines.

Trading Money

Exchanging dollars for baht or yen for marks is big business—more than $1 trillion a day.

A country's currency, like its language, is closely linked to its national identity. Some currencies dominate world markets and set standards of value at different points in history. Yet the prospect of any one of them becoming the international currency seems remote. One change on the horizon, though, is the European Union's goal of creating a single currency in 1999.

GERMANY
14.76 marks

CURRENCY TRADING

Money flows across national borders all the time, so foreign exchange—trading one currency for another—flourishes.

Daily trading volume in the foreign exchange, or **forex**, market has increased to more than $1 trillion, according to surveys by the Bank for International Settlements. This rise reflects in part an easing of restrictions on capital flows.

London and New York are the biggest centers for forex trading, followed by Tokyo, Singapore and Hong Kong.

JAPAN
1071 yen

AUSTRALIA
A$12.94

TRADING IN ASIA

The dollar, the mark and the yen—in that order—are the most actively traded currencies around the world, with New Zealand and Australian dollars key currencies in Asia. Currency trading was hugely profitable for banks in the 1980s. But in the 1990s, policy coordination among EU members has decreased market volume for major currencies. As a result, banks are looking more to Asian-Pacific currencies for trading opportunities.

For example, the Thai baht, the Indonesian rupiah, the Malaysian ringgit and other so-called exotic currencies are in increasing demand as bank traders expand their activities in the region.

Trading currency of emerging markets is considered riskier than trading currency of industrialized countries, in part because the economic systems are still developing and in part because there is often less information—or less reliable information—available on the overall financial picture of the countries involved.

INDIA
357.70 rupees

SOUTH KOREA
8124.50 won

THAILAND
252.54 baht

WADING IN
A **shallow currency market** is one where there isn't a lot of currency available to trade—which is often the case in Asia.

Currency rates as of Aug. 1, 1996.

Foreign Exchange

World currencies are traded regularly in the global foreign-exchange market.

Large-scale currency trading is carried out in three different ways:

- **Spot transactions**
- **Forward transactions**
- **Swap contracts**

In spot transactions, the trade occurs immediately and is settled within two days. Forward transactions and foreign exchange swaps are contracts to exchange currency at an agreed-upon price at a future date.

HOW TRADING WORKS

Most bank transactions are conducted over the telephone and registered in a computerized dealing system.

Make a market

If a bank wants to buy a particular currency, a trader calls for a quote from a bank that is a market maker for that currency. That means the bank specializes in handling it.

Get a bid

The bank responds with bid, or buy, and offer, or sell, rates since it doesn't know if the caller wants to buy or sell.

ON THE SPOT

Spot transactions take place in an over-the-counter market rather than at a central location such as an exchange. Trading is handled on the telephone or electronically through a network controlled by banks or other corporations.

Though they account for less than half of the total currency turnover, spot transactions are big-money deals, with minimum trades of $1 million.

The pace is intense. Trading goes on around the clock, throughout what's known as the global trading day, which begins when the New Zealand market opens and runs through the end of New York trading. Published rates are updated constantly, and must be constantly monitored. A good deal usually depends on split-second timing and small differences in price.

Most spot transactions are handled by traders working for large commercial banks, acting either for their corporate or fund clients, or for the banks' own accounts in what's called proprietary trading.

OTHER TRADING SYSTEMS

There are two other, smaller trading systems, a Reuters matching system and an electronic broking system created by banks themselves. Both display currencies and prices on computer monitors. Deals between buyers and sellers are conducted electronically rather than handled by traders on the telephone. The matching system in particular is used for smaller trades, perhaps $1 to $2 million.

This isn't a retail market. Individual investors who want to trade currency put their money into funds, which participate in the market as institutional investors.

EUROCURRENCY

Any major currency on deposit in banks outside the country of origin is known as Eurocurrency, such as **Eurodollars** or **Euroyen**. The money can earn interest, be used to make investments or settle transactions between trading partners, or be loaned. U.S. banks, in fact, borrow Eurodollars regularly.

Eurocurrency is popular in part because it's useful in international trade, where some bills have to be paid in a specific currency, often the dollar.

EURO¥EN

EURODOLLAR$

Stringent banking regulations in certain countries can also make using Eurocurrency more attractive.

Agree to terms

If the caller wants the deal, he or she says so. The bank that quoted a price confirms the details—what's being bought or sold and the price—and the caller verifies the terms.

Confirm deal

The caller who initiated the transaction enters the information in the dealing system and gets a confirmation.

The trade details are also entered in the bank's in-house system, and confirmed with the responding bank at the end of the day, either by phone, fax or messenger.

Transfer payment

Payment is sent by wire transfer to a corresponding currency bank. For example, a New York bank would send payment in yen to its Tokyo branch, or to a designated Japanese bank if it didn't have a branch there.

पचास रुपये

ELECTRONIC EFFECTS

Electronic broking systems are creating more competitive prices, reducing volatility and taking business away from some brokers. Less liquid forex markets are feeling the pinch.

Australia, which was ranked as the ninth-largest forex center in 1995, for example, has been losing its status as a so-called niche market because the systems have removed much of the need for overseas traders to seek a price there.

Australian dealing rooms had traditionally benefited during the period after New York trading winds down and before Tokyo, Hong Kong and Singapore become fully staffed. With the growing use of electronic systems, though, market participants are less likely to divert trades to the Australian market.

LEADING TRADING CENTERS

The top ten currency-trading centers in the world included four in the Asian-Pacific region, as of April 1995:

1. UNITED KINGDOM
2. UNITED STATES
3. JAPAN
4. SINGAPORE
5. HONG KONG
6. SWITZERLAND
7. GERMANY
8. FRANCE
9. AUSTRALIA
10. DENMARK

Stocks: Sharing a Corporation

Stocks are pieces of the corporate pie. When you buy stocks, or shares, you own a slice of the company.

- Owners share in success when company profits
- Owners at risk if company falters

When investors buy stock, or shares, they own a part of the corporation that **issued**, or created, the stock. A stock investment is also known as having **equity**, or an equity position. In general, the extent of equity that specific investors have in a corporation is measured by the number of shares they own.

Investors can buy stocks issued by companies in their native country and **traded**, or bought and sold, through stock markets there. In many cases, they can also buy stocks issued in other countries.

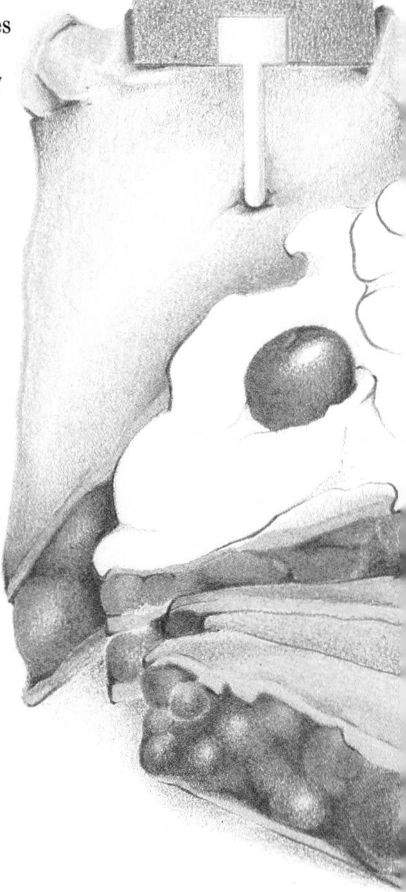

COMMON STOCK

Buying common stocks, sometimes known as ordinary shares, is the most typical way to invest in a corporation. The stocks, or shares, are issued initially by the corporation and sold to individuals or to institutions such as mutual funds or pension funds. After their initial offering, shares are traded regularly, and the price goes up or down in response to how much investors are willing to pay to own them.

Common stocks offer no performance guarantees, so an investor can never be sure of making money on a particular stock or on stock investments in general. At worst it is possible to lose an entire investment, though not more than that because shareholders aren't responsible for corporate debt. But in the U.S., where investment performance is tracked, stocks have, over time, produced better returns than other investments.

CLASSES OF STOCK

Corporations may issue different classes of stock, and list them separately on the stock market. Sometimes a class indicates ownership in a specific division or subsidiary of the company. Other times it indicates that the shares sell at different market prices, have different dividend policies, or impose restrictions on ownership. In Chinese markets, for example, Class A shares are sold to Chinese nationals and Class B shares are available to overseas investors. Class H shares, which trade in Hong Kong, are shares in mainland Chinese companies priced in Hong Kong dollars.

	101½	89	ConsPwr pfG		7.76	8.4	...	1	92½	9
	26⅛	24⅜	ConsPwr pfI		2.08	8.4	...	20	24¾	2
n	25⅞	23⅞	ConsPwr TOPrS		.39p	...	...	10	24⅜	2
n	**33**	**22¾**	**Contifnl**	**CFN**		...	...	**472**	**28⅞**	
s	31⅛	11⅞	ContlAirln A			...	4	31	25	
s	31⅜	11¾	ContlAirln B			...	...	4734	25	
	24¾	13⅛	ContlCan	CAN		...	dd	4	13	
	26	17¾	ContlHome	CON	.20	1.0	5	213	19	
	61¾	33				...	dd	430		

Classes of Stock

BLUE CHIPS

is a term borrowed from poker, where the blue chips are worth the most. When applied to stocks, it refers to the stocks of the largest, most consistently profitable corporations. The list isn't official—and it does change.

SONY
P&O

PREFERRED STOCK

- Dividend payment guaranteed
- Dividends don't usually increase if company prospers

SPLIT STOCK

- More shares created at lower price per share
- Stockholders profit if price goes back up

PREFERENCE SHARES

Preference shares, also known as preferred stocks, are also ownership shares issued by a corporation and traded by investors. They tend to be sold in some markets more frequently than in others.

They differ from common stock in several ways that can reduce investors' risks but may also limit the amount of money they can make. For example, in the U.S., the amount of the yearly dividend is fixed, and it is paid before dividends on common stocks. Preferred stockholders also have a greater chance of getting some of their investment back if the company fails.

But the fixed earnings aren't usually increased if the company makes more money than expected, and the price of preferred stock increases more slowly than common stock.

STOCK SPLITS

When the price of a stock gets too high, investors are often reluctant to buy. Corporations have the option of splitting the stock in an effort to stimulate trading. When a stock is split, there are more shares available at a more accessible price. Stocks can split three for one, three for two, ten for one, or any other combination.

That doesn't mean, however, that the value of the underlying asset has changed. If the company declares a two-for-one split, it gives every shareholder two shares for each one held. At the same time the price per share drops to half. An investor who owned 300 shares now has 600—but the market value is still the same.

REVERSE SPLITS

In a **reverse split** you exchange more shares for fewer—say ten for five—and the price increases accordingly. Reverse splits are sometimes used to raise a stock's price in order to attract institutional investors such as mutual funds or pension funds that may refuse to buy stock costing less than their minimum requirement—often $5.

The Value of Stock

A stock's value rises and falls depending on market conditions, investor perceptions and other factors.

A stock doesn't have a fixed value. Instead, there are several ways to gauge its worth. Price is one measure, with higher prices indicating greater value. Return on investment, or what you get back, is another. The larger your return, the greater the stock's value. Some investors also look for consistency, or a history of strong performance and steady growth. And stocks can also be compared to each other, to assess which is a wiser investment.

TRACKING A STOCK'S VALUE

The peaks and valleys of one stock's price illustrate how value can change over time.

Usually a stock climbs in price when the markets are strong, the company is well-managed and its products or services are in demand. When the three factors occur together, the increase can be rapid.

A stock's price generally moves up and down, even as it continues to increase in value overall. For example, stock market activity might decline, company management could change, or a competitor could introduce a popular new product.

Nothing ultimately dictates the highest price a stock can sell for. As long as people are willing to pay more for it, it will climb in value. But when investors unload shares or the market falls, prices can drop rapidly.

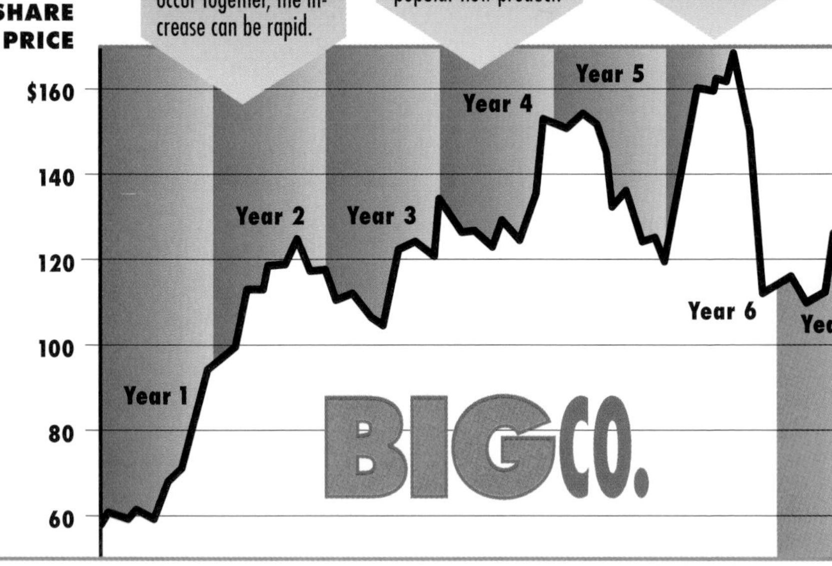

Stocks that pay dividends regularly are known as INCOME STOCKS, while those that pay little or no dividends while reinvesting their profit are known as GROWTH STOCKS.

CYCLICAL STOCKS

Stocks don't act alike. One basic difference is how closely a stock's value, or price, is tied to the condition of the economy. **Cyclical stocks** are shares of companies that are highly dependent on the state of the economy. When things slow down, their earnings fall rapidly, and so do their stock prices. But when the economy recovers, earnings rise rapidly and these stocks recover. Airline and hotel stocks are typically cyclical: people tend to cut back on travel when the economy is slow.

MAKING MONEY WITH STOCKS

Investors buy stocks to make money. One way is through **capital gains**, or making a profit by selling stock at a higher price than you paid for it.

If you buy 100 shares of a U.S. company at $50 a share (for a total investment of $5,000), and sell it for $75 a share (for a total of $7,500), you've realized a capital gain of $25 a share, or $2,500 before brokerage commission or taxes, if they apply.

Some people may also invest in stocks to get quarterly dividend payments. Dividends are the portion of the company's profit paid out to its shareholders. For example, if a company declares an annual dividend of $4 a share, and you own 100 shares, you'll earn $400 dollars a year, or $100 paid each quarter.

If you're buying stocks for the quarterly income, you can figure out the **dividend yield**—the percentage of purchase price you get back through dividends each year. For example, if you buy stock for $100 a share and receive $4 per share, the stock has a dividend yield of 4%. But if you get $4 per share on stock you buy for $50 a share, your yield would be 8%.

Annual Dividend		Purchase Price		Yield
$4	÷	$100	=	4%
$4	÷	$50	=	8%

A company's board of directors decides how large a dividend the company will pay, or whether it will pay one at all. Usually only large, mature companies pay dividends. Smaller ones need to reinvest their profits to continue growing.

Following a price collapse, a stock can recoup its value or continue to decline, depending on its internal strength and what the markets are doing. In this example, the price moved up and down for several years at about $100, the level it had reached several years before.

If a company is out of favor with its shareholders, has serious management problems, or is losing ground to competitors, its value can collapse quickly even if the rest of the market is highly valued. That's what happened here.

However, strong companies can cope with dramatic loss of value and can rebound if internal changes and external conditions create the right environment and investors respond with renewed interest.

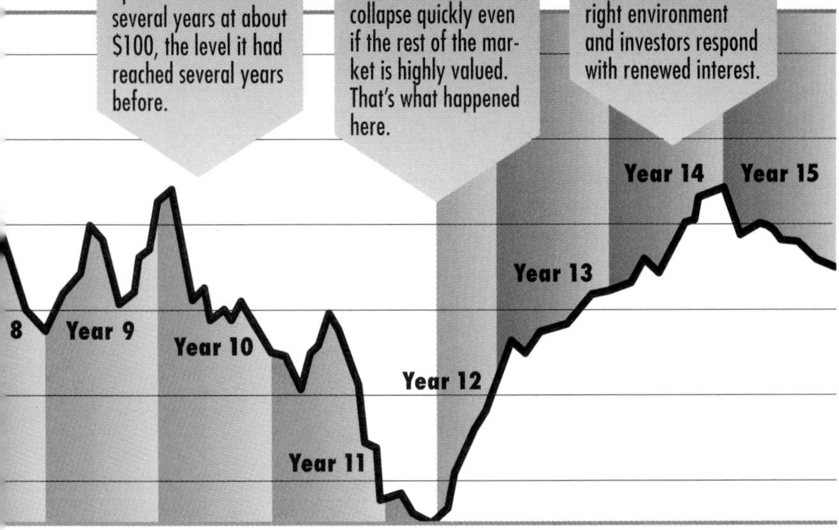

BETTING WITH THE ODDS

Investors who buy a stock believe other people will buy as well, and that the share price is going to increase. Investing is a gamble, but it's not like betting on horses. A long shot can always win the race even if everyone bets the favorite. In the stock market, the betting itself influences the outcome. If lots of investors bet on Atlas stock, Atlas's price will go up. The stock becomes more valuable because investors want it. The reverse is also true: if investors sell Zenon stock, it will fall in value. The more it falls, the more investors will sell.

TIMING IT RIGHT

The trick to making money, of course, is to buy a stock before others want it and sell before they decide to unload. Getting the timing right means you have to pay attention to:

- The rate at which the company's earnings are growing
- Competitiveness of its product or service
- The existence of new markets
- Management strengths and weaknesses
- The overall economic environment in which a company operates

Trading Around the Clock

Stock trading goes on around the world, around the clock, in an electronic global marketplace.

Stock trading goes on nearly 24 hours a day, on dozens of different exchanges on different continents in different time zones.

As the trading ends in one city, activity shifts to a market in another city, sweeping the changes in price around the world. The opening prices in Tokyo or Sydney are influenced by the closing prices in the U.S.—just as Asia's closing prices affect what happens in European trading, and what happens in Europe influences Wall Street. Before the New York markets close, for example, trading begins in Wellington. Two and a half hours after Tokyo closes, London opens. And with two and a half hours to go in London, trading resumes in New York.

The global market explains why a stock can end trading one day at a specific price and open the next day at a different price.

What's still evolving is the extent to which the markets are interrelated. One reason is the growing number of multinational companies that trade on several exchanges. Another is the increasing tendency for investors to buy in many markets, not just their own.

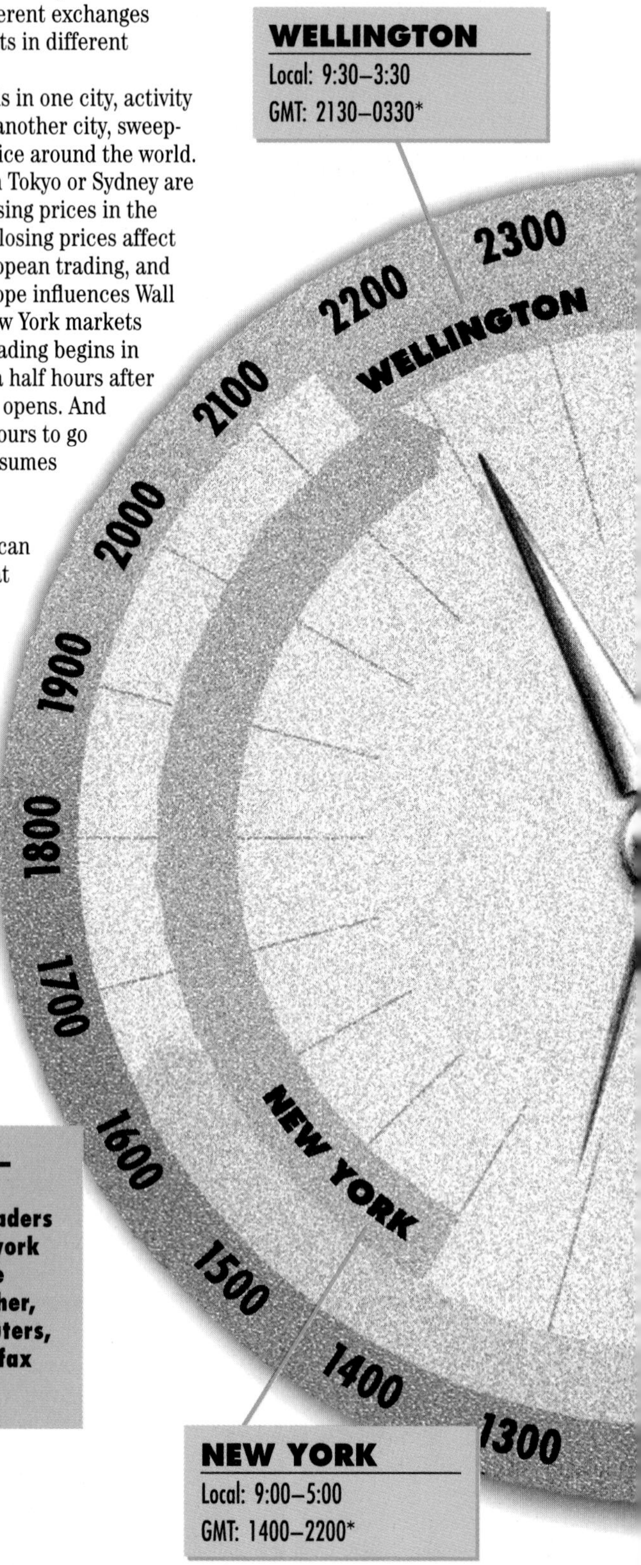

WELLINGTON
Local: 9:30–3:30
GMT: 2130–0330*

2300
2200
WELLINGTON
2100
2000
1900
1800
1700
1600
NEW YORK
1500
1400
1300

NEW YORK
Local: 9:00–5:00
GMT: 1400–2200*

ZONING OUT—OR IN
International traders can—and do—work in one time zone and live in another, thanks to computers, telephones and fax machines.

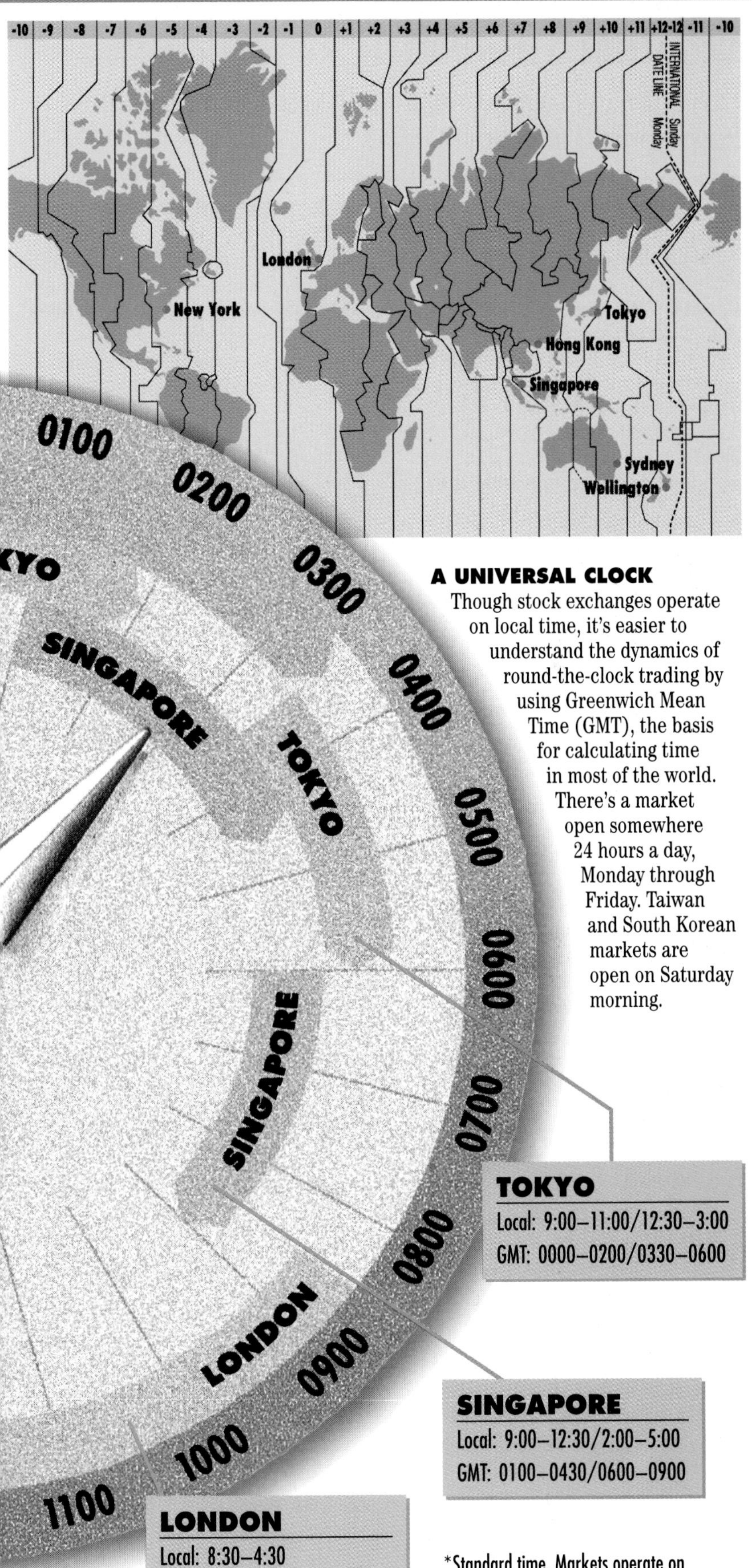

A UNIVERSAL CLOCK

Though stock exchanges operate on local time, it's easier to understand the dynamics of round-the-clock trading by using Greenwich Mean Time (GMT), the basis for calculating time in most of the world. There's a market open somewhere 24 hours a day, Monday through Friday. Taiwan and South Korean markets are open on Saturday morning.

TOKYO
Local: 9:00–11:00/12:30–3:00
GMT: 0000–0200/0330–0600

SINGAPORE
Local: 9:00–12:30/2:00–5:00
GMT: 0100–0430/0600–0900

LONDON
Local: 8:30–4:30
GMT: 0830–1630

*Standard time. Markets operate on daylight savings time part of the year.

Global Investing

Investors looking for ways to diversify their portfolios have a world of opportunity.

Investors who want to balance some of the risks of investing in their domestic stock market seek **diversification**, or variety, in their portfolios, and put money into equities in other countries. The assumption is that an economic downturn at home could be offset by profits in other, presumably better-performing, economies.

In the best of circumstances, investors benefit from such diversification in three ways—in what many investment professionals call the **triple whammy**:

- The stock rises in price, potentially providing **capital gains**
- The investment pays **dividends**
- The country's **currency rises** against the domestic currency, so that when investors sell they take more money home

In addition, many companies list stock on exchanges in other countries, making international investing easy. For example, about 400 companies based in other countries are traded on U.S. exchanges, and over 100 Malaysian stocks are listed in Singapore.

TAKING SOME RISKS

Buying stocks in other countries is no less risky than buying in your home market. Prices fall, economies sag and dividends get cut. And there are some additional pitfalls that can catch unwary investors, especially those investing in **emerging markets**, or countries that seem positioned to expand but may be less stable. Here are some of the common dangers to take into account:

- There may be large taxes on **capital gains**, or profits
- Accounting and trading rules may be weighted against certain investors
- Exchanging one currency for another may mean additional expense
- Unexpected changes in interest rates or currency values can cause major losses
- It may be difficult to get full disclosure of financial and management details

AMERICAN DEPOSITARY RECEIPTS

One way to invest in foreign companies in a well-regulated environment is through **American depositary receipts (ADRs)**. An ADR is a security that is sold in the U.S. that represents a specific number of shares in a non-U.S. company that have

The Currency Risk—and its Reward

One of the greatest variables in calculating the risks and rewards of international investing hinges on the change in currency values. If a currency shrinks in value, investors using

	STOCK PRICE IN YEN
BUY • A$ is strong	100 Shares @ **290** yen per share
SELL • Stock rises • A$ weak	100 Shares @ **348** yen per share
SELL • Stock rises • A$ is strong	100 Shares @ **348** yen per share
SELL • Stock drops • A$ weak	100 Shares @ **261** yen per share
SELL • Stock rises • A$ very strong	100 Shares @ **348** yen per share
SELL • Stock drops • A$ very strong	100 Shares @ **261** yen per share

been deposited in a bank in trust for the investor. The bank also pays dividends in dollars and handles tax payments.

About 30% of the roughly 1,200 ADRs in existence trade on a major U.S. stock market, accounting for about 5% of the listings. Only a few dozen of them are Asian. Exchange-listing requires the issuing company to provide an English-language version of its annual report, use U.S. accounting practices and extend certain shareholder rights. The remaining ADRs trade over the counter, and aren't required to provide the same level of financial information.

ADRs are traded the way stocks are, most of them changing hands among investors, with a smaller number sold in initial public offerings (see pages 42–43). There is an exception though: if demand for stock is strong in the home market, the ADR may be **unmade**, or broken into individual shares to be sold domestically. **GDRs**, or **global depositary receipts**, are similar investments that are sold in a variety of currencies world-wide. Indian companies have spearheaded the GDR drive to get around market rules at home.

that currency can benefit, especially if they hold stock sold in a stronger currency. Just the opposite happens if the currencies move in the opposite directions.

In this example, you can see the various outcomes of currency and stock market fluctuations for an Australian investor who buys Japanese stock when the Australian dollar drops 15% in value or gains 25%. In three situations, the result is a gain, or profit. In two others, when the A$ is strong against the yen, the result is a loss.

To figure the stock price, divide the price per share by the exchange rate.

$$\frac{\text{price per share}}{\text{exchange rate}} = \text{stock price}$$

To figure the gain or loss, divide the difference between the sale price and the initial cost by the initial cost.

$$\frac{\text{sales price} - \text{initial cost}}{\text{initial cost}} = \text{gain or loss}$$

EXCHANGE RATE	STOCK VALUE IN A$	GAIN OR LOSS	
A$ = 86 yen	A$337		
A$ = 73 yen	A$477	42% GAIN	The double advantage of a higher stock price and a lower A$ produced a A$477 sale price, for a A$140—or 42%—per share profit.
A$ = 86 yen	A$405	20% GAIN	Because the stock price increased and there was no change in the exchange rate, the A$405 sale price was A$68 more than the purchase price, or a 20% gain.
A$ = 73 yen	A$358	6% GAIN	Investors can make money on a dropping share price if the value of the A$ also drops. In this example the price drops to A$358, but there's a A$21—or 6%—profit.
A$ = 108 yen	A$322	4% LOSS	Investors can lose money when the A$ increases in value if they bought before the value increased. Here, the A$322 sale price means a 4% loss.
A$ = 108 yen	A$242	28% LOSS	The biggest losses occur when the value of the A$ increases and the share price drops. Here, a return of A$242 a share produces a 28% loss.

Value of A$ and yen as of July 18, 1996, rounded to nearest whole number.

Open Markets

In an open market, information is accurate and easily available and trading practices are fair.

Stock markets exist for many of the same reasons wherever they are: to raise investment capital, centralize buying and selling of shares, provide investors with financial incentives to put money into stock and in some places to create a marketplace for privatizing state assets. Those similarities mean that people can and do look for investment opportunities beyond their home markets.

At the same time, the structure and operation of stock markets vary. So do shareholder rights, corporate disclosure rules and accounting practices. That's why sophisticated investors are increasingly demanding the use of shareholder-friendly rules. And they put their money where their demands are met.

That's one reason the world-wide trend is toward more openness—**transparency** is the term of choice among investors—and less tolerance for insider trading and other abuses that have sometimes limited the appeal of certain stock markets. It also explains continuing reforms in market procedures, lower taxes and other moves to attract investors.

Among the reasons that full disclosure continues to be a problem in some markets are the perception that more information could lead to higher taxation or greater competition, and the reluctance of some managers to yield control over corporate decisions.

THE RIGHT TO VOTE

Investors who own U.S. stocks have the right to vote on major policy decisions, such as whether to issue additional stock, sell the company to outside buyers, or change the board of directors. In general, the more stock investors own, the more votes they have.

Most voting is done by **proxy**, an absentee ballot that's distributed to all shareholders before the annual meeting, though all shareholders have the right to attend and to vote there. The proxy contains detailed information about stock performance, executive salaries and shareholder proposals.

In the past, many shareholders simply voted as management suggested, but with more institutional investors owning large blocks of stock, corporate management has had to listen more closely to shareholder concerns not only in the U.S. but around the world.

AN UNOFFICIAL STANDARD

There is no official international regulatory standard for stock markets to meet, but unofficially the U.S. is considered the benchmark for accessibility and fair play. One reason is the steps the government has taken over the years to protect investors from abuses and to provide them with enough information so they can make well-reasoned decisions about where to put their money. For instance, annual reports are required.

Following the crash of 1929 and the stock-trading practices it exposed, the U.S. government created the Securities and Exchange Commission (SEC). Its mission is to regulate the activities of stock traders and administer the laws that govern the U.S. securities markets.

It also works to ensure that the markets operate honestly and fairly. When necessary, the SEC enforces securities law with various sanctions, from fines to prosecution.

SHAREHOLDERS' MEETING

INSIDER TRADING

In the U.S., the SEC monitors **insider trading**, which occurs when corporate officers or others with privileged information buy or sell stock in their own company or advise other investors to.

Insider trading is legitimate as long as it is done openly. In fact, knowing whether corporate officers are buying or selling their own stock can be a valuable forecaster of changes in the stock's price.

However, insiders can manipulate trading so that their own profits and other investors' losses are magnified. That's illegal in the U.S., as are efforts to hide trades by having a third party buy or sell. But in other markets, manipulation has been a recurrent problem despite efforts at increased government regulation.

SOKAIYA

The *sokaiya*, or gangsters who seek to extort money from Japanese companies by threatening to disrupt their annual meetings, have prompted companies, concerned about their image, to fight back. They hold their meetings at the same time, to make it harder for the sokaiya to make good on their threats. Of course, this kind of scheduling also makes it harder for activist shareholders to attend many meetings.

ONE CHANGING MARKET

Small and overseas investors have limited clout in Japan, partly due to the existence of **keiretsu**, large conglomerates or chains of affiliated companies.

Such a corporate alliance could involve, for instance, a bank, several manufacturers and a trading company, each of which owns part of the others, effectively excluding small shareholders—domestic and international—from exerting influence on share price or corporate policy.

But government regulations making payoffs illegal, simplifying rules allowing suits against corporations and requiring additional financial disclosures, particularly about the operation of subsidiary companies, have made the market operations more shareholder friendly.

Other signs that Japanese companies are becoming more aware of shareholder interests are moves to increase dividends, something allied companies wouldn't demand, and to buy back some of their own shares in order to boost the price.

But annual meetings still don't include voting on key decisions. Nor are insistent questions or persistent shareholders welcome.

Simply put, the SEC's role is twofold:

- **To see that investors are fully informed about securities being offered for sale**
- **To prevent misrepresentations, deceit and other types of fraud in securities transactions**

In addition to the SEC, most U.S. markets have their own regulatory bodies to monitor activities. They include the governing bodies of the major exchanges, the National Association of Securities Dealers (NASD), the Commodity Futures Trading Commission (CFTC) and the National Futures Association (NFA).

Buying Stocks

Buying stocks isn't hard, but the process has its own rules, its own distinctive language and a special cast of characters.

To buy or sell a stock in many countries, you usually have to go through a **brokerage house**, an investment firm that is a member of a **stock exchange**. Your deal is handled by a **stockbroker**. In some places, such as the U.S., the broker has to pass an exam on securities law and register with the body that regulates the investment industry.

Increasingly, though, you can buy stocks directly from certain companies, either through dividend reinvestment plans or on the Internet.

WHAT'S IN A NAME?

Though a broker is generally recognized as someone who buys and sells stocks, the financial markets use other, not so widely recognized, job descriptions to identify the various ways securities change hands and the people who get the job done.

Brokers act as agents to execute buy and sell orders from the investing public.

Dealers are people or firms that buy and sell securities as principals rather than agents, making their money on the difference between the cost of buying and the price for selling.

Traders, also called registered or competitive traders, buy and sell for their own accounts. People who buy and sell for broker/dealers or financial institutions are also called traders.

ROUND LOTS

When you buy through a broker, usually you buy or sell stock in multiples of 100 shares, called a **round lot**. Small investors can buy just a single share, or any number they can afford. That's called an **odd lot**. Brokers often charge more to buy and to sell odd lot orders.

A **broker**, originally, was a wine seller who broached—broke open—wine casks. Today's broker has a less liquid but often heady job as a financial agent.

CUSTOMER

PLACES ORDERS TO BUY AND SELL

When you tell your broker to buy or sell, you're giving an order. A **market order** tells your broker to act now to get the best buy or sell price available at the moment. Or you can give your broker more specific guidelines.

If you think the price of a stock you want to buy is going down, you can place a **limit order**. That way your broker will buy only when the price falls to the amount you've named.

Similarly, if you own a stock that's rising in value, you can place a **limit order to sell**. That means your broker will sell only if and when it climbs to the pre-established price.

Finally, if you own a stock that is declining in price, you might want to place a **stop loss order**. That tells your broker to sell if the price falls to a certain level, in order to prevent further losses.

TIMING YOUR ORDERS

Orders can specify time limits as well as price limits. When you give a stop order or a limit order, your broker will ask if you want it to be **good 'til cancelled (GTC)** or a **day order**. A GTC stands until it is either filled or you cancel it. A day order is cancelled automatically if it isn't filled that day.

RECORDING OWNERSHIP
Before the era of electronic record-keeping, you got securities, or written proofs of ownership, when you bought U.S. shares. These stock certificates are distinctive documents, some with elaborate designs that indicate your name, the number of shares, and various registration details. Today, most ownership records are stored in computer files, even though investments are still referred to as securities. You may even be charged a fee if you request a certificate.

BROKERAGE FIRM

HANDLES TRANSACTION

Some brokers spend a lot of time researching investments, helping clients develop goals and giving advice. They are often called **full-service brokers** and charge investors a **commission**, or fee, for their services.

Other brokers, called **discount brokers**, merely act as the agent for an investor, executing buy and sell orders, but offering no investment advice. But their commissions are usually much lower than a full-service broker's.

Finally, for investors who trade often or in large blocks of stock, there are **deep discount brokers**, whose commissions are lowest of all.

FREE-LANCE BROKERS
In Singapore, free-lance stock salesmen are active, working almost totally on commission, and personally assuming the risks their clients take in investing in particular stocks. That's different from the U.S. where, in most cases, brokers aren't held responsible for client losses.

These remisiers—the French word means to recruit business—are free to speculate in the market. But if their losses wipe out their clients and themselves, the firms they work for must ultimately bear the financial responsibility.

STOCK MARKET

REFLECTS ACTIVITY

Trading activity in individual stocks is reported daily in The Asian Wall Street Journal. Overall movement in the stock markets is tracked by a variety of indexes and averages. Investors can use that information to analyze the impact of their buy and sell decisions on their portfolios and to plan future trades.

STREET NAME
If you have a brokerage account with your broker's company, you can have your stocks registered in street name, or the name of the brokerage firm. One advantage is that if you want to sell shares, they're already in your broker's hands. You don't have to sign them and have them delivered before the sale can be confirmed. And you don't have to worry about losing them.

Some investors prefer to keep registration in their own names, though, in order to participate in dividend reinvestment programs without paying brokerage commissions on the purchases. With dividend reinvestment, anything you earn can be used to buy additional shares, including fractional shares. That way, your money is always invested.

Selling New Stock

The first time companies issue stock, it's called an **initial public offering**, or **IPO**.

To take a company public, which means making it possible for investors to buy the stock, the management registers the stock with a regulatory body, and makes an **initial public offering (IPO)**.

HOW IPOs WORK

If a small company finds its product or service in great demand, it quickly outstrips the ability of venture capitalists to provide money for rapid growth. That's when it decides to offer shares to the public.

The company goes to **investment bankers** who agree to **underwrite** the stock offering—that is, to buy all the public shares at a set price and resell them to the general public, hopefully at a profit. They sometimes also organize meetings between the company's management and large potential investors, such as managers of pension or mutual funds.

The underwriters help the company prepare a **prospectus**, a detailed analysis of the company's financial history, its products or services, and management's background and experience. The document also assesses the various risks the company faces.

SETTING A PRICE

The day before the actual sale, underwriters **price the issue**, or establish the price they will pay for each share. That's the amount the company receives from the stock sale.

When the stock begins trading, the price can rise or fall depending on whether investors agree or disagree with the underwriters' valuation of the new company.

FROM PRIVATE TO PUBLIC OWNERSHIP

The road to public ownership often begins with an **entrepreneur** who has come up with an idea for a product or service and borrows enough money to launch a start-up business. If the company grows, the entrepreneur can get funds for expansion in the **private equity market**.

There, sophisticated investors have assembled pools of money, called **venture capital**, that they're willing to risk on a new business in exchange for a role in how the company is run and a share of the profits.

A company gets the money only when stocks are issued. All subsequent trading means a profit or loss for the stockholder, but nothing for the company that issued it.

SELLING DIRECT

Some small companies are taking a short-cut to an IPO through direct offerings. A do-it-yourself offering saves them money by eliminating the role of underwriters. Companies still generally need to meet the regulator's filing rules. Because they're usually not listed on an exchange, or followed by market analysts, trading is often **thin**, or infrequent.

TRAVELING IPOs

When a company is considering an IPO, one of the considerations is finding the market that will provide the greatest amount of capital. That's why many Asian companies have chosen to go public in the U.S. rather than—or sometimes in addition to—their own country.

To sell shares in a market, the company must meet that market's listing requirements. Some companies, for example, choose to sell their stock as American depositary receipts, rather than seek full U.S. listing, because some of the rules are less stringent.

SECONDARY OFFERINGS

If a company has already issued shares, but wants to raise additional **capital**, or money, through the sale of more stock, the process is called a **secondary offering**.

Usually a company issues new stock only if its stock price is high. That helps minimize complaints from existing shareholders that their shares are being diluted, or reduced in value. Sometimes, if the company's management thinks the shares are too cheap, it will buy some back to boost the value of the remaining ones.

ASIAN IPO WATCH

INDONESIA

PT Kedawung Group—40 billion rupees. Opens: July 26. Bhakti Investama.

PT Bank BNI—1.8 trillion rupiah. Opens: July. Danareksa Sekuritas.

PT Selamat Sempurna—80 billion rupiah. 25%. Opens: August.

PT Krakatau Steel—1.2 trillion rupiah. Opens: October.

PT Sempati Air—200 billion rupiah. 15%-20%. Opens: October. Bahana Securities.

PT Bank Umum Servitia—16 billion rupiah. 10%. Opens: 1996. Makindo Securities.

Wan Hai 13. Listing
Univers 19.5%. Ope
Acer P June. Listi
Chiao T wan Intern
China C Listing: La
Ritek C ties.

Privatization

When governments sell their assets or sign contracts to provide public services, it's called privatization.

Privatization, which means selling part or all of government enterprises to individual and institutional investors, is a major economic trend around the world. Since the process can take different forms, other ways to describe it are as a transfer of ownership, called **denationalization**, or as a shifting of responsibility for providing goods and services from the public sector to the private sector.

Privatizations are taking place around the world. The largest single sale was of shares in Japan's Nippon Telegraph & Telephone in 1988. One of the most extensive campaigns was launched by New Zealand, beginning in 1987.

PUBLIC OWNERSHIP

Public ownership means that governments own and operate national enterprises.

WHY PRIVATIZE?

There are many motives to privatize, most of them economic. One theory, for example, is that privately run enterprises are more efficient than public ones, so that private ownership or operation provides better service or superior products at lower cost.

In addition, selling off attractive assets, such as telephone companies and natural resources, can raise substantial amounts of cash to offset financial problems brought on by public debt or provide cash infusions to bolster the economy and attract outside investors.

Another reason to privatize is to dispose of holdings that are a drain on public resources, such as hospitals or transportation systems, because they're expensive to operate and don't produce enough income to offset costs.

Political philosophy sometimes also plays a large role in the decision to privatize, with attitudes toward the role of government and free-market forces shaping action.

PROS AND CONS

In the privatization debate, there are strong arguments on both sides:

Pros

- Provides infusion of capital
- Introduces stronger management
- Eases or eliminates debt
- Brings nations and companies into the economic mainstream

Cons

- Potential loss of jobs and employee benefits
- Redistribution of wealth into fewer hands
- Potential outside control of national resources

NATIONAL TELECOMM

A GOLDEN SHARE

Governments sometimes like to keep a hand in the company being privatized by holding onto a special class of stock, called "golden share," with special voting privileges. The New Zealand government, for instance, kept a voice in the country's telecommunications company to insure that coverage remained universal.

TAKING SOME RISKS

In privatization, both governments and investors take some risks. From a government's perspective, there's always a question of whether it will raise enough money to justify the sale, what will happen to citizens if unemployment increases and services cost more, and how private ownership will affect its own power base.

Investors must consider the potential for government interference, especially when it remains a partial owner, and the impact of reserving shares for special interest groups or powerful families. They also have to factor in the impact of the enterprise's existing debts as well as the more traditional market and interest-rate risks that any equity purchase involves.

WHO BUYS?

The company being privatized and the bank doing the deal usually prefer selling to an institutional investor. A retail investor would have to be sophisticated and wealthy to get involved in that kind of offering. One option, though, is to put money into mutual funds that invest in a region or industry affected by privatization.

PRIVATE OWNERSHIP

When governments sell these assets, the ownership passes into private hands.

HOW PRIVATIZATION WORKS

Moving government assets into the private sector can be handled three ways, listed in order of popularity:

DIRECT SALES

Direct sales to strategic investors, often through an auction process. The new owners may then offer shares to the public, either domestically or internationally.

PUBLIC OFFERINGS

Public offerings, coordinated through one or more investment banks. In practice, it works much like an IPO in private industry (see page 42). However, most of the shares sold internationally go to institutional, rather than individual, investors.

OPEN SALES OR GIFTING

Sale or gifting of shares to citizens, who can hold them or sell to investment companies. Singapore, for example, sold shares in its telephone company through bank ATM machines.

One of the key debates in formulating a public offering focuses on the role of international investors, including whether there will be separate **tranches**, or groups of shares, sold domestically or elsewhere, whether or not the separate shares are **fungible**, or interchangeable, and how large a stake international investors can hold.

Among the things privatizing governments have learned are that if they're going to fulfill their goals, they must create a mechanism that allows the transfer to take place smoothly, protect the interests of the workers and strengthen the regulatory framework to prevent abuses. Some governments also offer incentives to make the shares more attractive to domestic investors, including discounts on pricing, the opportunity to buy on an installment plan and bonus shares if the investor holds the stock for a specific period of time.

Stock Buyers

All investors buy stock for the same reason: to make money. But they do their buying differently.

From China to Wall Street, the number of people investing in markets is climbing. But individual investors aren't the only participants. Institutional investors, including mutual funds and pension funds, have become major players in many markets. People with money in such funds have indirect stock investments, but no real role in what's bought and sold.

BUYING STYLES

There are two basic styles or approaches to buying stocks. Some individual investors look for quick profits in hot stocks. Called **day traders** or market timers, they buy stocks whose price they expect to rise dramatically in a short time. When the price goes up, they sell and buy something else.

Other investors take a longer-term view, preferring to **buy and hold** a stock—in some cases for years—until it gains substantially in price. They're also interested in the dividends they're earning.

Institutional investors, including those using sophisticated analytical computer programs, also have buying styles that help determine the kind of investments they make and how long they hold them. Pension funds, for example, need to have money available for payouts over a fixed schedule and must invest to meet those requirements.

In some Asian markets, there are daily high and low limits on stock prices to prevent sudden dramatic changes.

INSTITUTIONAL INVESTORS

An institutional investor is an organization that invests its own assets or those it holds in trust for others. Typical institutional investors are investment companies (including mutual funds), pension systems, insurance companies, universities and banks. For example, California's $100 billion public pension fund, Calpers, had $58 billion, or 58% of its assets, invested in stocks in mid-1996. Because they have so much money to invest, institutional investors trade regularly and in enormous volume.

In the U.S., a buy or sell order must be 10,000 shares or more to be considered an institutional trade. In some other markets, however, the figure is 5,000 shares. In either case, that's a small number for a big mutual fund eager to put its investors' money to work.

PROGRAM TRADING

Some institutional investors speed up the process of buying and selling stock by using program trading techniques that involve placing large orders by computer. The programs are sometimes triggered automatically, when prices hit predetermined levels.

Such sudden buying or selling can cause abrupt price changes or even dramatic shifts in the entire market. The stock market crash of 1987 occurred, at least in part, because of program trading triggered by falling prices. Rules have been crafted since then to slow down program trading in the U.S. after the key index drops by 50 points or more in a day. Much larger point drops can trigger a halt in all trading for a period.

ON-LINE TRADING

Investors typically trade stocks through traditional brokerage accounts, usually giving their instructions over the telephone. But electronic trading, which lets you buy and sell on-line, is an emerging force in the marketplace. Most experts expect that the number of these accounts—about 1% of the number of traditional ones in the U.S., though not yet handling 1% of the trading volume—will escalate as more brokerage houses offer the service and more computer-literate people move into investing.

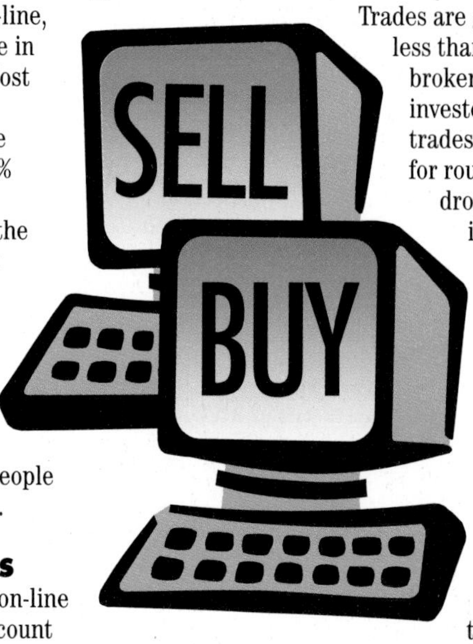

HOW IT WORKS

Investors establish on-line accounts with a discount broker offering the service, and access them either through the Internet's World Wide Web or by using software that works with a commercial service. Many of the brokerage houses provide access to research, including price histories, performance reports and portfolio tracking.

Most brokerage houses automatically search a number of exchanges to find the best price, and some of them provide price improvement, which means they find a lower buying price or a higher selling price than you gave in your order.

There are other big advantages to on-line investing. You can access your account from anywhere in the world. Trades are generally handled in less than a minute, and many brokers charge individual investors a flat fee for most trades. In fact, commissions for routine trades may drop as competition intensifies. So it always pays to shop around for the best deal.

In the same vein, some brokers make on-line investing easier than others, by displaying the current stock price at the beginning of the transaction and making the instructions easy to follow. Potential investors can usually visit the broker's Web site before opening an account, to get a sense of how it works.

SECURITY CONCERNS

All investors want to know that they'll actually own the stocks they pay for, and that they're the only ones that can make trades. That's one of the reasons that settling transactions efficiently is so important to a well-run stock market.

Trading on-line can raise some additional concerns. Most brokerage houses have developed electronic safeguards to protect accounts, usually requiring one and sometimes two passwords to execute an order. In addition, transactions are confirmed on the screen, and then again by e-mail or telephone as well as by mail.

Sifting Stock Information

Investors need to assess information about stocks and the companies that issue them.

Although the stock tables are the logical place to start, there is a lot of other information investors and investment professionals can use to evaluate stocks.

GETTING INFORMATION

In order to make smart buy and sell decisions, investors need information, including details of how a company is performing. Ideally, they should look at four sets of numbers that are good indicators of the shape a company is in—and whether its stock is likely to be a good investment.

- **The book value** is the difference between the company's assets and its liabilities. In the U.S., for example, stocks typically trade at 1½ times book value, while in some other countries they trade at 3½ times book value.
- **The earnings per share** are calculated by dividing the number of shares into the profit. If earnings increase each year, the company is growing.
- **The return on equity** is figured by dividing the company's earnings per share by its book value.
- **The payout ratio** is the percentage of net earnings a company uses to pay its dividend. The normal range in the U.S. is 25% to 50% of net earnings. A higher ratio can mean the company is struggling to meet its obligations.

DARTBOARD ANALYSIS

Some experts argue that unforeseen events at a company or in the economy at large can radically alter any stock's prospects, undermining the value of any kind of extensive analysis. In that vein, **dart board analysis** concludes that you make out just as well if you throw darts at the stock pages and buy what you hit. Results of a continuing competition between investment professionals and dart throwers are published bimonthly in the Hong Kong Week section of The Asian Wall Street Journal.

BIGCO.

Consolidated Financial Highlights

For the Year

Revenues
Operating earnings
Operating earnings per common share
Net income
Net income per common share
Dividends paid per common share

At Year-End

Total investments
Total assets
Common shareholders' equity
Book value per common share

Operating Earnings Per Common Share

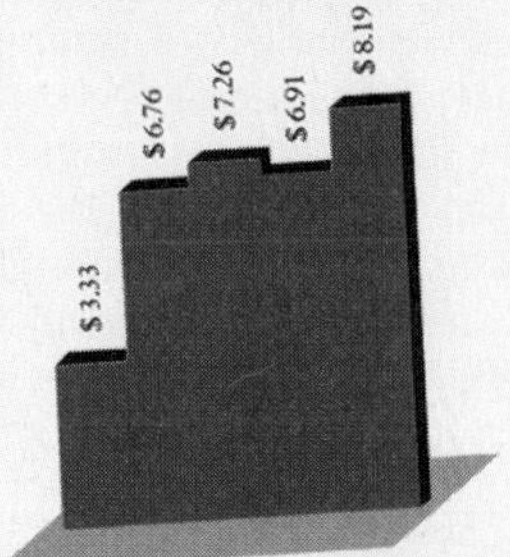

Record per share 1996 operating earnings (excluding realized investment gains) exceeded the previous high year by 13%.

Contents

ANALYTICAL METHODS

Investment professionals analyze stock information in different ways. Those who do **fundamental analysis** study a company's financial condition, its management and its competitive position in its industry, or sector. They may also look at the performance of the economy at large, including interest rates, unemployment and a range of other factors.

Those who do **technical analysis** chart past market performance to identify price trends and cyclical movements of particular stocks, industries or the market as a whole.

Some experts argue that research is overrated because individual stocks, as well as the broader markets, respond to such an unpredictable range of factors.

1996	1985	Percent Change
$ 4,005,237,000	$ 3,788,648,000	5.7
$ 385,458,000	$ 338,267,000	14.0
$ 8.19	$ 6.91	18.5
$ 391,270,000	$ 398,158,000	(1.7)
$ 8.31	$ 8.12	2.3
$ 2.35	$ 2.15	9.3
$ 8,467,668,000	$ 8,106,756,000	4.5
$12,203,990,000	$11,030,066,000	10.6
$ 2,196,371,000	$ 2,349,254,000	(6.5)
$ 52.00	$ 47.65	9.1

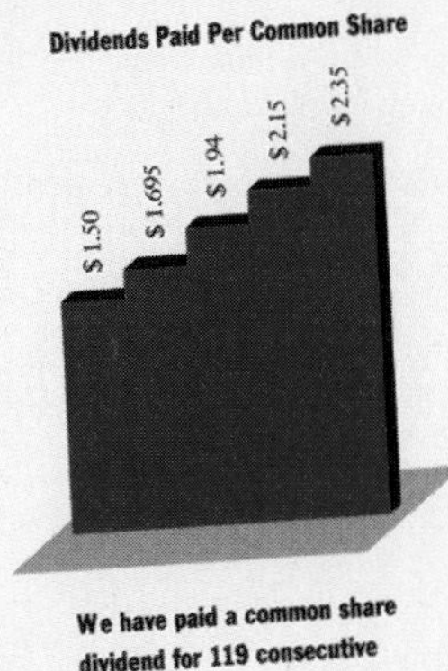

We have paid a common share dividend for 119 consecutive years.

d by
nings
nds) by
s' equity

SIZE MAKES A DIFFERENCE

A company's size can be a major factor when investors are deciding which stocks to buy. Size, usually calculated by **capitalization**, or the total value of the company's outstanding stocks, bonds and other securities, influences not only the amount of information that's available, but the ease with which the stock can be bought and sold, and the kinds of risks an investor takes in buying it.

In the U.S., companies are divided into three size categories: large, midsized and small. In general, the larger the company is, the easier it is to get detailed performance and management information. Because there's lots of information, more people are interested. That makes it easier to buy and sell shares. The smallest companies are often **thinly,** or infrequently, traded, which can make their stock difficult to sell quickly.

PUTTING NUMBERS TO USE

Using information wisely often depends on knowing why a number is the way it is. A small or low book value resulting from too much debt, for example, means that the company's profits will be limited even if it does lots of business. But sometimes a low book value means the company's assets are underestimated, making it a good investment.

THE ANNUAL REPORT

An annual report usually includes a section outlining the company's philosophy and detailed reports on each segment of its operations. Profit-and-loss statements and the annual balance sheet are also included, along with an auditor's letter verifying that the financial information is fair and accurate.

Stock Quotations

Up-to-date information is the lifeblood of stock trading, and price quotations are reported electronically.

When brokers and investors want the most up-to-date information on stock market activity, they refer to a band of rapidly moving price quotations on a Dow Jones Markets screen such as the one shown here on a computer. Stock prices and details of trading activity are relayed to brokerage firms and investment professionals in a constant, up-to-the-minute stream.

The prices that appear on electronic display boards in brokers' offices, on home computers via information retrieval services, or on cable network television are delayed in some markets. But electronic services such as Dow Jones Markets offer real-time pricing information.

SCROLLING NEWS

Brokers can search for past news stories, file important facts and react to important investment alerts from the minute-by-minute updating of world-wide financial news, such as the intervention sparked by the drop in the Canadian dollar highlighted here.

INDEX MOVEMENT

The current market indexes, the direction they're moving and their gain or loss are reported. Here the Dow Jones Industrial Average is at 5435 (see pages 74–75).

STOCK QUOTATIONS

Current stock prices and trading details for companies identified only by their trading symbols flow across the screen as issues are traded. In this example, 100 shares of this stock were just sold for $50 a share, up 1⅝, producing a dividend yield of 5.2%.

WATCHING THE SCREEN

Brokers keep one eye on the band and the other on the rest of the information on the screen. Modern computer terminals provide endless data about any single stock, the overall condition of the stock market and the latest breaking news on the economy—all at the touch of a few buttons.

For example, the terminal can be set to alert the broker to an unusual price move in a stock or to signal that a stock has hit a predetermined level for a buy or sell.

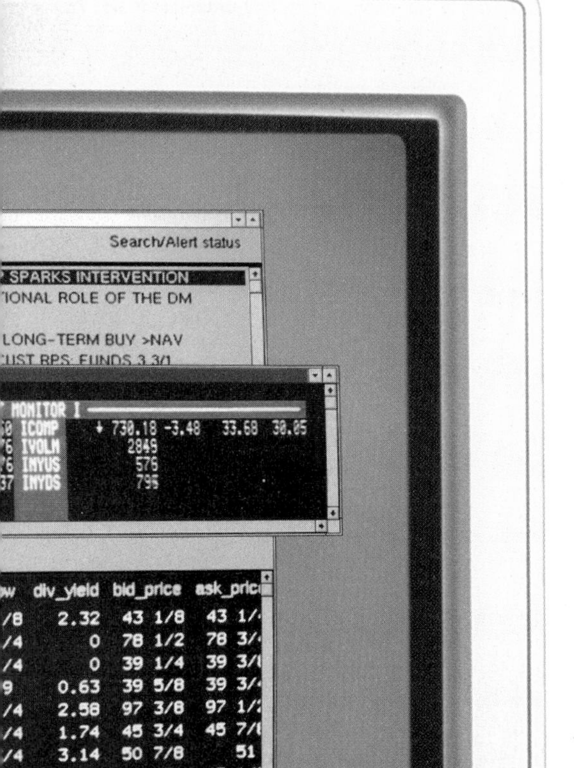

STOCK SYMBOLS

When a stock is listed in a U.S. market, it is identified by a **trading symbol**, a letter or combination of letters. Some symbols are easy to connect to their companies, such as IBM for International Business Machines or DJ for Dow Jones, but others can be harder to figure out. That often happens when companies have similar names or the logical symbol is already being used by another company.

The symbols for stocks listed on the New York and American exchanges range from one to three letters, with the briefest enjoying some added prestige. Those traded on the newer Nasdaq market have four- or five-letter designations. The one designation no company wants, though, is the letter Q. It's used for bankruptcies.

BEFORE ELECTRONICS

The impact of electronic information is being felt in stock markets around the world. For example, before Thailand's computerized order-matching system was inaugurated in 1991, traders used a "board knocking" system. As changing prices were written on a marker board, traders who wanted to buy or sell rapped on the board with a wooden stick. Confirmations that today are instantaneous took at least a day.

Ticker tape, once the primary method of reporting trading activity in the U.S., has disappeared too.

Selling Short

Some stock investors take added risks in the hope of greater returns.

Most stock transactions are fairly straightforward, with investors buying or selling shares at their current value. But investors can also **sell short** in some markets or **buy warrants**, trying to increase their gains. However, they have to be willing to take the risk of potentially greater losses that can occur. In each case, the approach is based on a calculated wager that a particular stock will have a marked change in value in the near future.

How Selling Short Works

Selling short is a way of participating in the stock market by borrowing and selling stocks you expect to decline in value. To sell short, you borrow shares from your broker, sell them and pocket the money. Then you wait, expecting the price of the stock to drop. If it does, you buy the shares at the lower price and return them to your broker to settle the loan (plus some interest and commission). For example, you sell short 100 shares of stock at $10 a share. When the price drops, you buy 100 shares at $7.50 a share, give them to your broker, and keep the $2.50-a-share difference as profit—minus commission. Buying shares back is called **covering the short position**. When the shares drop in price, your cost to replace them is less than the money you received from their sale, so you make a profit.

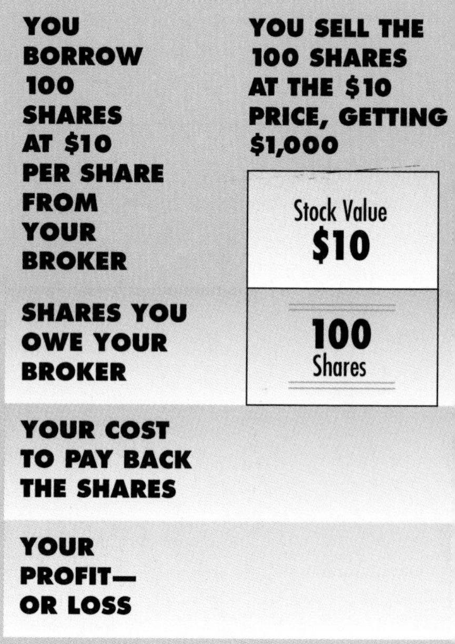

YOU BORROW 100 SHARES AT $10 PER SHARE FROM YOUR BROKER

YOU SELL THE 100 SHARES AT THE $10 PRICE, GETTING $1,000

Stock Value **$10**

SHARES YOU OWE YOUR BROKER

100 Shares

YOUR COST TO PAY BACK THE SHARES

YOUR PROFIT—OR LOSS

LIMITED APPEAL
Short selling is used more often in some markets than in others. But it is barred in some areas.

The frequency of short selling fluctuates noticeably even where it is customary. In general, interest in short sales increases when the market is booming but the economy isn't keeping pace. Sellers believe that a correction, or drop in the market, has to come, and that stocks will drop in value. They want to make money on those losses.

MARKET CYCLES
Stock markets rise when investors are putting money into shares, and fall when they are selling. A number of factors influence whether people buy or sell, as well as when and why they do so.

Changing market direction doesn't always mirror the state of a country's economy. In the U.S., the crash of 1987 occurred in a period of economic growth, and the market boomed in the 1990s despite the stubborn recession. But most of the time the strength or weakness of a stock market is directly related to economic and political forces.

MOVING WITH THE CYCLES
Pinpointing the bottom of a dropping market or the top of a hot one is almost impossible until after it has happened. But what most investors discover is that a market moves up and down in recurring cycles, gaining ground for a period and then reversing and falling for a time before heading up again. A rising market is known as a **bull market** and a

BUYING WARRANTS

Warrants are a way to wager on future prices—though using warrants is very different from selling short. Warrants guarantee, for a small fee, the opportunity to buy stock at a fixed price during a specific period of time. Investors buy warrants if they think a stock's price is going up.

For example, you might pay $1 a share for the right to buy PanAsia stock at $10 within five years. If the price goes up to $14 and you **exercise** (use) your warrant, you save $3 on every share you buy. You can then sell the shares at the higher price to make a profit, for example, $14 – ($10 + $1) = $3, or $300 on 100 shares.

Companies sell warrants if they plan to raise money by issuing new stock or selling stocks they hold in reserve. After a warrant is issued, it can be listed in the stock columns and traded like other investments. A **wt** after a stock table entry means the quotation is for a warrant, not the stock itself.

If the price of the stock is below the set price when the warrant expires, the warrant is worthless. But since warrants are fairly cheap and have a relatively long lifespan, they are traded actively.

WHAT ARE THE RISKS?

The risks in selling short occur when the price of the stock goes up, not down, or when the drop in price takes a long time. The timing is important because you're paying your broker interest on the value of the stocks you borrowed. The longer the process goes on, the more you pay and the more the interest expense erodes your eventual profit.

A rise in the stock's value is an even greater risk. If it goes up instead of down, you will be forced—sooner or later—to pay more to **cover your short position** than you made from selling the stock. Then you lose money on the transaction.

SQUEEZE PLAY

Sometimes, short sellers are caught in a squeeze. That happens when a stock that has been heavily shorted begins to rise. The scramble among short sellers to cover their positions results in heavy buying, which drives the price even higher.

falling one as a **bear market**. Generally, the market has to fall 15% before it's considered a bear market.

Sometimes market trends last a long time, even years, and overall, bull markets have lasted longer than bear markets. That doesn't mean, though, that markets always rise higher than they fall. It just means that drops tend to happen quickly, while rises tend to take a longer time. It's much like the law of gravity—it takes a lot longer to climb 1,000 feet than it takes to fall that distance.

INFLUENCES ON INVESTMENT

Some factors encourage investment and others discourage it.

Positive factors	Negative factors
Ample money supply	Tight money
Tax cuts	Increased taxes
Low interest rates	High interest rates offering better return in less risky investments
Political stability or domestic expectation of stability	Political unrest, turmoil
High employment	International conflicts
	Pending elections

Buying on Margin

Buying on margin lets investors borrow some of the money they need to buy stocks.

Investors who want to buy stock but don't want to pay the full price can **leverage** their purchase by buying on margin. They set up a **margin account** with a broker by depositing cash or eligible securities and maintaining a minimum balance. Then they can borrow part of the price of the stock and use the combined funds to make their purchase.

Investors who buy on margin pay interest on the loan portion of their purchase, but don't have to repay the loan itself until they sell the stock. Any profit is theirs. They don't have to share it.

For example, if you want to buy 1,000 shares of a stock selling for $10 a share, the total cost would be $10,000. Buying

How It Works

YOU OPEN A MARGIN ACCOUNT—$5,000 OF YOUR MONEY AND $5,000 OF YOUR BROKER'S MONEY

YOU PURCHASE 1,000 SHARES AT $10 EACH

YOU PROFIT IF STOCK PRICE RISES

	Stock Value $10	Stock Value $15
THE VALUE OF YOUR INVESTMENT	$5,000	$10,000
YOUR BROKER'S INVESTMENT	$5,000	$5,000

CLOSING THE BARN DOOR

Governments and regulatory agencies sometimes figure out ways to prevent financial disasters—after they happen. The rules and regulations that govern U.S. stock trading, for example, were devised in the wake of two major stock market crashes.

LEVERAGING YOUR STOCK INVESTMENT

Leverage is speculation. It means investing with money borrowed at a fixed rate of interest in the hope of earning a greater rate of return. Like the lever, the simple machine that provides its name, leverage lets the users exert a lot of financial power with a small amount of cash.

Companies use leverage—called **trading on equity**—when they issue both stocks and bonds. Their earnings may increase because they've expanded operations with the money raised by bonds. But they must use some of those earnings to repay the interest on the bonds.

on margin, you put up $5,000 and borrow the remaining $5,000 from your broker.

If the stock price rises to $15 and you sell, you get $15,000. You repay your broker the $5,000 you borrowed and put $10,000 in your pocket (minus interest and commissions). That's almost a 100% profit on your original investment.

Had you used all your own money and laid out $10,000 for the initial purchase, you would have made only a 50% profit: a $5,000 return on a $10,000 investment.

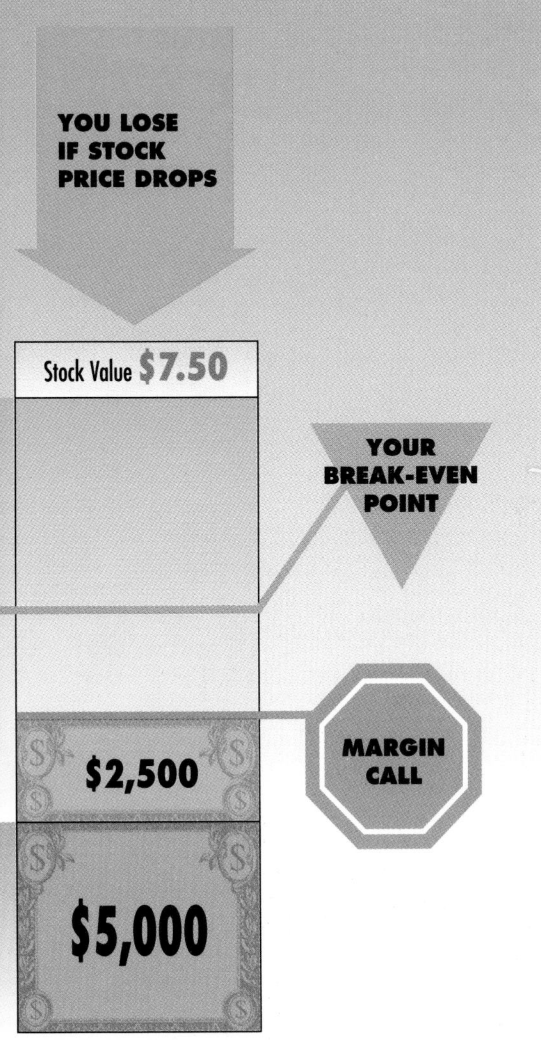

MARGIN CALLS

Despite its advantages, buying on margin can be very risky. For example, the stock you buy could drop so much that selling it wouldn't raise enough to repay the loan to your broker. To protect themselves in cases such as this, brokers issue a **margin call** if the value of your investment falls below a set percentage of its original value. That means you have to put additional money into your margin account. If you don't want to **meet the call**, or can't afford to, you must sell the stock, pay back the broker in full and take the loss even if you think the stock will rise again.

During crashes, or dramatic price decreases in the market, investors who are heavily leveraged because they've bought on margin can't meet their margin calls. The result is panic selling to raise cash, and further declines in the market. That's one reason the Federal Reserve Board instituted Regulation T, which limits the leveraged portion of any margin purchase in U.S. markets to 50%.

MARGIN MINIMUMS

To open a margin account in the U.S., you must deposit a minimum of $2,000 in cash or eligible securities (securities your broker considers valuable). All margin trades have to be conducted through that account, combining your own money and money borrowed from your broker.

Tracking World Markets

As investors buy more global stocks, they want to know more about how those markets are doing.

The change in price and the volume of trading in any single stock on a given day matters mostly to its shareholders. But what a market does overall—whether it climbs slowly, stays flat or drops sharply—is a gauge of an economy. That activity is reported in an **index** or **average**.

The performances of 15 major Asian-Pacific markets are provided daily in The Asian Wall Street Journal.

These statistical composites include the session's close, the net change from the previous day, as well as the change expressed as a percentage.

Here, for example, Australia's All Ordinaries Index closed at 2219.50, down 2.20 points, or 0.1% from the previous trading day, but up 16.50 points, or .75% for the year.

ASIAN-PACIFIC STOCK MARKETS 8/12/96

MAJOR STOCK INDEXES

	CLOSE	NET CHG	PCT CHG	END '95	PCT ON YR
Australia					
All Ordinaries	2219.50	-2.20	-0.10	+16.50	+0.75
All Mining	997.70	-2.10	-0.21	-0.60	-0.06
Bangkok					
SET	Closed	–	–	–	–
Bombay					
Sensitive	3458.98	-38.75	-1.11	+331.04	+10.58
China					
Dow Jones China 88	102.94	+1.03	+1.01	+53.97	+110.21
Dow Jones Shanghai	111.83	+1.48	+1.34	+48.13	+75.56
Dow Jones Shenzhen	111.11	+1.23	+1.12	+69.56	+167.41
Shanghai B Share	53.50	+0.28	+0.53	+5.81	+12.18
Shenzhen B Share	87.05	-7.38	-7.82	+27.57	+46.35
Colombo					
All Share	561.60	-0.90	-0.16	-102.10	-15.38
Hong Kong					
Hang Seng	11181.88	+77.85	+0.70	+1108.49	+11.00
Finance	11265.77	-27.15	-0.24	+1418.79	+14.41
Utilities	9564.41	+70.30	+0.74	-439.24	-4.39
Properties	20873.82	+290.78	+1.41	+3301.59	+18.79
Commerce	8285.69	+69.86	+0.85	+735.71	+9.74
All Ordinaries	5359.51	+34.11	+0.64	+588.94	+12.35
Dow Jones HK Small Cap	67.79	+0.08	+0.12	+11.11	+19.60
Jakarta					
Composite	543.95	-3.76	-0.69	+30.10	+5.86
Karachi					
KSE-100	1485.44	-1.74	-0.12	+14.57	+0.99
Kuala Lumpur					
Composite	1103.76	-1.44	-0.13	+108.59	+10.91
Manila					
Composite	3076.42	-11.77	-0.38	+482.24	+18.59
Seoul					
Composite	837.99	+1.22	+0.15	-44.95	-5.09
Singapore					
Straits Times	2115.65	-13.39	-0.63	-150.89	-6.66
DBS 50	549.10	-9.70	-1.74	-11.88	-2.12
Taipei					
Weighted Price	6317.62	+2.74	+0.04	+1143.89	+22.11
Tokyo					
Nikkei-225	20666.60	+115.55	+0.56	+798.45	+4.02
TSE-1st Section	1570.52	+3.08	+0.20	-7.18	-0.46
TSE-2nd Section	2041.31	-18.80	-0.91	-20.80	-1.01
Wellington					
NZSE-40	2120.34	-28.92	-1.35	-29.48	-1.3

OTHER MEASURES

Investors can compare stock market performance in seven major European markets and South Africa by consulting the Stock Market Indexes chart in The Asian Wall Street Journal. Each business day, it tracks the two previous days of trading activity and details gains or losses on ten separate indexes. In this example, more markets are up than down—five to three—though none of the movement was especially dramatic, which is typical in a short time frame.

Morgan Stanley Capital International's Europe Australasia Far East Index (EAFE) is a commonly used developed-country benchmark. It tracks activity in 20 nations, including six in Asia, and is weighted by market size.

EUROPEAN STOCK MARKETS

STOCK MARKET INDEXES

Exchange	Index	Monday Close	Previous Close	Change	% Change
London	FT-SE 100	3803.30	3810.70	- 7.40	- 0.19
	FT-SE Mid 250	4331.90	4324.50	+ 7.40	+ 0.17
Frankfurt	DAX	2528.18	2525.64	+ 2.54	+ 0.10
	FAZ	892.01	892.77	- 0.76	- 0.09
Paris	CAC 40	1978.17	1989.54	- 11.37	- 0.57
Milan	MIBtel	9452.00	9531.00	- 9.00	- 0.83
Amsterdam	CBS-General	372.40	370.50	+ 1.90	+ 0.51
Brussels	Bel 20	1744.65	1750.36	- 5.71	- 0.33
Johannesburg	Gold	1795.00	1781.00	+ 14.00	+ 0.79
Zurich	Swiss Market	3623.10	3643.20	- 20.10	- 0.55

DAILY NUMBERS

The daily numbers on a particular exchange have meaning only in relation to what has happened on that exchange in the past. For example, the Nikkei Stock Average, here 20666.60, reports only what has happened in that market; it is unrelated to the closing levels of indexes in Jakarta, Bombay, Singapore or elsewhere.

WORLD-WIDE STOCK MARKET PERFORMANCE

World-wide stock market performance can be compared by looking at the **percentage change**: knowing that Australia's All Ordinaries Index is up .75% means more to investors than saying it was up 16.50 points for the year.

For example, in the activity reported in this chart from Aug. 12, 1996, more of the key market indexes were down than up for the day, but the majority are up for the year. While political and economic situations at home have a major influence on stock performance, market forces around the globe are increasingly interrelated.

MARKET NAMES

The terms stock exchange and bourse are often used interchangeably. Bourse is the name of the stock exchange in Paris and in some other European cities and has over time become synonymous with exchange.

PICKING A MARKET

Financial analysts tend to evaluate markets from a top-down perspective, focusing on a country's or a region's financial environment rather than on the prospects of individual companies. Among factors that make a country's stocks attractive to investors are the underlying strength and stability of its economy, the value of its currency and its current interest rate. Growing economies, strengthening currencies and flat or falling interest rates are generally good indicators of economic growth. Conversely, countries whose currencies are weak, interest rates high and economies in recession don't attract equity investors.

The World Stock Index

The World Stock Index is a barometer of stock market performance around the world—measuring the ups and downs of more than 2,000 companies.

The Dow Jones World Stock Index—introduced in 1993—lets investors measure the performance of their global portfolios. This index includes results from more than two dozen countries grouped in three geographic regions: the Americas, Europe and Asia/Pacific. Eventually it will include every country where foreign investors can buy stocks.

A FIXED MARK

Indexes are always measured against a **benchmark**, a fixed value established at a specific time. The term originally referred to a surveyor's mark indicating a known height above sea level, but it has come to mean any standard that's used as a basis of comparison. In the World Stock Index, for example, it's a date 12 months prior.

DOW JONES WORLD STOCK INDEX

REGION/ COUNTRY	DJ GLOBAL INDEXES, LOCAL CURRENCY	PCT. CHG.	IN 4:00 P.M. INDEX	CHG.	PCT. CHG.	12-MO HIGH
Americas			150.88	+ 0.01	+ 0.01	153.90
Canada	137.58	+ 0.03	116.27	+ 0.02	+ 0.02	116.49
Mexico	226.18	+ 0.08	92.86	+ 0.18	+ 0.19	97.59
U.S.	609.53	+ 0.01	609.53	+ 0.04	+ 0.01	623.15
Europe/Africa			140.42	– 0.15	– 0.11	143.90
Austria	109.20	– 0.02	109.46	+ 0.24	+ 0.22	113.71
Belgium	141.95	– 0.27	142.72	– 0.62	– 0.43	148.48
France	129.03	0.00	129.74	– 0.62	– 0.48	132.63
Germany	141.01	– 0.16	140.48	– 0.60	– 0.43	147.79
Italy	142.98	– 0.56	113.37	– 0.53	– 0.47	121.02
Netherlands	181.48	+ 1.54	179.81	+ 2.27	+ 1.28	179.81
South Africa	205.96	– 1.64	126.31	– 1.74	– 1.36	160.95
Spain	158.77	+ 0.30	121.28	– 0.28	– 0.23	125.00
Sweden	216.67	– 1.38	177.07	– 1.96	– 1.10	183.93
Switzerland	210.73	– 0.43	230.46	– 1.95	– 0.84	249.58
United Kingdom	154.33	+ 0.58	125.77	+ 0.64	+ 0.51	129.26
Asia/Pacific			124.73	– 0.58	– 0.46	128.31
Australia	134.78	– 0.88	141.52	– 1.94	– 1.35	143.85
Hong Kong	235.05	– 0.58	236.10	– 1.36	– 0.57	260.15
Indonesia	225.79	+ 0.77	193.06	+ 1.34	+ 0.70	201.11
Japan	98.40	– 0.97	117.29	– 0.58	– 0.49	121.16
Malaysia	234.84	+ 1.14	256.64	+ 2.22	+ 0.87	264.21
New Zealand	139.74	– 0.07	177.95	+ 0.05	+ 0.03	189.29
Philippines	350.13	+ 1.32	347.78	+ 4.53	+ 1.32	347.78
Singapore	177.42	+ 0.06	204.71	+ 0.15	+ 0.07	224.73
South Korea	155.48	– 1.94	151.49	– 2.98	– 1.93	167.89
Taiwan	150.60	– 0.97	143.14	– 1.38	– 0.96	148.01
Thailand	220.96	– 0.13	206.55	– 0.19	– 0.09	227.64
Asia/Pacific (ex. Japan)			189.34	– 0.68	– 0.36	193.26
World (ex. U.S.)			129.64	– 0.38	– 0.29	132.46
DJ WORLD STOCK INDEX			138.95	– 0.24	– 0.17	141.61

Indexes based on 6/30/82=100 for U.S., 12/31/91=100 for World. ©1

INDEX	CLOSE	NET CHG	PCT CHG	12-MO HIGH	12-MO LOW	12-MO CHG	PCT	FROM 12/31	PCT
DJIA	5532.59	+ 45.52	+ 0.83	5689.74	3973.05	Closed	–	+ 415.47	+ 8.12
S&P 500	636.71	+ 5.53	+ 0.88	661.45	504.92	Closed	–	+ 20.78	+ 3.37
HONG KONG (HS)	10849.80	– 42.77	– 0.39	11594.99	8212.11	Closed	–	+ 776.41	+ 7.71
LONDON (FT 100)	3766.80	+ 22.60	+ 0.60	3781.30	3170.10	Closed	–	+ 77.50	+ 2.10
TOKYO (NIKKEI 225)	21660.47	– 33.96	– 0.16	21791.70	14485.41	+ 5612.58	+ 34.97	+ 1792.32	+ 9.02

The Asian Wall Street Journal regularly tracks international markets in comparison with the benchmark Dow Jones Industrial Average.

MAKING COMPARISONS

Each country's market index is computed in its own currency, and in four global currencies: dollars, pounds, marks and yen. Using global currencies ensures that the figures are comparable because the impact of exchange rates is figured in (see pages 24–25). The Asian Wall Street Journal uses versions of the index customized for different markets. For example, the edition used here gives the figures in dollars.

The composite, or benchmark, is reported in the last line of the chart. It provides the broadest picture of the international equity markets, and is a basis for comparing the different markets' performances.

S 12-MO CHG.	PCT. CHG.	FROM 12/31	PCT. CHG.
28.14	+ 22.93	+ 7.27	+ 5.06
17.23	+ 17.39	+ 8.02	+ 7.41
16.84	+ 22.15	+ 14.90	+ 19.11
114.69	+ 23.18	+ 28.11	+ 4.83
14.07	+ 11.14	+ 3.41	+ 2.49
1.36	+ 1.25	+ 8.17	+ 8.07
10.76	+ 8.15	+ 0.17	+ 0.12
5.97	+ 4.83	+ 9.72	+ 8.10
10.85	+ 8.37	+ 2.24	+ 1.62
1.43	– 1.24	+ 9.87	+ 9.53
30.36	+ 20.32	+ 12.51	+ 7.48
4.41	– 3.37	– 16.40	– 11.49
19.33	+ 18.96	+ 6.97	+ 6.10
44.79	+ 33.86	+ 13.93	+ 8.54
47.20	+ 25.76	– 2.17	– 0.93
10.43	+ 9.04	+ 1.28	+ 1.03
5.63	+ 4.73	+ 4.93	+ 4.11
25.24	+ 21.70	+ 13.62	+ 10.65
32.84	+ 16.16	+ 12.43	+ 5.56
22.67	+ 13.30	+ 20.58	+ 11.93
2.87	+ 2.50	+ 3.21	+ 2.82
24.09	+ 10.36	+ 33.56	+ 15.04
5.18	– 2.83	+ 1.79	+ 1.02
49.69	+ 16.67	+ 66.29	+ 23.55
18.49	+ 9.93	+ 8.79	+ 4.49
4.62	+ 3.15	+ 5.92	+ 4.07
1.71	+ 1.21	+ 23.69	+ 19.84
2.53	+ 1.24	+ 9.79	+ 4.97
23.24	+ 13.99	+ 15.88	+ 9.16
9.38	+ 7.80	+ 4.52	+ 3.62
16.78	+ 13.74	+ 5.49	+ 4.12

READING THE INDEX

The World Stock Index reports equity market performance in each country for the previous trading day and the percentage change from the day before in local currency. Then the same information is computed in dollars, adding the amount it has gained or lost. In Indonesia, for example, the closing index in rupiah was 225.79, up .77% from the previous trading day. Computed in dollars for the benefit of U.S. investors, it was $193.06, up $1.34 or .70% from the previous numbers.

The markets are also tracked over the past 12 months, and since the beginning of the current year. Investors can compare the year's high and low to the current performance. Note that in this example performance in the Americas was stronger—with a 22.93% increase—than either Asia/Pacific at 4.73% or Europe/Africa at 11.14%.

However, the biggest gain reported for a single market since Dec. 31 is the 23.55% registered in the Philippines.

MARKET SNAPSHOTS
Information about the Asian-Pacific markets that are included in the Dow Jones World Stock Index is provided on pages 62–71.

Asian-Pacific Stock Markets

Stock markets in the region have carved out a place on the global equities map.

Over the last decade, stock market activity in the Asian-Pacific region has boomed. Small markets have expanded, and new ones have opened. Buyers from all over the world can and do own shares in most of them.

Technologically, the markets are sophisticated. Trading is handled electronically in most of the markets, and many of them are actively working toward paperless settlement systems. Most of them are increasingly transparent, with management and performance information available and regulatory measures in place. Others are working to meet international standards.

ASIAN-PACIFIC

BOMBAY

ISSUE	Vol(N/A)	Close	Chg.
ASSOCIATED CEMEN		2414.20	−34.80
BOMBAY DYEING		224.70	−2.50
BHARAT FORGE		178.00	+2.00
BALLARPUR INDUST		162.20	+0.20
CEAT TYRES		95.00	−0.50
CENTURY TEXTILES		5425.00	−75.00
E I HOTELS		720.00	+30.00
GREAT EASTERN SH		50.50	−0.70
GLAXO INDIA		237.20	−0.50
GRASIM INDUSTRIES		572.20	+0.20
GUJARAT FERTILIS		110.70	+0.70
HINDUSTAN LEVER		821.50	−16.00
HINDALCO		1255.20	+14.00
HINDUSTAN MOTORS		30.70	−0.50
INDIAN HOTELS		826.00	−3.00
INDIAN ORGANIC		20.50	−0.50
INDIAN RAYON		493.00	+1.00
ITC		311.70	−5.50
KIRLOSKAR CUMMINS		398.00	−6.20
LARSEN & TOUBRO		289.50	−3.70
MAHINDRA & MAHIN		360.50	−2.50
MUKAND		140.00	Unch
NESTLE		407.20	−7.80
PREMIER AUTO		55.00	+0.50
PHILIPS INDIA		129.20	−0.30
RELIANCE INDUSTR		212.00	−6.50
SIEMENS		609.70	+9.70
[illegible]		[illegible]	[illegible]

MARKET RESTRICTIONS

Some markets are open to all, while others limit participation by nonresidents. That can be done by setting a cap on the percentage of a company or class of companies that can be owned by overseas investors, by limiting investment to a fixed percent of market capitalization, or by selling different classes of shares, one for citizens and another for everyone else, as the markets in China do.

The issue of encouraging overseas investment, which brings in added capital, can be in conflict with worries about losing domestic control or having to respond to demands of investors who expect greater levels of information or corporate responsibility. Overseas investment can also increase a market's volatility, broadening the scope of influencing factors.

TRANSPARENT MARKETS

As markets grow in the region and attract more overseas investors, there has been a parallel demand for greater accountability—more information, and more uniform standards—often described as transparency (see page 38). Most of the markets are moving toward greater openness and greater security, often based on U.S. practices. Typical of the reforms are systems for settling transactions and recording ownership of shares, which can be and often are handled electronically.

Recent upheavals in various markets have quickened the pace of this trend as well. But problems such as poor accounting methods, insider trading and unreliable stock transactions can persist, despite efforts of regulatory agencies to change them.

SAFE HARBOR

Singapore is known as Southeast Asia's safest haven for equity investors, a reputation that is both the island's strength and its weakness. When other regional markets lose steam, money flows into Singapore. But when other markets have their periodic wild bursts, Singapore languishes by comparison.

SELLING RIGHTS

When a company wants to raise more capital by selling additional shares, it sometimes offers its stockholders the right, or opportunity, to buy some of those shares before they're offered for general sale. Usually, it means paying less than the current market price.

Rights, or the written offer for these shares, have a market value of their own and are actively traded on many stock markets around the world, including the Asian-Pacific region. Usually, they must be exercised, or acted on, within a relatively short period, or they lose their value.

TOCK TRANSACTIONS

...ue	Vol(1000)	Close	Chg.
ELL ELECTRIC	4907	4.825	+0.050
ENZHEN INTL	625	0.137	+0.008
CHINA IND	...	8.200	Unch
CO	2205	2.800	−0.100
CONVERTIBLE	100	6.650	Unch
INDUSTRIES	5368	0.540	+0.010
PROP	1031	78.250	−0.250
GANG CENT	1066	0.660	Unch
GANG GRAND	964	0.700	Unch
GANG INTL	4434	1.220	−0.010
GANG TECH	3220	0.380	+0.005
HING	2	5.000	+0.100
CHEONG	...	0.233	Unch
HO CONS	1266	0.430	+0.010
HO RES	30	0.405	−0.015
HING HOLD	280	0.235	+0.002

SEOUL

	Vol(100)	Close	Chg.
NDL	167	142	Unch
FIRE INS	28	5200	−120
TORS	465	70	+1
PUSAN	315	90	+1
SEC	49	100	−1
ANK	144	97	+1
IFC	50	144	Unch
ODS	255	530	Unch
OL TEXT	209	144	+2
BANK			

Issue	Vol(1000)	Close	Chg.
UNILEVER IND	70	34400	−200
UNITED TRACTOR	6320	3675	−50
UNITEX	5	7000	−6000
VOKSEL ELETRIC	50	1300	−50

KUALA LUMPUR

ISSUE	Vol(1000)	Close	Chg.
ACIDCHEM MAL	594	6.05	+0.05
AFFIN HLDGS	129	5.85	+0.05
ALUMINUM CO (M)	61	4.02	+0.06
AMAL IND ST	47	7.05	−0.10
AMMB HOLDINGS	556	35.00	+1.25
ANSON PERDANA	6606	6.60	−0.25
ANTAH HLDGS	391	3.10	−0.04
AOKAM PERDANA	1279	4.18	−0.02
ARAB MALAY DEV	82	1.60	Unch
ARAB MALAY FIN	2	9.40	Unch
ARAB-MALAY CORP	6	9.80	+0.25
ASIA PAC LAND	64	1.40	Unch
ASIATIC DEV	42	2.56	Unch
AUSTRAL ENTER	155	5.05	Unch
AUTOWAYS HOL	221	6.45	−0.20
AYER HITAM PLANT	34	41.00	−0.50
AYER HITAM TIN	251	5.35	+0.25
BANDAR RAYA DEV			
BANK ISLAM (...			
BATU KAWAN			

Issue
MANIL
MANIL
MANIL
MANIL
MANIL
MEGA
METR
METR
MONC
ORIE
ORIE
PETR
PETR
PETR
PHIL
PHIL
PHIL
PHI
PHI
PH
PH

TRADING INFORMATION

Trading activity in 14 Asian-Pacific markets is reported daily in The Asian Wall Street Journal. Information on shares is listed in alphabetical order, followed by the **volume**, or number of shares traded, the closing price and the price change from the previous trading day.

In this example from the Kuala Lumpur Stock Exchange in Malaysia, Aokam Perdana was actively traded, with 1.279 million shares changing hands. Its price fell two sen. But Arab-Malay Corp. was more thinly traded, with 6,000 shares bought and sold. In this case, its price rose 25 sen.

STILL EMERGING

India is focusing on the issue of share-transfer delays, trying to bring its cumbersome paper-driven settlement process more in line with international standards.

Prolonged delays in transferring shares from one owner to another have often frustrated investors and fund managers. As a result, some foreign investors prefer to buy global depositary receipts issued abroad by Indian companies.

The establishment of share depositories, which is under way, is expected to help reduce the delays and the tons of paper that in the past led to market flaws and inefficiencies.

Market Snapshots: Australasia

AUSTRALIA

The Australian Stock Exchange (ASX) lists 1,180 domestic stocks and 60 from overseas, including eight from China-based companies. The ASX is a national computer-based market, with a share settlement system to rival the best.

Mining stocks amount to about a third of the domestic listings on the exchange, reflecting the dominance of that sector in the Australian economy. Among them are a number of highly speculative investments.

IN THE MARKET

About 18% of Australians own shares directly or through managed equity funds—lower than in many other industrialized countries. The government is trying to encourage participation with a tax break on dividends earned on equity investments. Overseas investors, especially those from the U.S. and the U.K., are active in the market, accounting for about 22% of the total turnover. There are few restrictions on overseas investment, except in a few specific companies.

CURRENT ISSUES

The exchange is actively working to build its base in Asia and enlarge its role in the region, and has considered extending its trading hours to be more competitive. It does have an active derivatives section, trading options and warrants, and has invented a product called **share-ratio contracts**. Share ratios are based on the performance of individual stocks compared with a share-price index.

REGULATION

The Australian Securities Commission and the exchange have worked to restore the market's image, which suffered amid transparency problems in the 1980s. But there is continuing pressure to insist on tougher corporate governance standards to match the best practices elsewhere.

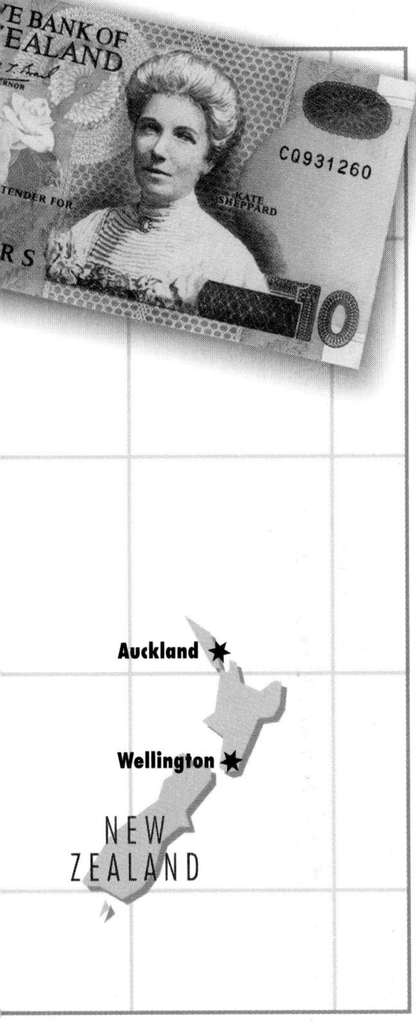

NEW ZEALAND

The New Zealand Stock Exchange (NZSE), which enjoys the distinction of kicking off the global trading day because it is the first across the international date line, lists about 203 equity and 14 debt issues, including 65 overseas-based companies. There's a wide variety of shares traded, including ordinary shares, preferred shares, rights, equity warrants, convertible notes and share options.

The exchange, having eliminated its trading floor in 1991, uses a screen-based trading system that makes it a national market. The bourse has worked toward a paperless cash settlement system. Companies listed on the NZSE must re-register by July 1997, providing more open disclosure of their ownership and corporate structure, and making the market even more transparent.

IN THE MARKET

The NZSE is open to all investors, and some overseas investors own large—sometimes majority—stakes in many of the companies that have been privatized since 1987. Forestry concerns dominate the market. But the largest company in terms of market capitalization is telephone utility Telecom Corp.

CURRENT ISSUES

New Zealand's government projects continued budget surpluses, and is using the money to cut taxes, reduce debt and spur domestic investment in the stock market. It also provides a sizable comfort level for overseas investors looking for profits and stability at the same time. Overseas investors living in countries that have tax treaties with New Zealand are subject to a dividend withholding tax at the reduced rate of around 15%, instead of 33%.

REGULATION

The NZSE is an independent body that operates under its own bylaws with little government supervision. Among the exchange's new rules is one requiring companies to notify shareholders when any investor increases ownership above a certain percentage, and another obligating member firms to separate client funds from other assets of the firm.

Market Snapshots: East Asia

SOUTH KOREA

The Korea Stock Exchange (KSE) is the fourth largest in Asia and the 17th largest in the world, with about 738 companies listed in two sections. The first trades big companies—80% of the listed stock—and the second trades newly listed companies.

The KSE inaugurated a computerized order-routing system in 1983 to send orders directly to the trading floor, and introduced Smats, a computerized trading system, in 1988. Since 1991, Smats has handled more than 95% of the total trading volume.

IN THE MARKET

Domestic individual investors hold about 36% of the shares traded on the KSE and domestic institutional investors, about 33%. Overseas investors account for a little more than 10%, with the number rising, though the market has been open to them only since 1992.

There are limits on overseas ownership for both institutional and individual investors, with some business sectors closed entirely. Stocks that have reached their limit can be traded among international investors on the over-the-counter market.

CURRENT ISSUES

The KSE is controlled in a number of ways. Daily price limits prevent stocks from moving more than a fixed percent up or down from the previous day's closing price.

Withholding taxes are heavy on investors from countries that don't have tax treaties with Korea. This includes Japan and most other Asian countries.

But there are increasing moves toward liberalizing restrictions and at the same time providing greater transparency and accountability, in part prompted by investor pressure.

REGULATION

Most financial decisions and regulations are handled by the government's Ministry of Finance and Economy.

DELISTING

Stocks that have been listed on a particular market may also be delisted, or no longer traded on that exchange. Sometimes a company delists voluntarily, either because the management feels it isn't receiving the market attention it deserves, the expense of listing isn't justified by the trading volume, or it can gain added prestige by listing elsewhere.

Sometimes, however, a stock market requires the delisting because the company no longer meets the minimum requirements for being included.

JAPAN

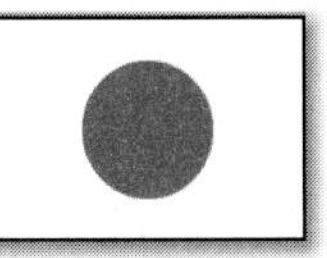

The Tokyo Stock Exchange (TSE), the second largest market in the world, is divided into two sections. The first section lists around 1,235 companies, and the second specializes in about 465 smaller capitalization issues. The 150 most active first-section stocks are traded on the floor of the exchange, and the rest are handled by an automated system.

Stocks are also traded on seven other exchanges and on an over-the-counter market operated by the Japan Securities Dealers Association. A second OTC market, the Frontier Market, was launched in 1995 but had no listings by mid-1996. Designed to raise funds for fast-growing, small companies with little earnings history, it has looser listing requirements.

IN THE MARKET

More than two-thirds of the outstanding shares traded on the TSE are owned by domestic financial institutions and industrial corporations. Individual Japanese investors—who seem to favor cash over equity investments—own about 23.5%, and 7.4% are held by overseas investors.

CURRENT ISSUES

The Tokyo Stock Exchange has been hit by a rash of prominent foreign delistings, or stocks withdrawn from trading on the exchange. Issuing companies have complained about high fees and low levels of trading in the foreign section. In response, the TSE has been promoting new rules that allow small, unlisted Asian companies to gain a first listing in Tokyo, and has partially deregulated brokerage commissions.

The market is considerably more opaque than Wall Street, and Japanese financial accounts are often difficult to decipher. However, the exchange is working to enhance stockholder rights, in part as a response to increased demands for information from institutional investors and in part to encourage broader individual participation in the market (see page 39). **Churning**, or excessive trading in client accounts, is coming under greater scrutiny. Efforts are also being made to insure that share prices are determined by fundamental valuation, or what they're really worth, rather than being held artificially high because large blocks of shares are held by linked companies (see page 39).

Companies are more likely to buy back their own shares since the removal in 1995 of a tax rule that made the practice prohibitively expensive. **Buybacks**, common in other countries, can boost a company's stock price.

REGULATION

In 1992, Japan wrote clear securities laws and regulations and set up its first full-time regulator, the Securities and Exchange Surveillance Commission. It can raid offices, confiscate evidence and request that prosecutors indict a suspected offender. The Japanese Securities Dealers Association has also adopted a code of conduct similar to the ones used in the U.S. and Europe.

Market Snapshots: East Asia

HONG KONG

The Stock Exchange of Hong Kong, the second largest in Asia, was created in 1986 by merging four decentralized trading centers. The bourse serves as a fund-raising center for the mainland. It first included state-owned Chinese companies in mid-1993 and lists more than 20 such shares, known as Class H shares.

Electronic order matching has been introduced, and eventually all members will be equipped for trading from their offices rather than on an exchange floor. For the present though, floor trading continues. The electronic system will also allow for linkage with mainland markets.

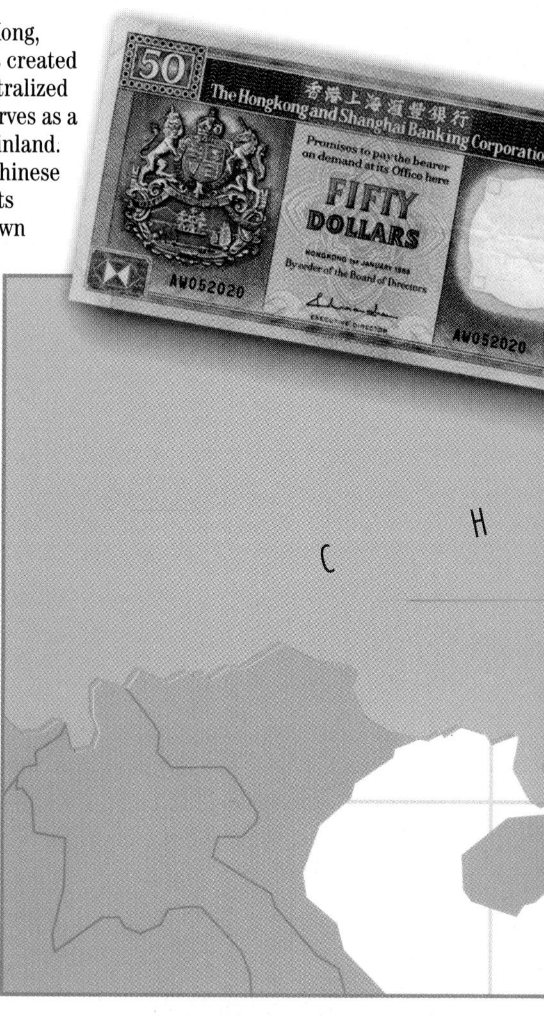

IN THE MARKET

Both domestic and overseas investors trade in the Hong Kong market. While Hong Kong has made some efforts to reduce its high commissions and fees, institutional investors are increasingly trading Hong Kong shares in London and New York, where costs are lower.

CURRENT ISSUES

The overriding issue for the Hong Kong bourse is the impact of the July 1, 1997, resumption of Chinese sovereignty over Hong Kong, although Chinese officials maintain that the financial system will not change. In the meantime, both the stock and futures exchanges continue to introduce new products, with mixed results. Index futures and warrants are extremely popular, but options on individual stocks haven't caught on. Corporate bonds aren't actively traded, and mutual funds are less popular than straightforward stock trading.

REGULATION

The Securities and Futures Commission, created in 1989, oversees the Hong Kong Stock Exchange. Its mandate is to make the market fair and efficient, and to keep investors informed.

TRACKING THE CHINESE MARKETS

Trading in the Shanghai and Shenzhen stock markets is tracked daily in The Asian Wall Street Journal using three indexes, one for each market and the Dow Jones China 88 Index. The latter is based on 88 shares selected from both markets on the basis of market

TAIWAN

The Taiwan Stock Exchange conducts business electronically, trading approximately 370 listed shares with a fully automated computerized system. It has extremely limited trading hours—from 9 to noon during the week and from 9 to 11 on Saturdays.

CURRENT ISSUES

Taiwan's tense relationship with mainland China has had a negative effect on the stock market, which in turn dented domestic consumption and business sentiment in Taiwan in 1996. Even if more overseas investing were allowed, some experts think buyers might hesitate to commit money to the market.

REGULATION

The Securities and Exchange Commission was set up in 1960 to create guidelines for the stock market. It continues to oversee its activities and impose restrictions on trading.

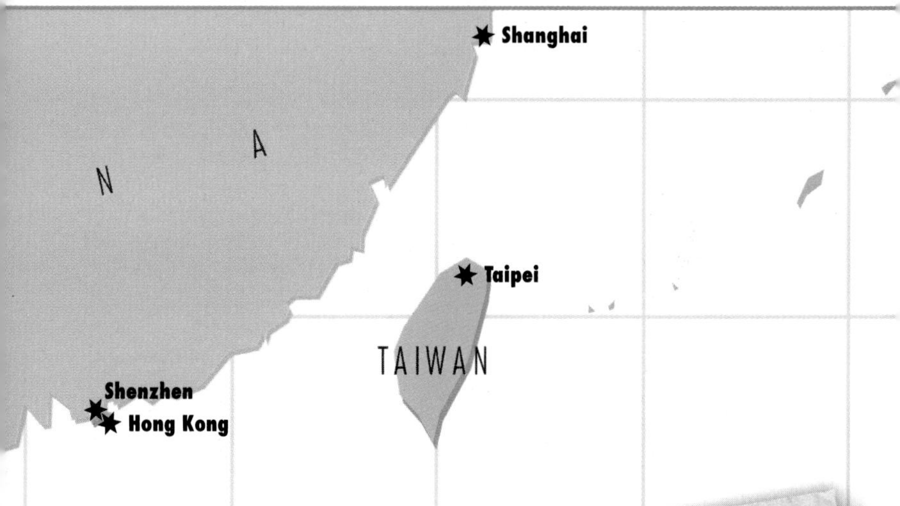

Shanghai
N A
Taipei
TAIWAN
Shenzhen
Hong Kong

capitalization, liquidity and the extent to which they represent their respective industries.

All three indexes track Class A shares, which are available to Chinese citizens, but not Class B shares, which are available to overseas investors. Separate indexes for the two Class B markets are also listed.

Though they weren't included in the Dow Jones World Stock Index when they were introduced in 1996, the Dow Jones indexes charting activity in China are based on the same standards used to track markets in countries and regions that are covered. That means, for example, that all three indexes are calculated on a capitalization-weighted basis. Each stock's price movement influences the indexes in proportion to its relative market value.

IN THE MARKET

More than 90% of the market activity is from retail domestic investors, in part because Taiwan is a semi-closed market. Overseas institutions have been permitted to participate since 1991, and account for less than 2% of overall trading. In 1996, individual overseas investors were also permitted to buy shares up to a total value of $5 million a year. Overseas investors have also been subject to elaborate currency and other regulations imposed by the Ministry of Finance, though the trend toward relaxing the rules seems to be continuing.

Market Snapshots: Southeast Asia

INDONESIA

The Jakarta Stock Exchange (JSX) has grown dramatically since 1987 when the government opened it to international investment, removed the 4% limit on daily price changes and relaxed listing requirements. Nearly 250 companies are traded on JSX, but fewer than 30 stocks dominate trading. In addition, new rules have relaxed listing requirements to make it easier for small companies to participate.

Since 1995 the exchange has operated with a computerized order-matching system, eliminating much of the frenzy that characterized earlier trading, and more than doubling its transaction capacity.

IN THE MARKET

Overseas institutional investors have generally driven the market, as few individuals buy shares, and domestic pension funds are prohibited by law from investing more than 10% of their assets in equities. Most own closer to 5%.

Currently, overseas shareholders may own no more than 49% of a listed company. If that limit has been reached, they may have to buy shares from other overseas investors on the foreign board, usually at a premium over the main board's prices.

CURRENT ISSUES

While the market has succeeded in drawing international attention, it hasn't yet attracted broad domestic participation. Indonesians can earn high interest on savings accounts, and potential investors may have been discouraged by earlier upheavals in the market. In addition, many listed stocks are illiquid, in part because up to 85% of the shares are owned by founding families and do not change hands.

The government is trying to encourage more participation by offering incentives on privatization purchases.

REGULATION

Bapepam, the regulator, has authority under the Capital Markets Act of 1995 to investigate possible violations of security law and seek civil and criminal penalties.

The new regulations also make JSX increasingly transparent, providing for stricter accounting standards, more regulation of exchange trading and fuller disclosure.

PHILIPPINES

The Philippine Stock Exchange, initially a computerized linking of the Manila and Makati Stock Exchanges, has expanded electronically into other parts of the country to allow trading from regional centers. The first move was a successful attempt to attract more overseas participation in the market by establishing uniform opening and closing prices for all traded stocks. The second is aimed at encouraging more local participation.

The exchange lists common stock of about 200 companies, and has had a number of IPOs. Preferred shares, bonds and warrants are thinly traded.

IN THE MARKET

Both domestic and overseas investors participate in the market. In the past, the latter were limited to trading B shares, while A shares were reserved for local buyers. Recently, though, a number of companies have declassified their shares, allowing more overseas ownership. That has meant greater infusions of capital.

CURRENT ISSUES

Changes in the financial markets and increased stability of the government have bolstered stock market activity. One mark of that increasing interest is that the cost of an exchange seat shot up 70% in less than a year.

REGULATION

The Philippine Securities and Exchange Commission has been working toward requiring full disclosure of corporate actions and policies by all publicly listed companies. However, the exchange is self-regulating and has sometimes imposed stricter standards for listing than the commission would have allowed.

THAILAND

The Stock Exchange of Thailand (SET) opened in 1975 with just nine listed stocks, but now lists over 400 companies and 70 mutual funds. Two-thirds of all trading, though, is in the 100 stocks with the biggest market capitalization. An over-the-counter market for small- and medium-sized firms was launched in 1995.

Floor trading doesn't exist. Traders buy and sell using a computerized order matching system that provides instant confirmations and allows buyers and sellers to remain anonymous until the transaction is complete.

Though seats on the exchange are expensive, the 50 member brokerage houses share the large fees generated by the typically active trading.

IN THE MARKET

Individual domestic investors account for about 60% of the trading activity and overseas investors, about 30%. The bourse is trying to increase the role of institutional investors.

There is a 49% cap on international ownership of most companies, with a 25% cap for financial institutions. A foreign board handles overseas trades in companies that have reached their limit—sometimes at a stiff premium to the price on the regular board.

CURRENT ISSUES

Stocks traded on the exchange are prohibited from moving up or down by more than 10% each day, in an effort to control volatility. There are no such restrictions on the foreign board.

The SET, in the hope of limiting fluctuations in the index, is trying to encourage institutional investor activity, which may be more stable than individual investment.

REGULATION

The Thailand Securities and Exchange Commission is responsible for monitoring the SET, which also polices itself.

Market Snapshots: Southeast Asia

MALAYSIA

The Kuala Lumpur Stock Exchange (KLSE), one of the largest markets in Southeast Asia, split from the Singapore exchange in 1990. Trading is fully automated, with delivery and settlement slated to be handled by a paperless, book-entry system. There are about 510 shares listed, on two boards. The main board requires earnings records for three to five years, and the second—currently with 152 listings—requires records for two to three years.

To attract even more business, the exchange has lowered transaction costs and restructured its fee system, and it lists a variety of securities, including ordinary and preference shares, warrants and bonds. To increase local participation, the KLSE allows sales of small lots of stock, to make trading in blue-chip issues more affordable.

REGULATION

The Securities Commission was set up in 1993 to provide regulation for the industry and to advise the Minister of Finance on financial markets. Among the rules that aim toward creating more openness in the market, any shareholder owning more than 5% of a company's issued share capital must declare the holding. Otherwise investors can remain anonymous.

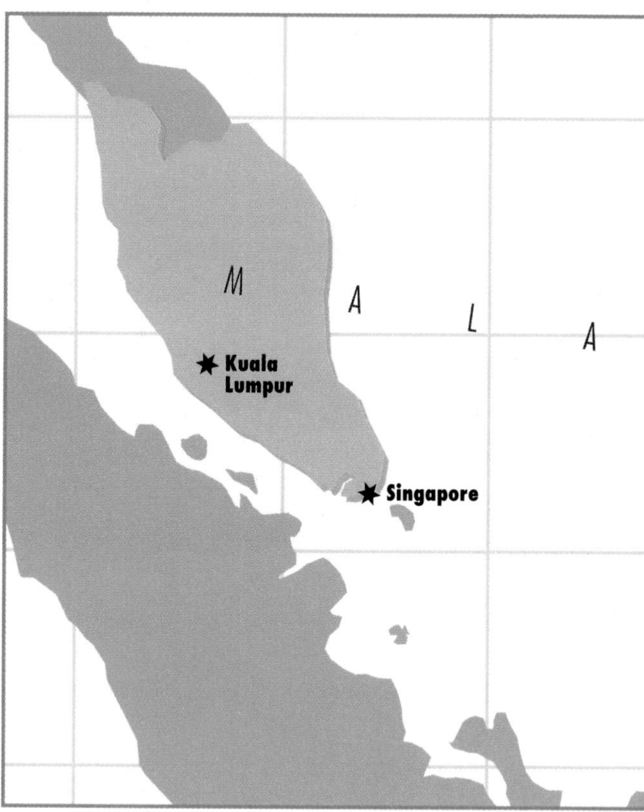

IN THE MARKET

Overseas investors can trade freely in all listed securities. About 100, mostly blue-chip stocks, attract consistent overseas interest, though some smaller companies are drawing attention. Sometimes the companies create separate foreign issues with the same rights as domestic shares, but that are traded only among overseas investors.

CURRENT ISSUES

Malaysian authorities continue to aggressively introduce new markets and products for local and global investors in an effort to make Kuala Lumpur a premier financial center. Following the establishment of a futures market and money-market exchange, officials announced plans to set up an OTC market for high-technology companies. Authorities continue to mull steps to attract global fund-management houses.

SINGAPORE

The Stock Exchange of Singapore (SES), one of the biggest and most modern stock exchanges in Asia, is a floorless market with a fully automated, screen-based trading system. Trades are handled over the telephone or through a computer system, which automatically matches bids and offers and sends confirmations to the brokers. Settlement is also computerized, and all actively traded stock certificates are held in a central depository.

There are about 275 domestic and overseas companies listed on the main board, and another 43 listed on Sesdaq, for small-capitalization companies with shorter earnings records. In addition, about 130 regional stocks, primarily from Malaysia, are traded in Singapore dollars in an over-the-counter market called CLOB International, though they're not formally listed. Frequently, half the exchange's volume comes from trading in these shares.

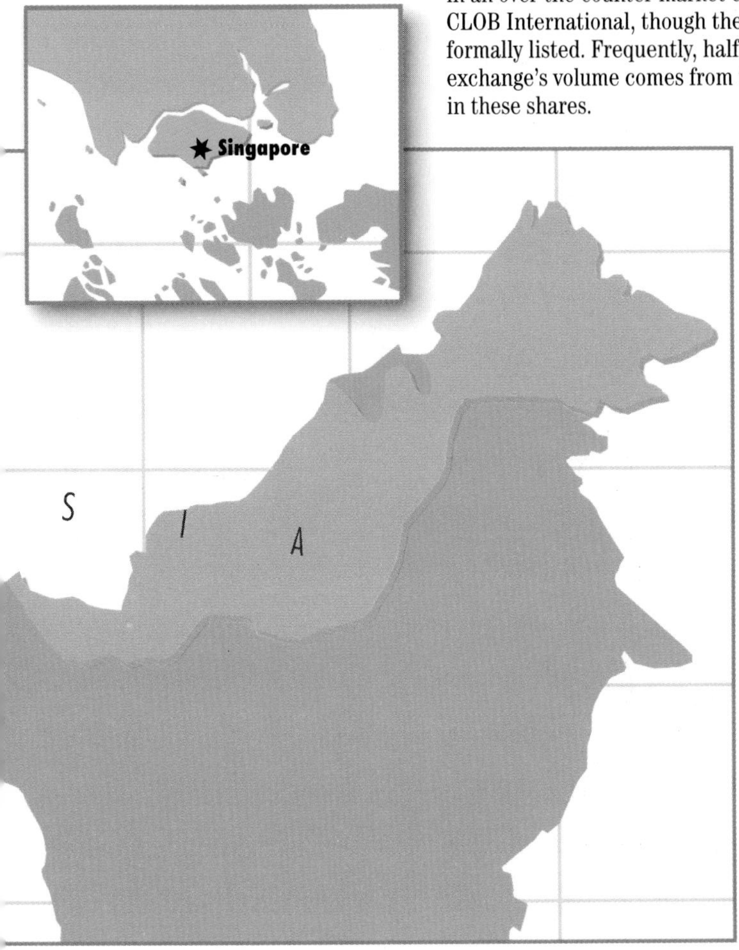

Singapore

S I A

IN THE MARKET

Almost every adult in Singapore has owned some stock, mostly because of a huge public campaign when the national telephone company was privatized in 1993. The government holds a golden share in some strategic companies, giving it veto power over major decisions.

Shareholdings of more than 5% in a company must be registered, at least by nationality, though it is possible to remain anonymous. There are few barriers for international investors, except for some limits on overseas ownership of banks and certain other companies.

REGULATION

In Singapore, financial markets are increasingly transparent. The stock exchange itself sets the standards for trading. In 1996, for example, the SES instituted new rules to monitor stock trading by interested parties, specifically a director, executive or major shareholder of the company. All transactions over S$500,000 must be announced, and if the transaction is large enough, it must get shareholder approval. The move to monitor this type of insider trading has been widely interpreted as good news for investors, as an example of the openness of the market.

Watching Wall Street

What happens on Wall Street has the potential of moving markets from Bangkok to Brussels.

New York is the financial center of the U.S., and the site of its major stock markets. As more and more trading is conducted by telephone and computer, the original stock exchanges and their live trading have come to be known as traditional markets, in contrast with the newer electronic markets. In fact, though, the exchanges increasingly combine modern technology with customary methods.

The first stock exchange in America was organized in Philadelphia in 1790. But by the time the traders who met every day under the buttonwood tree on Wall Street adopted the name **New York Stock Exchange** in 1817, New York had become the center of market action.

The rival **New York Curb Exchange** was founded in 1842. Its name said it all: trading actually took place on the street until it moved indoors in 1921. In 1953, the Curb Exchange became the **American Stock Exchange**.

A STREET BY ANY OTHER NAME

Wall Street, which got its name from the stockade built by early settlers to protect New York from attacks from the north, was the scene of New York's first organized stock trading. Now it lends its name to the financial markets in general—though lots of traders never set foot on it.

OTHER U.S. MARKETS

Traditionally stocks are listed on only one of the major U.S. markets, but stocks listed on the NYSE or AMEX may also be traded on one of the **regional exchanges** located in other U.S. cities. These smaller markets, including the San Francisco-based Pacific and exchanges in Chicago, Boston and Philadelphia, are linked with the two in New York but trading can be faster and sometimes cheaper.

Trading results for stocks listed on both the NYSE and regional exchanges are combined at the end of every business day, as NYSE **composite trading** figures. Though stocks continue to be traded after the official exchanges have closed for the day—including large transactions in the U.S. "third" or afterhours market—combining U.S. exchange results helps maintain price stability.

LOOKING AT LONDON

The London Stock Exchange is a leading center for trading foreign shares. As a result, activity in the City of London, as the financial district is known, draws attention around the world.

Trading is entirely electronic, handled through two systems: the Stock Exchange Automated Quotation (SEAQ) system is for British and Irish shares, and SEAQ International is for all other listings.

Japanese and Hong Kong stocks attract significant activity. And trading in South Korean and Taiwanese shares has been growing in recent years.

THE NASDAQ STOCK MARKET

The Nasdaq Stock Market, a sophisticated electronic network, allows brokers to trade thousands of stocks from their offices all over the country.

Unlike traditional exchanges, there's no central location and no exchange floor. Instead, brokers match buy and sell orders, monitoring continuously updated prices on their computer screens, and conducting business over the telephone.

The Nasdaq Stock Market is the largest market, listing 5,500 companies—from small, emerging firms to corporate giants such as Microsoft, Apple Computer and Intel. Trading in the largest and most active Nasdaq stocks is reported in NASDAQ National Market Transactions, published every trading day in The Asian Wall Street Journal.

OVER-THE-COUNTER TRADING

Thousands of stocks aren't traded in an established market. Instead, they're bought and sold over the counter (OTC). The term originated at a time when U.S. investors actually bought stock over the counter at their local broker's office. Today, though, transactions are actually handled by telephone or computer.

Many OTC stocks are low-priced or infrequently traded, so their prices aren't reported regularly. Brokers receive daily trading results, called the pink sheets, for these stocks or subscribe to an electronic listing service that provides information on selected pink-sheet issues.

SEATS, AT A PRICE

The NYSE and AMEX are private associations that sell memberships, or seats, permitting member brokers to trade on the exchange. The NYSE has 1,366 members and the AMEX has 661. Generally, the value of a seat rises as stock prices and trading volume rise. But when there is turmoil in the markets, or when competition increases and commissions decrease, the price fluctuates. For example the price for a seat on the NYSE was $1.1 million in 1987, $295,000 in 1990, and $1.45 million in mid-1996. In Thailand, in contrast, an exchange seat costs about $12 million.

REQUIREMENTS FOR STOCK MARKET LISTING

The major U.S. stock markets impose specific requirements that companies must meet before their stock can be listed, or traded on that market. If they qualify for all three, the companies can choose where they wish to be traded.

Exchange	Requirements*	Typical daily volume*	Number Listed*
NYSE New York Stock Exchange	1.1 million publicly held shares minimum; $40 million minimum market capitalization	415.1 million shares	2,755
NASDAQ® The Nasdaq Stock Market	500,000 publicly held shares minimum; $3 million minimum market capitalization. 100,000 publicly held shares minimum; $1 million market capitalization for Nasdaq Small-Cap market	557.1 million shares	5,500
AMEX American Stock Exchange	500,000 publicly held shares minimum; minimum market capitalization of $3 million	23.8 million shares	796

*As of July 31, 1996

Gauging the U.S. Market

Investors track several averages and indexes to get a sense of American market trends.

The Dow Jones Industrial Average (DJIA) is the best known and most widely reported U.S. market indicator—one that is watched all over the world. But it isn't the only gauge for the huge U.S. stock market. A number of other indexes bear watching, too.

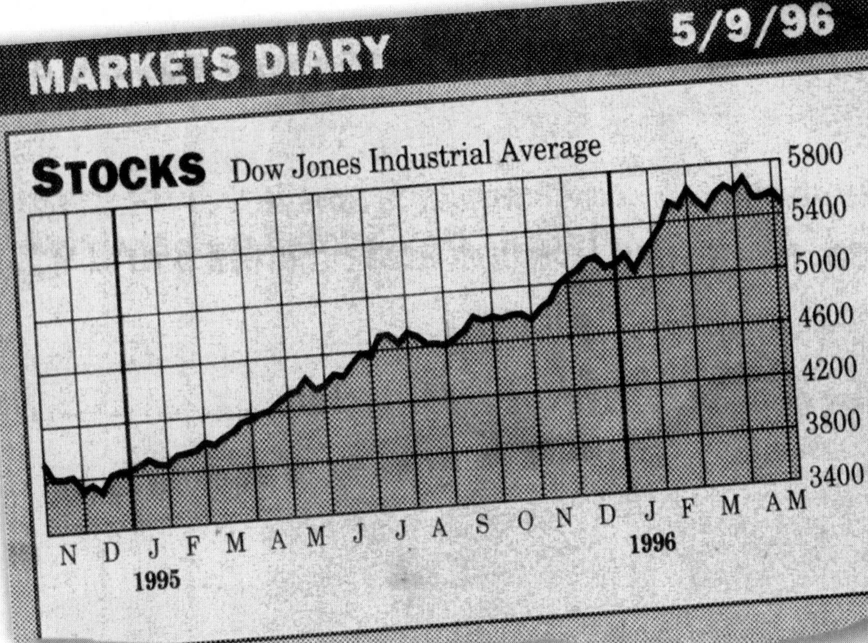

THE DOW JONES AVERAGE

The industrial average, sometimes referred to as the Dow, is often used as a synonym for the whole U.S. market. In fact, when people say, "The market was up 15 points today," they mean the Dow rose 15 points.

Originally, the Dow was a simple average of a group of stocks, and was figured by dividing the total price by the number of stocks. Today, the Dow is computed by adding the stock prices of 30 major industrial companies and dividing by a factor that adjusts for distortions caused by stock splits over the years.

As a result, the Dow is more of an index than an average. It's a yardstick by which to measure the market performance of its 30 component stocks over time. Investors who want to know what actually happened to the average price of the 30 stocks in the DJIA look at the percentage change in the Dow on a given day, not at the average itself.

GOOD BETS
Investors diversifying in stock markets around the world have reason to continue that approach. Since 1982, Morgan Stanley's Europe Australasia Far East Index (EAFE) has outperformed the Standard & Poor's 500-stock index of U.S. stocks eight years out of 14.

THE DOW'S RELIABILITY

The Dow accurately measures what it claims to measure: the performance of 30 key companies that make up about 25% of the total value of all stocks listed on the NYSE. To the extent that those companies represent key sectors of the economy, their performance indicates how the economy as a whole is doing. However, other sectors of the U.S. economy perform differently, and indexes that report on a broader range of companies sometimes give a clearer picture of the markets.

WHY WATCH THE INDEXES

The DJIA and other U.S. stock indexes, such as the Nasdaq Composite Index and Standard & Poor's 500-stock index, serve as important tools for measuring the overall health of the stock market. By comparing current market performance with how stocks behaved in the past, investors can draw better conclusions about when to buy and sell. The indexes also serve as benchmarks against which investors can measure the performance of their own portfolios. For example, if all the indexes are going up and an investor's portfolio is losing ground, it's probably time to reevaluate.

The U.S. stock market's every move is reported daily in indexes that track highs and lows, the changes from yesterday, last month and last year, plus the volume of trading and many other details.

The NYSE Composite Index includes all stocks traded on the New York Stock Exchange.

Standard & Poor's 500 Index incorporates a broad base of stocks, including industrial companies, transportation companies, utilities and financial companies. Because some of its stocks have a greater influence on the direction of the market than others, the S&P 500 is calculated by giving greater weight to those stocks.

The Nasdaq Composite Index tracks the performance of stocks traded through its electronic system. The Nasdaq index usually shows more volatility than the other indexes because of the kinds of companies it covers.

The AMEX Market Value Index monitors the performance of the companies listed on the American Stock Exchange.

Value-Line, the most widely distributed independent investment information service, tracks the performance of 1,700 common stocks.

The Russell 2000 is an index that tracks small-company stocks, including a great many of the initial public offerings of the last few years.

The Wilshire 5000, the broadest index, includes all stocks traded OTC and on exchanges, including the S&P 500.

Other Market Indicators

	1996	-- Change	--	1995
N.Y.S.E. Composite	351.76	+0.77	+0.22 %	305.47
Industrial	447.09	+1.63	+0.37 %	384.46
Utility	239.06	-1.34	-0.56 %	225.94
Transp.	318.52	-2.40	-0.75 %	292.96
Financial	300.00	+0.65	+0.22 %	255.69
Am. Ex. Mkt Val Index	557.79	-1.89	-0.34 %	536.91
Nasdaq Composite	1142.29	+0.79	+0.07 %	1039.30
Industrial	1047.61	-3.31	-0.31 %	975.11
Insurance	1288.50	-7.44	-0.57 %	1126.19
Banks	1111.74	+0.62	+0.06 %	955.96
Nasdaq Natl Mkt Comp	512.66	+0.51	+0.10 %	465.29
Industrial	428.20	-1.22	-0.28 %	397.68
Standard & Poor's 500	654.72	+2.73	+0.42 %	569.17
Industrial	773.94	+3.55	+0.46 %	672.94
Value Line Index (geom)	344.69	-0.45	-0.13 %	329.13
Wilshire 5000 Equity	6,444.684	+10.658	+0.17 %	5674.12
		Tuesday		Friday
Philadelphia Gold/Silver		126.67		124.55
Russell 2000		333.38		333.88
Toronto 300 Composite		5151.89		5143.43

READING THE INDICATORS

Each index is tracked in comparison to the previous trading day and the previous year. In the first column, the current index is reported, followed by the change from the previous trading day in numbers and as a percentage. Here, for example, the NYSE Composite is up 0.77 points or 0.22%.

Although the indexes track different combinations of stock and reflect daily differences, the overall trends, or patterns, tend to be alike. All of the indexes in this chart are up for the year even though some are down from the previous trading day.

Trading on the New York Stock Exchange

The Big Board is a popular name for the largest and most influential exchange in the U.S.

The New York Stock Exchange, like other traditional exchanges, provides the facilities for stock trading and rules under which the trading takes place. The exchange has no responsibility for setting the price of a stock. That is the result of supply and demand, and the trading process.

Stock trading on the NYSE occurs **auction style**: in each transaction, stock is sold to the highest bidder and bought for the lowest offer.

THE TRADING FLOOR
The NYSE's trading area is known as the **trading floor**.

1 The trading day begins (at 9:30 a.m. local time) and ends (at 4:00 p.m.) when the bell is rung from **the podium**.

8 **Confirmation** is made when the floor broker sends the successful trade details back to the branch office where the order originated.

7 After every deal, a reporter marks an **optical scanner card** with the stock symbol, the price and the initiating broker. The scanner transmits the information within seconds to the Exchange's electronic tape. The card also begins an **audit trail** in the event that something about the trade is suspicious.

COMPUTERIZED TRADING
Smaller orders of less than 1,200 shares are filled using a computerized system called the **Designated Order Turnaround (DOT)**. Frequently, more than 50% of any day's trades are completed this way.

6 **Post Display Units** show the day's activity at the post. They report the stocks traded, the last sale price and the order size.

Action on the exchange floor often occurs at a furious pace. People wear different colored jackets to indicate they're doing specific jobs:

Light blue jackets with orange epaulets for messengers

Green jackets for floor supervisors or traders

Navy jackets for exchange "reporters"

2 The Exchange rents **booths** to brokerage houses. Each booth is home base for a firm's floor brokers. When an order is received from one of its brokerage offices, a floor broker takes the order to the appropriate **specialist** post to carry out the transaction.

3 The Exchange rents space to **specialist** firms—the brokers to brokers. A specialist keeps a list of unfilled orders. As buy and sell orders move in response to price changes, the specialist facilitates transactions.

The specialists' other job is to maintain an orderly market in a stock. If the **spread** between the **bid** and **ask** (the gap between the highest price offered by a buyer and the lowest price asked by a seller) becomes too wide, specialists turn into dealers themselves, buying and selling stock. This narrows the spread and stimulates trading—a good thing for the vitality of the exchange and for the specialists as well, since the more they trade, the more commission they earn.

4 Various stocks or groups of stocks are traded at **trading posts** near the specialists' positions. Each company's stock trades at only one post on the floor of the Exchange, so the trading can be tracked accurately. However, the stock of several different companies may be traded at the same post. The number of companies assigned depends on the combined volume of business they generate.

5 Floor brokers can use a specialist if they choose. But many trades actually occur between two floor brokers who show up at the post at the same time.

On a typical day a floor broker walks—or runs—an average of

19 KM,

crisscrossing the floor.

Reading U.S. Stock Tables

The stock tables keep investors up to date on what's happening in the market.

Information summarizing Big Board trading appears daily in The Asian Wall Street Journal. **Highest and lowest prices** for the past 52 weeks are included. When there's a new high or low, it's indicated with an arrow in the margin, such as the one next to Deere in the second column below. The range between the prices is a measure of the stock's volatility, or price movement. The stock with the most volatile price here is Chrysler, where the range of movement is from 18⅞ to 47⅞—about 150%.

Percent yield is one way to evaluate the stock's current value. It tells you how much dividend you get as a percentage of the current price. For example, the yield on Chrysler is 1.4%

Percent yield also lets you compare your earnings on a stock with earnings on other investments. But it doesn't tell you your total return, which is the sum of your dividends plus increases (or decreases) in stock price. When there's no dividend, yield can't be calculated, so the column is left blank.

NYSE

Close	Net Chg		52 Weeks Hi	52 Weeks Lo	Stock	Sym	Div	Yld %	PE	Vol 100s	Hi	Lo	Close	Net Ch
39⅜	+ ⅝		47⅞	18⅞	Chrysler	C	.60	1.4	8	12256	43¾	43⅛	43¼	–
19¼	+ ⅛		96⅜	73½	Chubb	CB	1.72	1.9	13	763	93	92¼	92¾	+
16⅛	– ⅛		35¾	23⅝	Church&Dwt	CHD	.44f	1.9	16	240	24¼	23¾	23¾	
17½	+ ⅛		1¼	½	Chyron	CHY		...	...	1526	½	½	½	–
68⅞	+ ⅝		43¾	37	Cilcorp Inc	CER	2.46	5.8	18	12	42⅝	42⅜	42⅝	+
34⅜	– ⅛		24⅜	15⅜	CincBell	CSN	.80	4.1	28	513	19¾	19¼	19⅝	–
467⅝	+1¾	s	28⅝	23¼	CincGE	CIN	1.66	6.0	14	974	27⅝	27⅜	27⅝	
28⅜	– ¼		62	50½	CincGE pfA		4.00	6.7	...	z110	59½	58	59½	+1
48	+2		**29⅝**	**12⅝**	**CincMilacron**	**CMZ**	**.36**	**1.5**	**32**	**1384**	**24⅝**	**23⅜**	**24⅝**	**+1**
19⅝	+ ½		3⅜	1⅛	CineplxOde	CPX		...	dd	493	2¾	2½	2⅝	
51	+ ¼	s	33⅞	14⅛	CircuitCty	CC	.08	.3	22	5653	27⅝	26¾	27	–
8⅛	– ⅛	s	41½	27½	Circus	CIR		...	26	3083	38¼	37⅛	37⅜	–
38¼	+ ¼		33⅝	14⅜	Citicorp	CCI		...	14	9615	32⅞	32½	32⅝	–
19½	...		89¼	68¼	Citicorp pf		6.00							+
27	+ ¼		100½	80¾	Citicorp pfA									
26⅛	+ ¼		27[illegible]											
25¼	+ ⅜													

Corporations are listed alphabetically—sometimes in shortened versions of the actual name—and followed by their trading symbol. An **s** in the left margin indicates a stock split, such as the one at Circus (see page 31).

Cash dividends per share is an estimate of the anticipated yearly dividend per share in dollars and cents. Notice that the prices of stocks that pay dividends tend to be higher than the prices of stocks with no dividend. Chubb's yearly dividend is estimated at $1.72 a share. If you owned 100 shares, you'd receive $172 in dividend payments, probably in quarterly payments of $43.

MOVING AVERAGE

A moving average is created by charting 52 weeks of weekly average stock prices. It's moving because the chart is updated every week by dropping the oldest number and adding the newest one. The result is a smoother curve than you would get by recording the daily ups and downs of the market.

Price/earnings ratio (P/E) shows the relationship between a stock's price and the company's earnings for the last four quarters. It's figured by dividing the current price per share by the earnings per share—a number the stock table doesn't provide as a separate piece of information. Here, for example, Dayton Hudson's P/E ratio of 14 means its price is 14 times its annual per share earnings.

Since stock investors are interested in earnings, they use P/E ratios to compare the relative value of different stocks. But the P/E ratio isn't foolproof. It reports past earnings, not future potential. Two companies with the same P/E may face very different futures: one on its way to posting higher earnings and the other headed for a loss.

There's no perfect P/E ratio, though some investors avoid stocks if they think the ratio is too high. A small company growing rapidly can have a high P/E, yet still be an attractive investment. On the other hand, a profitable, mature company could be a poor investment because its high P/E means the likelihood of a reduced return on investment.

Volume refers to the number of shares traded the previous day. Unless a **Z** appears before the number in this column, multiply by 100 to get the number of shares. (The Z indicates the actual number traded.) An unusually large volume, indicated by underlining, usually means buyers and sellers are reacting to some new information. In this example, 827,800 shares of Data General were traded in this session.

COMPOSITE TRANSACTIONS

52 Weeks Hi	52 Weeks Lo	Stock	Sym	Div	Yld %	PE	Vol 100s	Hi	Lo	Close	Net Chg
36⅝	21⅛	Danaher	DHR	.06e	.2	25	536	35⅝	35¼	35⅝	...
14¾	10½	DanielInd	DAN	.18	1.2	43	112	14¾	14⅝	14¾	+ ¼
13⅞	7⅝	DataGen	DGN		...	dd	8278	8¼	8	8¼	+ ¼
7⅜	1⅜	Datapoint	DPT		...	dd	540	6⅜	6	6⅜	+ ¼
9⅛	6⅛	Datapoint pfA		1.00	12.5	...	66	8⅛	8	8	...
7¼	5	DavisW&W	DWW		...	cc	17	6¼	6⅛	6⅛	– ⅛
85	61⅛	DaytnHud	DH	1.60	2.3	14	1429	69⅛	68⅛	68⅝	+ ⅝
29⅞	23⅛	DeanFood	DF	.64f	2.3	16	457	27⅝	27⅜	27½	– ⅛
9½	8¾	DeanWtGvTr	GVT	.72	7.9	...	804	9¼	9⅛	9⅛	– ⅛
39¼	30⅝	DeanWtDscvr	DWD	.10p	.3	...	3622	38⅜	37¼	37¼	–1
67½	36¾	Deere	DE	2.00	3.0	cc	3073	67⅝	66⅞	67⅛	+ ⅜
2⅝	5/16	DelValFnl	DVL		...	dd	107	1⅜	1⅜	1⅜	– ⅛
15⅛	13⅝	DelGpDivInco	DDF	1.06	7.4	...	276	14½	14⅜	14⅜	+ ⅛
24½	21½	DelmarPL	DEW	1.54	6.3	15	2501	24½	24¼	24½	+ ⅛

	52 Week Hi	Lo
s	45	20
	18½	12
s	40¾	29
	33½	30
	24⅜	11
	10½	7
	8⅛	4
	8	4
	14⅜	6
	49	31
	34½	21
n	18	13
▲	3⅝	15
	34⅞	17

High, low and **close** reports a stock's highest, lowest and closing price for the previous day. Usually the daily difference is small even if the 52 week spread is large. One of the largest spreads here is for Deere, which was as high as 67⅝ and as low as 66⅞ before closing at 67⅛.

Net change compares the closing price in the chart with the previous closing price. A minus (–) indicates a lower price, and a plus (+) means it's higher. Here, Dayton Hudson closed at 68⅝, up ⅝ point from the day before. Prices that change 5% or more are in **boldface**, as CincMilacron is here.

Stock prices are given in fractions of dollars, from ⅛ to ⅞:

⅛	¼	⅜	½	⅝	¾	⅞
12½¢	25¢	37½¢	50¢	62½¢	75¢	87½¢

Bonds: Financing the Future

Bonds are loans that investors make. The borrowers get the cash they need while the lenders earn interest.

Bonds appeal to many investors because they promise to pay a set amount of interest on a regular basis. That's why they're called **fixed-income securities**.

Another attraction is that the issuer promises to repay the loan in full and on time. So bonds seem less risky than investments that depend on the ups and downs of a stock market.

A bond also has a fixed **maturity date** when the loan expires and must be paid back in full, at **par value**, or the amount it cost when it was issued. The interest a bond pays is also set when the bond is issued. The rate is competitive, which means the bond pays interest comparable to what investors can earn on other investments of similar term and risk.

THE LIFE OF A BOND

The life, or **term**, of any bond is fixed at the time of issue. It can range from **short-term** (usually a year or less), to **intermediate-term** (two to ten years), to **long-term** (ten to 30 years or more). Generally speaking, the longer the term, the higher the interest rate that's offered to make up for the additional risk of tying up money for so long a time. The relationship between the interest rates paid on short-term and long-term bonds is called the **yield curve**.

ISSUING BONDS

The corporations, governments and supranational organizations that issue bonds all want to raise money from investors, though not for the same reasons.

Corporations often need large amounts of cash to finance growth and development, and use bonds to provide those infusions. The issuers believe that the borrowed money will help build the business, and the increased earnings will be available to repay the loans.

Governments aren't profit-making enterprises, so bonds are the primary way they can raise money to fund capital projects such as roads or airports. Bonds also provide the money to keep everyday government operations running when other revenues (primarily taxes) aren't sufficient to cover the cost. When governments have an operating deficit, they may need to borrow increasing amounts from investors, creating added fiscal problems.

Supranational organizations issue bonds to raise funds internationally that can be used for infrastructure and other projects in developing nations, which may have difficulty raising capital on their own.

MAKING MONEY WITH BONDS

Conservative investors use bonds to provide a steady income. They buy a bond when it's issued and hold it, expecting to receive regular, fixed-interest payments until the bond matures. Then they get the principal back to reinvest.

SELECTING BONDS

Investors choose among the three basic bond types, and from a variety of issuers within each category. For example, they can buy domestic bonds, which are issued in their own country and sold in their

When interest rates fluctuate, as they do in certain economic conditions, some investors try to make money by trading bonds rather than holding them. Bonds that are issued when interest rates are high become increasingly valuable when interest rates fall. That's because investors are willing to pay more than par value for a bond with a 10% interest rate if the current rate is 7%.

In this way, an increase in the price of a bond, or **capital appreciation**, often produces more profits for bond sellers than holding the bonds to maturity.

But there are also risks in bond trading. If interest rates go up, buyers may lose money because the bonds they hold don't pay as well as the newer ones being issued. And they won't be able to get back the full amount that they've paid for the bond if they sell (see pages 88–89).

The other risk bondholders face is rising inflation (see pages 22–23). Since the interest amount they earn on a bond investment doesn't change, the value of that money can be eroded by inflation. For example, if an investor has a 30-year bond paying $5,000 annual interest, the money would buy less in 1999 than it did in 1979.

THE INSTITUTION AS BORROWER

CORPORATE BONDS

Corporations use bonds
- To raise capital to pay for expansion, modernization
- To finance corporate takeovers or other changes in management structure

GOVERNMENT BONDS

Governments use debt issues
- To pay for a wide range of government activities
- To pay off the national debt

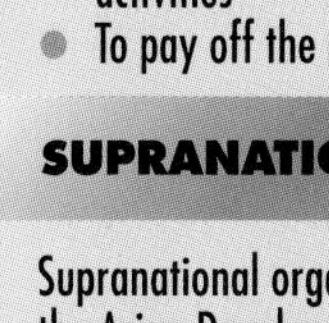

SUPRANATIONAL DEBT

Supranational organizations such as the Asian Development Bank and the World Bank tap international credit markets to raise funds and provide capital for projects in developing nations

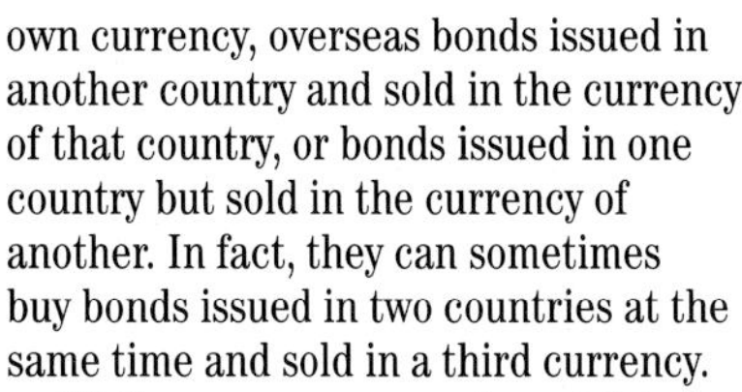

own currency, overseas bonds issued in another country and sold in the currency of that country, or bonds issued in one country but sold in the currency of another. In fact, they can sometimes buy bonds issued in two countries at the same time and sold in a third currency.

While some governments restrict who is eligible to buy their domestic bonds, other countries, including the U.S., sell bonds to all buyers. In fact, the U.S. Treasury estimates that at the end of 1995 about 26% of all privately held Treasury bonds were held overseas, nearly 7% by Japanese investors.

MAKING CHOICES

The choices individual and institutional investors make among available bonds are usually based on one or more of the following:

- **Where they can earn the most**
- **What the bond would cost them**
- **How confident they are in the issuer's ability to pay**
- **The diversity they can achieve by owning different bonds**

Issuers, on the other hand, are usually most concerned with raising as much money as they can for the least expense.

A World of Bonds

Despite some differences in the details, the role bonds play is decidedly universal.

Bonds are issued around the world to provide businesses and governments with money that might be difficult or impossible to raise any other way. And, as the globalization of financial markets increases, issuers offer their debt not only at home but also in countries where they can share the benefits of low interest rates and/or the strength of the currency. Issuers are also looking for demand, or markets where investors have cash reserves that they are willing to invest in debt.

Some large bond issues—ones trying to raise $2 billion, for example—are sometimes offered in three time zones simultaneously, usually in London, New York and either Tokyo or Hong Kong. These **global bonds** seek the largest possible investor base, often for supranational agencies such as the World Bank.

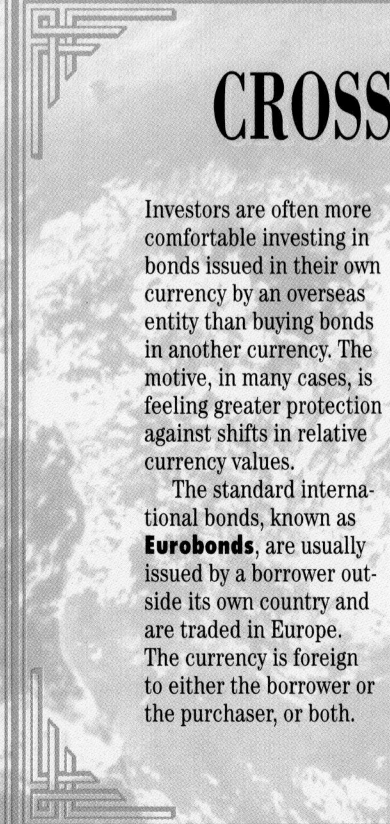

CROSS

Investors are often more comfortable investing in bonds issued in their own currency by an overseas entity than buying bonds in another currency. The motive, in many cases, is feeling greater protection against shifts in relative currency values.

The standard international bonds, known as **Eurobonds**, are usually issued by a borrower outside its own country and are traded in Europe. The currency is foreign to either the borrower or the purchaser, or both.

GROWING MARKETS

Asian-Pacific bond markets are expanding, fostered in part by attention from the governments in the region. For them to grow, experts agree that issuers must tap the capital that's available locally and build an investor base. They also suggest that when more bonds available in Asia are offered by Asian issuers there may be added interest.

Some markets also remain closed to overseas investors, or are subject to government intervention. Plus, some areas lack a strong **secondary market**, where bonds trade after they're issued, or a regional settlement system.

Currently, Japan has the largest bond market in the region, followed by Australia and New Zealand. Hong Kong has a thriving market, and markets in South Korea, Malaysia and Thailand are developing. Singapore's local-currency bond market remains small, although foreign-currency bonds are traded actively in what is known as the Asian dollar market.

BORROWER AND LENDER

The Asian Development Bank is both a borrower and a lender. The Manila-based bank is owned by its 56 member countries, 46 from the Asian-Pacific region. The bank raises money through international debt offerings. It also offers interest-free loans to developing nations through the Asia Development Fund. About one-third of its total lending falls into that category.

CHINA'S BOND MARKET
In 1996, China was developing a new national bond law to strengthen issuing and trading regulations in that market and to allow greater diversity in the types of debt the government issues. The law is also designed to make it easier to introduce auction-style sales, the norm for most government bonds, and give the overall market a boost.

BORDER INVESTING

Yankee bonds are issued by an overseas borrower for U.S. investors. They're payable in dollars and registered with the U.S. Securities and Exchange Commission.

Samurai bonds are yen-denominated bonds issued in Japan by overseas governments or companies. The bonds can be settled only in Japan, though they may be **dual-currency** issues. That means the payment and the interest are in yen, but the redemption is in another currency, such as the dollar or the Australian dollar. In a **reverse dual-currency** issue, the payment and redemption are in yen, but the interest is paid in another currency. Dual-currency Eurobond issues are also available.

Other bonds, sometimes called **dragon bonds**, are launched and priced in Asia for non-Japanese Asian investors, and traded primarily in Asian time. The debt is usually but not always issued in dollars and is frequently listed on at least two stock exchanges in the region, usually Hong Kong and Singapore.

THE WORLD BANK

The World Bank, or more formally the International Bank for Reconstruction and Development (IBRD), is an investment bank that raises money by issuing bonds to individuals, institutions and governments in more than 100 countries. The bonds are guaranteed by the governments of the 178 countries who own the bank.

The World Bank lends the money from its investors to the governments of developing countries at affordable interest rates, to help finance internal projects and economic policy reforms. The poorer the country, the more favorable terms the bank offers. In fact, long-term loans to the poorest nations through its International Development Association (IDA) are interest-free.

Its International Finance Corporation (IFC) finances private enterprise in the developing world, provides advice and technical services, and helps stimulate additional financing from other investors. And its affiliate Multilateral Investment Guarantee Agency promotes private investment in developing countries. One approach it takes is to provide guarantees to protect investors from political risks such as war or nationalization that might otherwise make them reluctant to participate.

Types of Bonds

The words that are used to describe bonds have very specific meanings.

Like the word **security**, which once meant the written record of an investment, the word **bond** once referred to the piece of paper that described the details of a loan transaction. Today the term is used more generally to describe a vast and varied market in debt securities.

The language that describes a specific bond tells potential investors its distinctive characteristics. Sometimes the terminology applies only to nongovernment bonds, but in some cases it may apply to certain government bonds as well. The ones described on these pages are primarily domestic bonds, sold within a country's border in its own currency.

BOND

How Bonds Are Backed Up

ASSET-BACKED BONDS, created in the U.S. in the mid-1980s and growing in popularity in Asia, are secured, or backed up, by specific holdings of the issuing corporation, such as equipment or real estate. An asset-backed bond can be created when a securities firm **bundles** some type of debt, such as mortgages, and sells investors the right to receive the payments that consumers are making on those loans.

DEBENTURES are the most common corporate bonds. They're backed by the credit of the issuer, rather than by any specific assets. Though they sound riskier, they're generally not. The debentures of reliable institutions are often more highly rated than asset-backed bonds.

MORTGAGE-BACKED BONDS are backed by a pool of mortgage loans. They're sold to brokers by government agencies and private corporations, and the brokers resell them to investors.

In the U.S., mortgage-backed bonds are **self-amortizing**. That means each payment an investor gets includes both principal and interest, so that there is no lump-sum repayment at maturity.

Mortgage-backed securities are becoming increasingly popular in Australia, with banks becoming more active as issuers. There's also interest in this type of security in Hong Kong and in Malaysia.

Bonds With Conditions

A SUBORDINATED BOND is one that will be paid after other loan obligations of the issuer have been met. **Senior** bonds are those with stronger claims. Corporations sometimes sell senior and subordinated bonds in the same issue, offering more interest and a shorter term on the subordinated ones to make them more attractive.

CONVERTIBLE BONDS give investors the option to convert, or change, their corporate bonds into company stock instead of getting a cash repayment. The terms are set at issue; they include the date the conversion can be made, and how much stock each bond can be exchanged for. The conversion option lets the issuer offer a lower initial interest rate, and makes the bond price less sensitive than conventional bonds to changes in the interest rate.

CALLABLE BONDS don't always run their full term. The issuer may **call** the bond—pay off the debt—before the maturity date. It's a process called **redemption**. The first date a bond is vulnerable to call is named at the time of issue.

Issuers may want to call a bond if interest rates drop. If they pay off their outstanding bonds, they can float another bond at the lower rate. Sometimes only part of an issue is redeemed, rather than all of it. In the U.S., the ones that are called are chosen by lottery.

Callable bonds are more risky for investors than noncallable ones because an investor whose bond has been called is often faced with reinvesting the money at a lower, less attractive rate. To protect bondholders expecting long-term steady income, call provisions usually specify that a bond can't be called before a certain number of years.

Popular Innovations

ZERO-COUPON BONDS are a popular variation on the bond theme for some investors. Since **coupon**, in bond terminology, means interest, a zero-coupon by definition pays out no interest while the loan is maturing. Instead, the interest **accrues**, or builds up, and is paid in a lump sum at maturity.

Investors buy zero-coupon bonds at **deep discount**, or prices far lower than par value. When the bond matures, the accrued interest and the original investment add up to the bond's par value.

Organizations like to issue zeros because they can continue to use the loan money without paying periodic interest. Investors like zeros because they can buy more bonds for their money, and time the maturities to coincide with anticipated expenses. Zeros have some drawbacks: they are extremely volatile in the secondary market, so investors can't be sure how they'll make out if they need to sell; and, in the U.S., investors have to pay taxes every year on the interest they *would have received* had an actual payment been made.

INFLATION-INDEXED BONDS
The U.S. Treasury now issues **inflation-indexed bonds** specifically designed to offer returns that would protect investors from the negative effects of inflation on fixed-income investments. Australia, Britain and Canada offer similar bonds.

The bonds have their yields pegged, or linked, to some measure or measures of inflation so that their value will remain relatively constant over time no matter what inflation does. They may be offered in denominations as small as $100 to make them accessible to more people. But from the government's point of view, their greatest appeal is being able to lock in long-term debt payment at a rate likely to be lower than the going rates.

MARKET MAKERS
Most nations have an organized group of bond dealers, known as primary dealers or sometimes market makers, that handles sales and takes responsibility for maintaining a certain level of liquidity in the market.

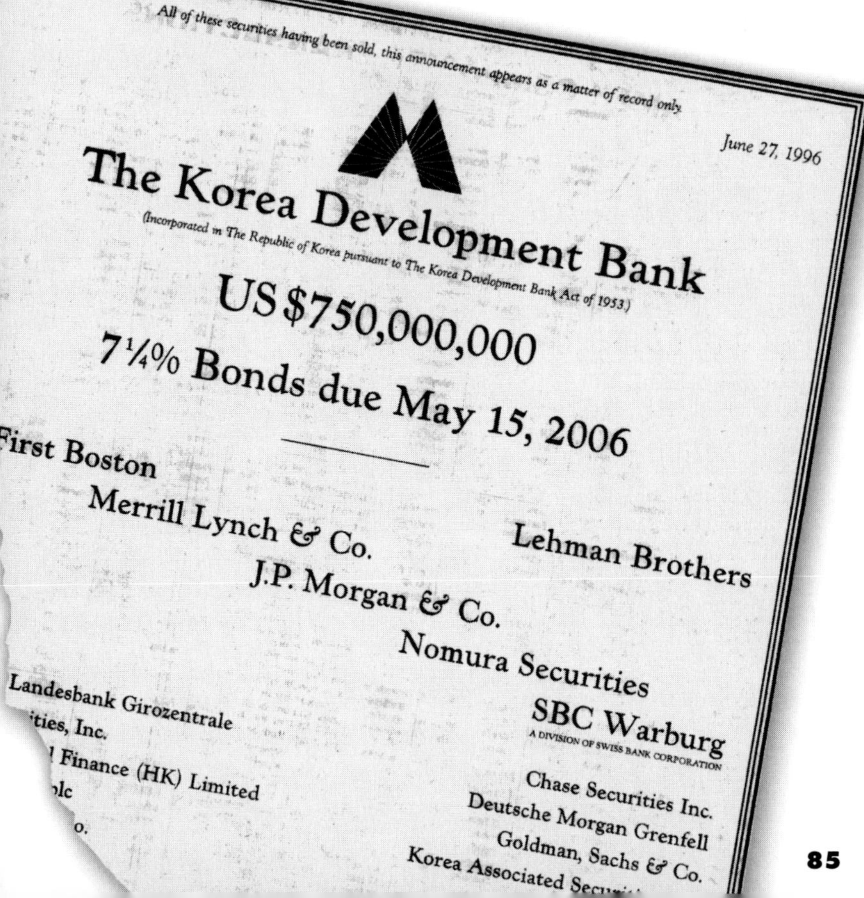
All of these securities having been sold, this announcement appears as a matter of record only.

June 27, 1996

The Korea Development Bank

(Incorporated in The Republic of Korea pursuant to The Korea Development Bank Act of 1953)

US $750,000,000

7¼% Bonds due May 15, 2006

First Boston

Merrill Lynch & Co. Lehman Brothers

J.P. Morgan & Co.

Nomura Securities

SBC Warburg
A DIVISION OF SWISS BANK CORPORATION

Landesbank Girozentrale

ities, Inc.

Finance (HK) Limited

lc

o.

Chase Securities Inc.

Deutsche Morgan Grenfell

Goldman, Sachs & Co.

Korea Associated Secu

The Bond Certificate

A bond certificate is a record of the loan and the terms of repayment.

Unlike stockholders, who have **equity**, or part ownership, in a company, bondholders are **creditors**. The bond is an IOU, or a record of the money they've lent and the terms on which it will be repaid.

Until 1983, all bonds in the U.S. were issued as certificates. **Bearer bonds** had coupons attached to the certificate; when it was time to collect an interest payment, the investor, or bearer, detached the coupon and redeemed it. That's why a bond's interest rate is known as its **coupon rate**.

Though new bonds aren't usually issued in certificate form, there are thousands of investors still holding certificates for bonds issued in the U.S. Today most new bonds are registered and stored electronically, the way stock purchases are. They're called **book-entry bonds**.

SURVIVING BEARERS
Eurobonds, or bonds issued by a borrower outside its own country, continue to be *bearer bonds*. They're not registered with any regulatory authority, and can be traded or redeemed by whoever holds them. They're often used by governments looking for cheaper ways to raise money than issuing a domestic bond.

Bonds are registered by the issuer and carry an **identifying number**. The owner's name also appears.

The issuer is the corporation, government or agency that issues the bond. It is identified by name and often by a symbol or logo. Its **official seal** authenticates the bond's validity. When a company issues bonds, the documents have the same design as the company's stock certificates. And they are protected against counterfeiting in the same way, with special paper, elaborate borders and intaglio printing.

LONG

The 30-year U.S. Treasury bond is popularly known as the long bond. But the longest bonds around are

Interest rate is the percentage of par value that is paid to the bondholder on a regular basis. For example, a $1,000 bond that pays 9.5% yields $95 a year. If the original buyer holds the bond to maturity, the **yield**, or return on investment, is also 9.5% a year. However, if the bond is traded, the yield could change even though the interest rate stays the same. For example, if an investor buys the bond for $1,100 in the secondary market, the interest will still be $95 a year, but the yield will be reduced to 8.6%, because the new owner paid more for the bond (see page 89 about figuring yield).

Par value, or the dollar amount of the bond at the time it was issued, appears several times on the face of the bond. Par value is the amount originally paid for the bond and the amount that will be repaid at maturity. Many bonds are sold in multiples of $1,000.

A **baby bond** has a par value of less than $1,000. Bonds of $500 or less are sometimes issued by local governments to involve a larger number of people in the fund-raising process.

Maturity date is the date the bond comes due and must be repaid. A bond can be bought and sold in its lifetime for more or less than par value, depending on market conditions. Whoever owns the bond at maturity is the one who gets par value back.

22222

REGISTERED

ONLY, THE
N THE NOTE
E IS JUNE 6,
MPOUNDED
. HOLDERS
COME TAX
NAL ISSUE
NAL ISSUE
ME BY THE
6, 1989 AND
FERRED TO
SCOUNT ON
THE YIELD

IBLE

CUSIP 121212 AA 0

SEE REVERSE FOR CERTAIN DEFINITIONS

CUC INTERNATIONAL INC.

nal Inc., a Delaware corporation (the "Issuer"), for value received hereby promises to pay to

JOHN B. HOLDER

DUE 1999

DOLLARS

e in New York, New York on June 6, 1996 in such coin or currency of the United States of America as at the time of payment shall be legal tender for the payment of public and private debts. ear interest except in the case of a default in payment of principal upon acceleration, redemption or at maturity and in such case the overdue principal of this Security shall bear interest at the yment of such interest shall be legally enforceable), which shall accrue from the date of such default in payment to the date payment of such overdue principal has been made or duly provided s of a 360-day year of twelve 30-day months. Interest on any overdue principal shall be payable on demand. Payment of the principal of and any such interest on this Security will be made at the hat purpose in New York, New York.
ns set forth on the reverse hereof including without limitation provisions subordinating the payment of principal of and interest on overdue principal, if any, on the Securities to the payment in re dated as of May 25, 1989 (the "Indenture") between the Issuer and Morgan Guaranty Trust Company of New York, as Trustee (the "Trustee"), and provisions giving the holder hereof the tock, par value $.01 per share ("Common Stock"), of the Issuer on the terms and subject to the conditions and limitations referred to on the reverse hereof, as more fully specified in the

poses have the same effect as though fully set forth at this place.
atory until the certificate of authentication hereon shall have been duly signed by the Trustee acting under the Indenture.

hereof, the Issuer has caused this instrument to be duly executed under its corporate seal.

CUC International Inc.

HENTICATION
ribed in the within-mentioned

MPANY OF NEW YORK,
as Trustee

Authorized Officer

Attest:

Secretary

By:

Chairman of the Board

100-year corporate bonds, including those introduced in 1993 by Walt Disney Co. The first ones come due in 2093.

Figuring a Bond's Worth

The value of a bond is determined by the interest it pays and by what's happening in the economy.

A bond's interest rate never changes, even though other interest rates do. If the bond is paying more interest than is available elsewhere, investors will be willing to pay more to own it. If the bond is paying less, the reverse is true.

Interest rates and bond prices fluctuate like two sides of a seesaw. As the table below illustrates, when interest rates drop, the value of existing bonds usually goes up. When rates climb, the value of existing bonds usually falls.

Several factors—including **yield** and **return**—affect whether or not a bond turns out to be a good investment.

PAR FOR THE COURSE

If the bond investor buys at par, and holds the bond to maturity, **inflation**, or the shrinking value of the currency, is the worst enemy. The longer the maturity of the bond, the greater the risk that at some point inflation will rise dramatically and reduce the value of the money that the investor is repaid.

If the bond pays more than the rate of inflation, the investor comes out ahead. For example, if a bond is paying 8% and the annual rate of inflation is 3%, the bond produces real earnings of 5%. But if inflation shoots up to 10%, the interest earnings won't buy what they once did. And in either case, the principal invested in the bond also shrinks in value.

UNDER (AND OVER) PAR

But many bonds, particularly those with maturities of five or more years, aren't held by one investor from the date of issue to the date of maturity. Rather, investors trade bonds in the secondary market. The prices fluctuate according to the interest rate, time to maturity, the degree of certainty of repayment and overall economic conditions—especially the rate of inflation—that influence interest rates.

SELLERS / BUYERS

At Issue

U.S. bond issuer is selling bond

AT PAR VALUE

Par value:	$1,000
Term:	10 Years
Interest rate:	6%

6% Prevailing interest rate

BUYING AT PAR VALUE

- Pay par value at issue and keep till maturity
- Receive ten annual interest payments of $60
- Receive par value—$1,000—at maturity

2 Years Later

If bondholder sells two years after issue when interest rates are high, the bond is

SELLING AT A DISCOUNT

Market value	$ 800
Interest (x2)	+$ 120
	$ 920
Less original cost	–$1,000
LOSS	**$ 80**

8% Prevailing interest rate

BUYING AT A DISCOUNT

- Pay $200 less than par value
- Receive eight annual interest payments of $60
- Receive par value—$1,000—at maturity

3 Years Later

If bondholder sells three years after issue when interest rates are low, the bond is

SELLING AT A PREMIUM

Market value	$1,200
Interest (x3)	+$ 180
	$1,380
Less original cost	–$1,000
RETURN	**$380**

3% Prevailing interest rate

BUYING AT A PREMIUM

- Pay $200 more than par value
- Receive seven annual interest payments of $60
- Receive par value—$1,000—at maturity

HOW IT WORKS

Generally, when inflation is up, interest rates go up. And conversely, when inflation is low, so are interest rates. It's the change or anticipated change in interest rates that causes bond prices to move up or down.

If a corporation floats a new issue of bonds offering 6% interest, it seems like a good deal; so you buy some bonds at the par value price of $1,000. Three years later, interest rates are up. If new bonds costing $1,000 are paying 8% interest, no buyer will pay you $1,000 for a bond paying 6%. To sell your bond you'll have to offer it at a **discount**, or less than you paid. If you must sell, you might have to settle for a price that wipes out most of the interest you've earned.

But consider the reverse situation. If new bonds selling for $1,000 offer only a 3% interest rate, you'll be able to sell your 6% bonds for more than you paid—since buyers will agree to pay more to get a higher interest rate. That **premium**, combined with the interest payments for the last three years, makes a tidy profit.

The fluctuations in interest rates, and therefore in bond prices, produce much of the trading that goes on in the bond market as investors try to get out of low-interest-rate bonds or try to make profits on high-interest-rate bonds.

CHANGING YIELD

Yield is what you actually earn. If you buy a 10-year $1,000 bond paying 6% and hold it until it matures, you'll earn $60 a year for ten years—an annual yield of 6%, or the same as the interest rate.

But if you buy in the secondary market, after the date of issue, the bond's yield may not be the same as its interest rate. That's because the interest rate stays the same, but the price you pay may vary, changing the yield.

Most bond charts express current yield as a percentage. For example, if a bond's yield is given as 6%, it means your interest payments will be 6% of what you pay for the bond today—or 6% back on your investment. Investors use the yield to compare the relative value of bonds.

Return is what you make on the investment when the par value of the bond, the profit or loss from trading it and the yield are computed.

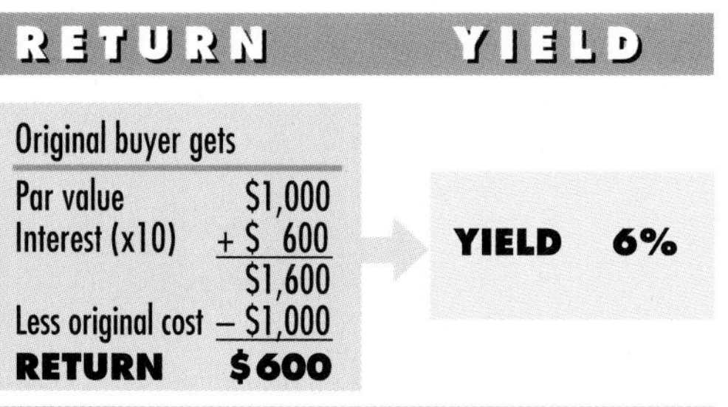

RETURN		YIELD
Original buyer gets		
Par value	$1,000	
Interest (x10)	+ $ 600	YIELD 6%
	$1,600	
Less original cost	– $1,000	
RETURN	**$600**	

New buyer gets		
Par value	$1,000	
Interest (x8)	+ $ 480	YIELD 7.5%
	$1,480	
Less original cost	– $ 800	
RETURN	**$680**	

New buyer gets		
Par value	$1,000	
Interest (x7)	+ $ 420	YIELD 5%
	$1,420	
Less original cost	– $1,200	
RETURN	**$220**	

HOW TO FIGURE A BOND'S YIELD

$$\frac{\text{Annual interest}}{\text{Price}} = \text{Yield}$$

for example

$$\frac{\$60}{\$1000} = 6\%$$

YIELD TO MATURITY

There's an even more precise measure of a bond's value called the **yield to maturity**. It takes into account the interest rate in relation to the price, the purchase price vs. the par value and the years remaining until the bond matures. If you paid $200 less than par value for a bond, that discount will be added to your interest in calculating the yield to maturity. Yield to maturity is a way to predict return over time.

Yield to maturity is calculated by a complicated formula—and it isn't often stated in bond tables. Brokers have access to the information, and computers can be programmed to provide it.

Rating Bonds

Investors want to know the risks in buying a bond before they take the plunge. Rating services measure those risks.

Bond investors want to be reasonably sure that they'll get their interest payments on time and their principal back at maturity. It's almost impossible for an individual to do the necessary research. But rating services make a business of it.

The best-known services are **Standard & Poor's Corp.** and **Moody's Investors Service Inc.** These companies investigate the financial condition of a bond issuer rather than the market appeal of its bonds. They look at other debt the issuer has, how fast a company's revenue and profit are growing, the state of the economy, and how well other companies in the same business (or comparable national economies) are doing. Their primary concern is to alert investors to the risks of a particular issue.

Issuers rarely publicize their ratings, unless they are top of the line. So investors need to get the information from the rating services themselves, from the financial press or their own brokers.

WHAT BONDS GET RATED?

The rating services pass judgement on all kinds of corporate and international bonds. Asian Development Bank debt is rated triple-A, for instance. U.S. Treasurys are not rated—the assumption is that they're absolutely solid since they're obligations of the U.S. government, backed by its full faith and credit. This means the government has the authority to raise taxes to pay off its debts.

JAPAN'S RATING AGENCIES

Three Japanese credit-rating agencies, Japan Bond Research Institute (JBRI), the Japan Credit Rating Agency (JCR), and Nippon Investors Service (NIS), are active in assigning rates.

Rating a Bond: A Key to the Code

Moody's	Standard & Poor's
Aaa	AAA
Aa	AA
A	A
Baa	BBB
Ba	BB
B	B
Caa	CCC
Ca	CC
C	C
•	D

The ratings of the Japanese agencies are often higher than S&P's or Moody's, and there has been some criticism that their rating criteria aren't as strict. International investors may give those ratings less weight as a result.

Japanese Corporate Bond Ratings

Rating	Issuer	Type		Amount	Due	Guarantor
AA	UNY Co., Ltd.	Unsec	Deb	Yen 10 Billion	2002	
A	Mitsubishi Estate	Unsec	Deb	Yen 15 Billion	2003	
A	Mitsubishi Estate	Unsec	Deb	Yen 10 Billion	2006	
A	Trusco Nakayama	Unsec WW	Deb	Yen 0.425 Billion	2000	
*A	Nakamichi Leasing	Unsec	Deb	DM 40 Million	2001	(P.P.) IBJ
*A	Toyo Radiator Co.	Unsec WW	Deb	SF 60 Million	2000	(P.P.) DKB
BBB	Taisei Corporation	Unsec	Deb	Yen (E) 5 Billion	2002	(P.P.)
*BBB	Goto Co., Ltd.	Unsec WW	Deb	SF 25 Million	2000	(P.P.) Tokai Bk
BB	Hankyu Realty Co.	Unsec	Deb	Yen 5 Billion	2001	
B	Marubeni Corporation	Unsec	Deb	Yen (E) 5.6 Billion	2004	(P.P.)

Conv Deb—Convertible Debenture; Conv Price—Convertible Price; Deb—Debenture; Dtd—Issuing Date; Exc Rate—Exchange Rate; Exer Price—Exercise Price; Unsec—Unsecured; WW Deb—With Warrants Debenture.

Source: Mikuni & Co.,

THE RISK OF DOWNGRADING

One danger bondholders face—and one they can't anticipate—is that a rating service may **downgrade** its ratings of a company or government during the life of a bond, creating a **fallen angel**. That happens if the issuer's financial condition deteriorates, or if the rating service predicts a business decision might have poor results. If downgrading occurs, investors instantly demand a higher yield for the existing bonds. That means the price of the bond falls in the secondary market. It also means that if the issuer wants to float new bonds, the bonds will probably have to be offered at a higher interest rate to attract buyers.

The rating systems of two major services are similar, but not identical, in the ways they label bond quality. Both services also make distinctions within categories Aa/AA and lower. Moody's uses a numerical system (1,2,3) and Standard & Poor's uses a plus or minus.

Meaning	
Best quality, with the smallest risk; issuers exceptionally stable and dependable	**INVESTMENT GRADE BONDS**
High quality, with slightly higher degree of long-term risk	
High to medium quality, with many strong attributes, but somewhat vulnerable to changing economic conditions	
Medium quality, currently adequate but perhaps unreliable over long term	
Some speculative element, with moderate security but not well safeguarded	
Able to pay now but at risk of default in the future	**JUNK BONDS**
Poor quality, clear danger of default	
Highly speculative quality, often in default	
Lowest-rated, poor prospects of repayment though may still be paying	
Interest payments are in default	

Investment grade generally refers to any bonds rated Baa or higher by Moody's, or BBB by Standard & Poor's.

Junk bonds are the lowest-rated corporate bonds. There's a greater-than-average chance that the issuer will fail to repay its debt. The highly-publicized U.S. corporate mergers and takeovers of the 1980s were financed with junk bond issues. Investors were willing to take the risk because the yields were so much higher than on other, safer bonds.

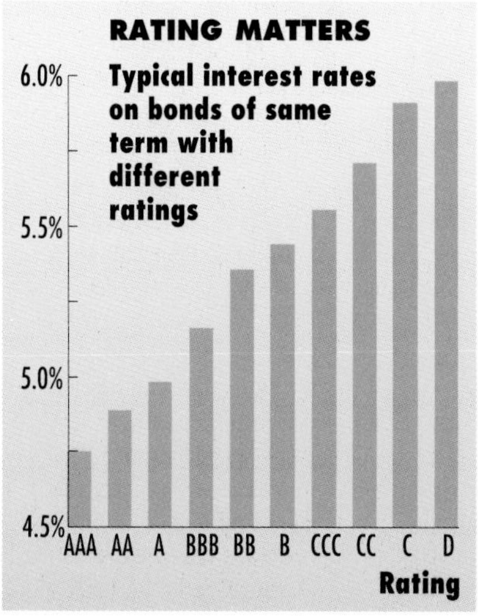

RATING MATTERS

Typical interest rates on bonds of same term with different ratings

6.0%
5.5%
5.0%
4.5%
AAA AA A BBB BB B CCC CC C D
Rating

RANKINGS INFLUENCE RATES

As the chart to the left shows, a credit rating not only indicates an issuer's ability to repay a bond, but it also influences the yield on a bond. In general, the higher the bond's rating, the lower its interest rate will tend to be. For example, issuers of higher-rated bonds don't need to offer high interest rates; their credibility does part of the selling for them.

But issuers of lower-rated bonds need to offer higher rates to entice investors. Junk bonds, for example, pay high interest because of their risk.

Bonds in the Marketplace

Investors can buy bonds when they're issued or when they're already on the market.

To bring a bond to market, the issuer selects a lead manager or co-lead managers, usually a bank or two, to handle the details. The lead manager **underwrites**, or buys up, the issue and organizes a syndicate of securities houses to sell the bonds at a set price, known as a **reoffer price**, which is usually the issue price less fees. The manager also generally tries to build interest in the issue, so that it will sell. Sometimes, in fact, an issue sells out immediately.

The lead manager also arranges for a clearing house to handle the paperwork the sale generates. While some governments have their own clearing houses, most debt is cleared through one of two European houses, Euroclear in Brussels or Cedel in Luxembourg.

Investors who want to buy bonds at issue can contact the lead manager, call a bank or broker to see if they're handling part of the sale, or participate in a bond fund that buys the issue.

INTERNATIONAL DEBT ISSUES

EURODOLLAR BONDS

Issuer	Cpn.%	Mat.	Price	Chg.	Yld.%
Abbey Ntl PLC Gl	6.9	17/10/05	94 13/16	+2/16	7.48
African Dev Bank	7⅜	06/04/23	94 10/16	nc	7.71
Asian Dev Bk Glb	6¼	24/10/05	93 14/16	+2/16	7.16
Rep. of Austria	6¼	19/05/08	91 3/16	+2/16	7.26
King. of Belgium	8¼	14/02/00	104 2/16	nc	6.78
King. of Belgium	5½	05/11/03	86 4/16	nc	7.88
Peoples Rep China	6½	17/02/04	92 8/16	+2/16	7.82
Euro Inv. Bank	6½	03/02/00	99 8/16	+1/16	6.53
Euro Inv. Bank	6⅝	30/06/99	100	nc	6.52
Euro Inv. Bank	7¾	15/12/98	102 6/16	nc	6.53
Euro Inv. Bank	8¼	20/12/04	105 15/16	+2/16	7.14
Exp.Imp. Bk Japan	6¼	25/05/05	93	+2/16	7.21
Rep. of Finland	6¾	24/11/97	100 11/16	nc	6.22
Int. Amer Dev Bk	6⅝	18/02/03	97 14/16	nc	6.91
Int. Amer Dev Bkn	7½	05/04/05	101 3/16	+2/16	7.17
Int. Bk Rec & Dev	8½	26/06/16	108 12/16	nc	7.49
Int. Bk Rec & Dev	6¾	16/01/02	101 5/16	nc	6.47
Int. Bk Rec & Dev	7⅝	19/01/23	101 2/16	nc	7.53
Int. Bk Rec & Dev	6⅜	21/07/05	95 3/16	+2/16	7.10
[illegible]	[illegible]	27/10/99	101 11/16	nc	6.54

Issuer
King. of Spain
King. of Sweder
United Kingdon

Issuer
IBRD Global
Sweden
Belgium
JDB
EIB
IBRD Global
Italy
JDB
IBRD Global
IBRD Global
Exim
IBRD Global
Exim
Austria

TRACKING BOND PERFORMANCE

Actively traded Eurobonds are tracked regularly as International Debt Issues in The Asian Wall Street Journal. Eurobonds are issued by a borrower outside its own country and are often denominated in a different currency. The most common Eurobonds are dollar, yen and mark issues.

The **issuer** is identified by name, or an abbreviated version of the name. The People's Republic of China or the Export-Import Bank of Japan are clear here, for example.

The **Cpn (coupon) %** is the interest rate at which the bond pays. In most cases, it is set at issue. In this example, the Asian Development Bank is paying 6¼%. **Mat(urity)** is the date on which the bond comes due and the principal is repaid to the current owner. Here, the ADB 6¼% bond matures in October 2005. The last two digits in the date are for the year. You supply 19 or 20, as appropriate.

Price is the amount the bond closed at on the previous trading day.

Change is the price compared to the previous

UNDERSTANDING BOND PRICES

Bond prices are quoted in increments of points and partial points, using a par value of 1,000. When the prices are given in dollars, the value of each point is $10 and each fraction 62.5¢.

1/16 = 62.5¢	6/16 = $3.75	11/16 = $6.88
2/16 = $1.25	7/16 = $4.38	12/16 = $7.50
3/16 = $1.88	8/16 = $5.00	13/16 = $8.13
4/16 = $2.50	9/16 = $5.63	14/16 = $8.75
5/16 = $3.13	10/16 = $6.25	15/16 = $9.38

So a bond quoted at 85 9/16 would be selling for $855, and one quoted at 105 14/16 would be selling for $1058.75.

Cpn.%	Mat.	Price	Chg.	Yld.%
6½	29/09/99	99 8/16	nc	6.56
6½	04/03/03	97 2/16	nc	7.05
7¼	09/12/02	101 9/16	nc	6.81

EUROYEN BONDS

Cpn.%	Mat.	Price	Chg.	Yld.%
4½	22/12/97	104.91	– .01	1.14
4⅝	04/02/98	105.20	+ .02	1.30
6	16/12/98	110.40	+ .05	1.64
5	01/10/99	109.63	+ .08	1.91
6⅝	15/03/00	115.95	+ .05	2.10
4½	20/06/00	108.96	+ .04	2.14
3½	20/06/01	103.62	+ .04	2.73
6½	20/09/01	119.20	+ .08	2.53
5¼	20/03/02	113.66	+ .14	2.67
4½	20/03/03	109.55	+ .05	2.94
4⅜	01/10/03	108.20	+ .05	3.09
4¾	20/12/04	111.90	+ .08	3.16
2⅞	28/07/05	96.75	+ .05	3.30
4½	28/09/05	109.65	+ .05	3.27

Source: IBJ International Plc, London

trading day. In this example, ADB 6¼ sold for 93 14/16, or $938.75, a gain of 2/16, or $1.25. That's $61.25 below par, or $1,000.

Yld (yield) % is the percentage of interest an investor would earn if buying the bond at its current price. If the price is lower than par, the yield is higher than the stated rate. If the price is higher, as the IBRD 8½% bond due in 2016 is, at 108 12/16, or $1,087.50, the yield is lower than the stated interest rate.

However, investors are still sometimes willing to pay a higher price, or what is known as a **premium**, for a bond with a high coupon rate because they will often earn more.

BREAKING THE SYNDICATE

When the issue no longer sells briskly, or if it doesn't generate much interest, the lead manager can decide to break the syndicate, and allow the bond to sell for whatever price it commands. At that point, the debt is part of the secondary, or resale, market.

BOND FEES

The lead manager takes a portion of the issue price as underwriting and management fees, and splits selling fees, or commissions, with members of the selling group.

In some cases, the underwriter also gets a precipium, or extra fee, as a reward for dealing with the slower process of a retail-targeted issue and a greater degree of underwriting risk.

ISSUING GOVERNMENT BONDS

In some nations, the central bank issues bonds, and in others it's a special agency. In much of the world, including most of Asia and the U.S., the issuing authority is the finance ministry—Japan's Ministry of Finance, for example, or the U.S. Department of the Treasury.

Most governments sell their bonds **auction-style**, to the highest bidder, sometimes on a regular schedule. In fact between 80% and 90% of public debt reaches the market this way. The U.S. Treasury, for example, sells short-term debt every Monday (see page 95). Generally, the government is committed to selling at whatever price the issue raises.

An alternative is to use a **tap issue**. The government announces a sale and issues a small amount of debt for investors to bid on. There's no set amount of debt and no predetermined time frame. The sale might last only a brief period, or over the course of a month. And the tap can be turned off, or ended, when it suits the issuer.

Trading in One Market

The huge, liquid U.S. debt market often influences prices on other bond markets.

In the U.S., newly issued bonds and those trading in the secondary market are available from stockbrokers and from some banks. U.S. Treasurys, though, are sold at issue directly to investors without any intermediary—or any commission—through the Federal Reserve Banks. To buy through the Federal Reserve, an investor establishes a **Treasury Direct** account that keeps records of the transactions and pays interest directly into the investor's bank account. When the Treasury issue is held to maturity, the par value is repaid directly as well. However, investors can't use Treasury Direct to sell before maturity; bonds bought directly must be transferred into a brokerage account before they are traded.

HOW TRADING WORKS

Most already-issued bonds are traded **over the counter** (OTC)—a term that usually means over the phone. Bond dealers are connected via electronic display terminals that give them the latest information on bond prices. A broker buying a bond uses a terminal to find out which dealer is currently offering the best price and calls that dealer to negotiate.

U.S. brokerage houses also have inventories of bonds that they want to sell to clients looking for bonds of particular maturities or yields. Sometimes investors make out better buying bonds their brokers already own—or **make a market in**—as opposed to bonds the brokers have to buy from another house.

The New York Stock Exchange and American Stock Exchange, despite their names, also list a number of bonds. Their **bond rooms** are the scene of the same kind of brisk auction-style trading that occurs on the stock-trading floor.

Activity in the NYSE bond trading room is every bit as intense as a busy day on the floor of the exchange, although most U.S. bonds are sold over the counter.

THE COST ISSUE

While many newly issued U.S. bonds are sold without commission expense to the buyer—because the issuer absorbs the cost—all bond trades incur commission costs. The amount an investor pays to buy an older bond depends on the **commission** earned by the stockbroker involved and the size of the **markup** that's added to the bond.

Markups are not officially regulated in the U.S., and the total amount is not reported on confirmation orders, so charges can be excessive. A broker should reveal the markup, if asked. Or you can figure it out by finding the current selling price of the bond and subtracting the buying price. The difference is the markup.

However, investors who trade bonds to take advantage of fluctuating interest rates may find that their profit outweighs the costs of trading.

THE PRICE OF BONDS

Price is a factor that may keep individual investors from investing heavily in bonds. While the par value of a U.S. bond is usually $1,000, bonds are often sold in bundles, or packages, that require a much larger minimum investment. High individual bond prices also limit the amount of diversification an investor can achieve. As a result, many people prefer bond funds (see page 103), and many of the bonds themselves are bought by large institutional investors.

THE TREASURY BILL AUCTION PROCESS

HOW AUCTIONS WORK

9AM T-bills on offer every Monday

10AM

1 The U.S. Treasury offers 13-week and 26-week T-bills for sale every Monday.

2 Institutional investors (such as pension funds and mutual funds planning to buy at least $500,000 worth of T-bills) buy up a major part of the issue by submitting competitive bids. Their bids must arrive at the Federal Reserve Bank by 1:00 p.m. Monday, the auction deadline, and state how much less than $10,000 they'd be willing to pay for each T-bill. For example, one fund might offer $9,800 and another $9,600.

11AM

NOON

3 At the same time, individual investors can submit a noncompetitive tender, or offer, by filling out a Treasury Direct form available at local banks. Investors indicate how many T-bills they want to buy and enclose a check for that number times $10,000. For example, someone wanting three bills would enclose a check for $30,000.

1PM — Deadline for all bids!

2PM

4 All tenders, competitive and noncompetitive, received by the Federal Reserve before the deadline are forwarded to the Treasury Department.

5 The Treasury accepts bids beginning with those closest to $10,000 until its quota is filled. That way, they raise the most possible revenue with the least possible debt.

3PM — Cut-off announcement

4PM

6 On Monday afternoon the Treasury announces the cut-off point, for example perhaps $9,700. News services report the information, and some bidders learn that they've bought T-bills, while others find out they bid too little.

7 The Treasury computes the average of the accepted bids and sells T-bills to all noncompetitive bidders for that price. It refunds to investors the difference between the $10,000 par value and the price paid. For example, if the price was $9,850, the refund would be $150 per bill or $450 for three.

PM

8 When the bill matures, the buyers get back the full value—$10,000—of each bond they bought.

U.S. Treasury Bonds, Notes and Bills

The U.S. Treasury offers three investment choices: bonds, notes and bills.

Since investors consider the U.S. government the most reliable borrower in the world, they refer to the latest 30-year Treasury bond as the **benchmark** against which all other bonds are measured. Bonds, notes and bills issued by the Treasury almost always yield less than any other debt of the same maturity—despite the fact that interest on Treasurys is federally taxable, although it is exempt from state and local taxes.

Treasury bills with maturities of 13 and 26 weeks (three and six months) are auctioned every Monday, so investors can buy new issues regularly. Notes, bonds and 12-month bills are sold less frequently, usually quarterly, and are announced well in advance.

Like other bonds, Treasurys are traded in the secondary market after issue. Treasury bond prices are measured in 32nds rather than 16ths of a point. Each $\frac{1}{32}$ equals 31.25 cents, and the fractional part is dropped when quoting a price. For example, if a bond is at 100:2 (or 100 + $\frac{2}{32}$), the price translates to $1,000.62.

READING THE TABLES

Trading information on representative Treasury bonds and notes, listed in order of maturity, appears in a daily table in The Asian Wall Street Journal.

U.S. TREASURY ISSUES

GOVT. BONDS & NOTES

Rate	Maturity Mo/Yr	Bid	Asked	Chg.	Ask Yld.
7⅛	Sep 99n	101:17	101:19	+ 5	6.57
6	Oct 99n	98:13	98:15	+ 5	6.52
7½	Oct 99n	102:20	102:22	+ 4	6.59
7⅞	Nov 99n	103:25	103:27	+ 4	6.59
7¾	Nov 99n	103:14	103:16	+ 4	6.59
7¾	Dec 99n	103:15	103:17	+ 3	6.61
6⅜	Jan 00n	99:07	99:09	+ 5	6.61
7¾	Jan 00n	103:17	103:19	+ 4	6.61
8½	Feb 00n	105:29	105:31	+ 5	6.63
7⅛	Feb 00n	101:17	101:19	+ 4	6.63
6⅞	Mar 00n	100:24	100:26	+ 5	6.63
5½	Apr 00n	96:08	96:10	+ 6	6.61
6¾	Apr 00n	100:09	100:11	+ 6	6.65
8⅞	May 00n	107:15	107:17	+ 4	6.65
6¼	May 00n	98:18	98:20	+ 5	6.65
5⅞	Jun 00n	97:07	97:09	+ 5	6.66
6⅛	Jul 00n	98:00	98:02	+ 4	6.67
8¾	Aug 00n	107:11	107:13	+ 4	6.67
6¼	Aug 00n	98:13	98:15	+ 5	6.68
6⅛	Sep 00n	97:29	97:31	+ 5	6.68
6¼	Jan 97n	100:11	100:13	....	5.55
7½	Jan 97n	101:02	101:04	....	5.57
4¾	Feb 97n	99:11	99:13	....	5.71
6¾	Feb 97n	100:22	[illegible]		
6⅞	Feb 97n	[illegible]			
6⅝	Mar 97n				

Rate	Maturity Mo/Yr	Bid	Asked	Chg.	Ask Yld.
6¼	Feb 03n	96:30	97:00	+ 6	6.82
10¾	Feb 03	120:16	120:20	+ 6	6.83
10¾	May 03	120:31	121:03	+ 6	6.86
5¾	Aug 03n	93:24	93:26	+ 5	6.86
11⅛	Aug 03	123:17	123:21	+ 4	6.88
11⅞	Nov 03	128:11	128:15	+ 5	6.89
5⅞	Feb 04n	94:00	94:02	+ 6	6.89
7¼	May 04n	101:31	102:01	+ 5	6.91
12⅜	May 04	132:19	132:23	+ 6	6.92
7¼	Aug 04n	101:29	101:31	+ 5	6.93
13¾	Aug 04	141:24	141:28	+ 8	6.93
7⅞	Nov 04n	105:26	105:28	+ 4	6.94
11⅝	Nov 04	129:12	129:16	+ 6	6.93
7½	Feb 05n	103:17	103:19	+ 6	6.94
6½	May 05n	97:01	97:03	+ 6	6.94
8¼	May 00-05	104:00	104:04	– 4	7.02
12	May 05	132:30	133:02	+ 8	6.95
6½	Aug 05n	96:30	97:00	+ 6	6.95
10¾	Aug 05	125:03	125:07	+ 6	6.97
5⅞	Nov 05n	92:18	92:20	+ 5	6.96
5⅝	Feb 06n	91:05	91:07	+ 6	6.89
9⅜	Feb 06	116:26	116:30	+ 5	6.94
6⅞	May 06n	[illegible]	[illegible]	+ 4	6.95

Rate is the percentage of par value paid as annual interest. The bond maturing in February 2000 pays 7⅛% interest.

Maturity date is the month and year the bond or note comes due. An **n** after the month means it is a note. Notes usually mature in two to ten years; bonds mature in ten to 30 years.

Prices for Treasury issues are quoted as **bid** and **asked** instead of as a closing price. That's because Treasury issues are traded over the counter, in thousands of private, one-on-one telephone transactions instead of on

FIGURING COUPON YIELD

$$\frac{\text{dollar return on T-bill}}{\text{cost of T-bill}} = \text{coupon equivalent yield}$$

for example

$$\frac{\$400}{\$9{,}600} = 4.16\%$$

STRIPS AND BILLS

Trading in **U.S. Treasury Strips** and **Bills** are reported in separate sections of the table. They're also listed by maturity date, and provide information on prices and yield. Since bills are short-term debt, the table also provides days to maturity.

Because strips are sold at **deep discount**, or a fraction of their par value, the ones with distant maturity dates sell for very little money, while the ones coming due are sold close to par value. Compare the 97.29 bid price on the strip maturing in Nov. '96 with the 46:14 bid for the strip maturing in 2007.

Bid and **asked** prices for T-bills are stated in such small numbers because they're sold at discount, a price lower than par value. T-bills don't pay periodic interest, but repay full par value at maturity. The difference between the discount price paid and the par value received equals the interest. For example, if an investor pays $9,500 for a $10,000 T-bill, that's 5% less than the payback—or 5% interest.

Dealers trade in T-bills by bidding and asking discount percents. For example, for the bill due on Aug. 1, the highest bid was 4.91. That is, the offer was to pay $9,509 to buy a $10,000 bill, yielding 4.98% in interest.

Ask yield is the **yield to maturity**. As with bonds and notes, it represents the relative value of the issue. The figure that gives the most accurate sense of what an investor makes on a T-bill is the **coupon equivalent yield**, or the percentage return resulting from dividing the dollar return by the amount paid. For example, a $10,000 bill sold for $9,600 has a coupon equivalent yield of 4.16% (see box above).

U.S. TREASURY STRIPS

Mat.	Type	Bid	Asked	Chg.	Ask Yld.
Aug 96	ci	99:09	99:10	+ 1	5.05
Nov 96	ci	97:29	97:29	+ 1	5.47
Nov 96	np	97:29	97:29	+ 1	5.49
Feb 97	ci	96:14	96:14	+ 1	5.73
May 97	ci	95:00	95:00	+ 1	5.84
May 97	np	94:31	95:00	+ 1	5.85
Aug 97	ci	93:16	93:17	+ 1	5.95
Aug 97	np	93:14	93:15	+ 1	6.01
Nov 97	ci	91:29	91:30	+ 1	6.14
Nov 97	np	91:29	91:30	+ 1	6.15
Feb 98	ci	90:12	90:13	+ 2	6.25
Feb 98	np	90:11	90:12	+ 2	6.27
May 98	ci	88:29	88:30	+ 2	6.30
May 98	np	88:29	88:31	+ 2	6.29
Aug 98	ci	87:13	87:14	+ 2	6.36
Aug 98	np	87:11	87:13	+ 2	6.39
Nov 98	ci	85:29	85:31	+ 2	6.43
Nov 98	np	85:29	85:31	+ 2	6.43
Feb 99	ci	84:13	84:16	+ 3	6.49
Feb 99	np	84:13	84:16	[illegible]	[illegible]
May 99	[illegible]	[illegible]	[illegible]	[illegible]	[illegible]
...					
Nov 06	ci	48:07	48:12	+ 3	7.11
Feb 07	ci	47:10	47:15	+ 3	7.13
May 07	ci	46:14	46:19	+ 3	7.14

TREASURY BILLS

Maturity	Days to Mat.	Bid	Asked	Chg.	Ask Yld.
Jun 27 '96	2	4.82	4.72	+0.01	4.80
Jul 05 '96	10	4.71	4.61	+0.02	4.69
Jul 11 '96	16	4.71	4.61	−0.03	4.70
Jul 18 '96	23	4.18	4.08	+0.01	4.16
Jul 25 '96	30	4.81	4.77	+0.02	4.87
Aug 01 '96	37	4.91	4.87	+0.01	4.98
Aug 08 '96	44	4.96	4.92	....	5.03
Aug 15 '96	51	4.99	4.95	−0.02	5.07
Aug 22 '96	58	5.01	4.99	−0.02	5.11
Aug 29 '96	65	[illegible]	[illegible]	[illegible]	[illegible]
Sep 05 '[illegible]	[illegible]	[illegible]	[illegible]	[illegible]	[illegible]

the major exchanges. So it's not possible to determine the exact price of the last transaction. The best information that's available is the highest price being bid, or offered, by buyers and the lowest price being asked by sellers as of late afternoon in New York.

For example, the bond paying 10¾% that matures in May 2003, had a bid price of 120:31 and an asked price of 121:03. The .31 in the price refers to $\frac{31}{32}$ of a point, or $9.6875. So the bid price was $1,209.69 and the asked price was $1,210.94.

Change represents the change in the bid price given here and the bid price given in the tables for the previous trading day. The change is stated as a percent and preceded by a + if it went up and a – if it was down. For example, the bid price on the May 2003 bond is .6% of a point higher than on the previous day.

Mutual Funds: Putting It Together

A mutual fund is a collection of stocks, bonds or other securities owned by a group of investors and managed by a professional investment company.

Most investment professionals agree that it's smarter to own a variety of stocks and bonds than to gamble on the success of a few. But diversifying can be tough because buying a portfolio of individual stocks and bonds may be expensive. And knowing what to buy—and when—can be a full-time job.

Mutual funds, also known as **unit trusts**, offer one solution: when investors put money into a fund, it's pooled with money from other investors to create greater buying power than they would have investing individually.

Since a fund can own hundreds of different securities, its success isn't dependent on how one or two holdings do. And the fund's managers keep constant tabs on the markets, adjusting the portfolio to reflect changing conditions.

How Mutual Funds Work

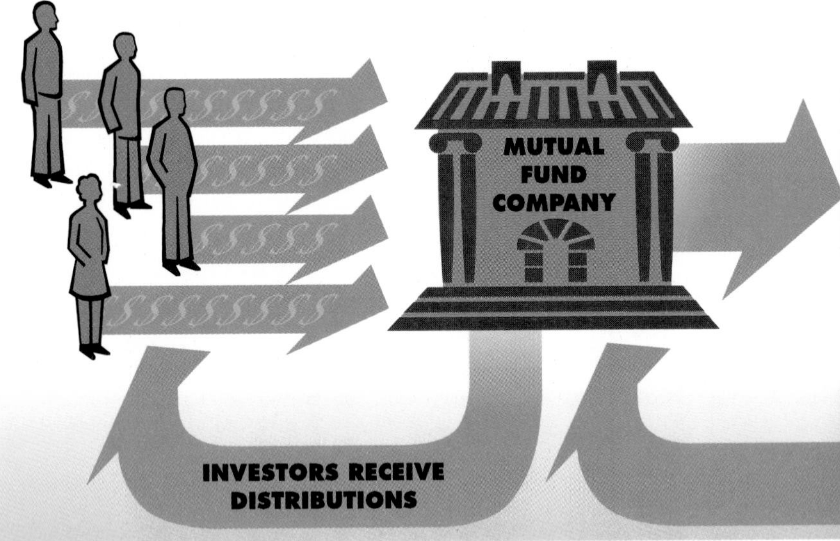

ALMOST INFINITE VARIETY

Investors shopping for mutual funds have an enormous variety from which to choose an investment suited to their goals. In mid-1996, there were more than 36,000 funds available world-wide. That includes more than 7,500 in the U.S. and thousands in Hong Kong, which is Asia's fund-management capital.

A fund's legal base isn't always an indicator of its geographical focus. In two typical examples, some U.S.-based funds invest in the Asian-Pacific region, while some funds based in Hong Kong invest in Latin America. Nor is its base necessarily an indication of the currency in which the fund is traded. A single investment firm may offer unit trusts denominated in one of as many as nine different currencies.

Investors can choose from a variety of fund types. For instance, the focus could be on stocks, bonds, warrants or real-estate investment trusts (REITs), which are publicly traded companies that own, operate, buy and develop commercial properties.

HOW A MUTUAL FUND IS CREATED

A mutual fund company decides on an investment concept

Then it issues a prospectus

Finally, it sells shares

CREATING FUNDS

Mutual funds are created by investment companies (sometimes called mutual-fund companies), brokerage houses and banks. A company frequently offers a range of funds—from as few as one or two to more than 100—with different objectives to appeal to people with specific investment goals. In some cases, companies offer funds in more than one market or establish legal bases in more than one country to increase their market share. Many U.S. banks, for example, sell funds in Asia in addition to those they sell in the U.S. Because certain countries have more liberal tax policies than others, investment companies often prefer to use them as a legal base. Funds based in tax havens are often called offshore funds.

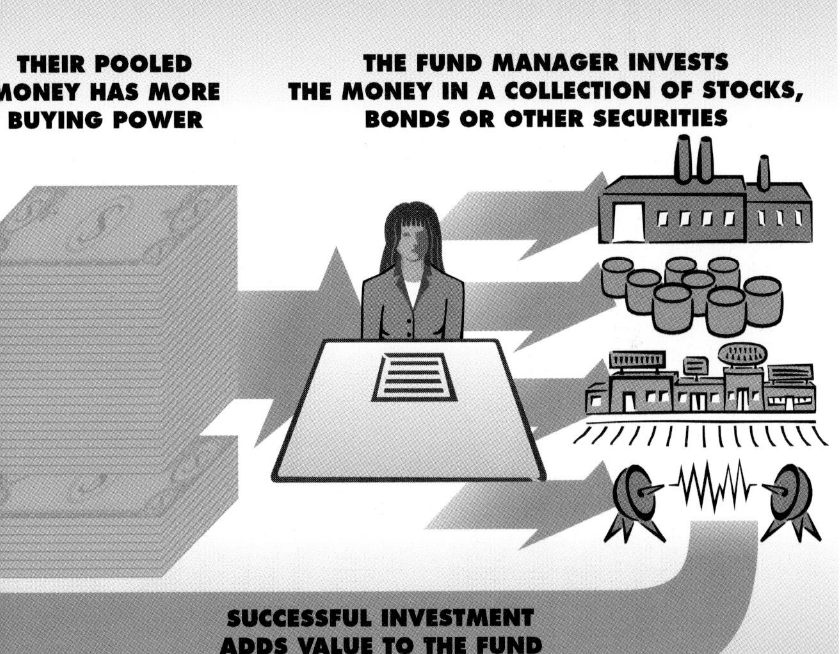

OPEN- AND CLOSED-END FUNDS

The term **mutual fund** is used to describe investment funds in general, but technically they are **open-end funds**. That means the fund sells as many shares as investors want. As money comes in, the fund grows. If investors pull money out, the number of outstanding shares drops. Sometimes open-end funds aren't available to new investors when they grow too large to be managed effectively—though current shareholders can continue to invest money. When a fund is closed this way, the investment company often creates a similar fund to capitalize on investor interest.

Closed-end funds, or investment trusts, more closely resemble stocks in the way they are traded. While these funds do invest in a variety of securities, they raise money only once, offer only a fixed number of shares and are traded on an exchange (hence the name **exchange-traded** funds) or over the counter. The market price of a closed-end fund fluctuates in response to investor demand as well as to changes in the value of its holdings.

Funds Around the Globe

If someone needed to invent a reason for the existence of mutual funds, investing abroad might be the best one.

Mutual funds that invest in overseas markets offer investors diversity, professional management and greater ease of investing. These funds also give small investors access to markets they couldn't enter on their own. There are overseas stock funds, bond funds and money-market funds to appeal to a variety of interests. There are three basic categories of funds: global, regional and country. The Asian Wall Street Journal also tracks a number of funds investing in developing, or emerging, markets. In some cases, the markets may be concentrated in a single region, but in others there's a broader geographic mix.

GLOBAL FUNDS invest in numerous stock or bond markets. By spreading investments throughout the world, these funds can balance risk by owning securities not only in mature, slow-growing economies, but also in the booming economies of many developing nations. The funds can also survive economic and political volatility more easily because of the greater portfolio variety.

Single-country funds that buy big blocks of shares in a country's industries can influence share prices and sometimes corporate policy, just as institutional investors may in buying a particular company's stock.

REGIONAL FUNDS concentrate on a particular geographic area, such as the Asian-Pacific region. Many mutual-fund companies offer regional funds to capitalize on the growing investor interest in overseas markets and on the strength of particular parts of the world economy.

Like the more comprehensive funds, regional funds invest in several different countries so that even if one market is in the doldrums, the others may be booming.

Regional funds work well when the markets they include are small—such as that of New Zealand—and may not offer enough securities to justify a single-country fund.

SOUTHEAST ASIA

CLOSED-END FUNDS

Closed-end funds can be well-suited to investing in international markets. Because they don't have to keep money on hand to redeem shares when an investor sells, they can be fully invested at all times. Nor do they have to sell off investments if a market drops quickly. They also tend to be smaller than open-end funds, so their managers often have more flexibility.

CLOSED END FUNDS

Fund Name	Stock Exch	NAV	Market Price	Prem /Disc	52 week Market Return	Fund
General Equity Funds						
Adams Express	N	23.01	19 1/8	– 16.9	18.8	ASA
Alliance All-Mkt	N	23.14	19 3/8	– 16.3	25.6	All S
Avalon Capital	O	10.57	9 3/4	– 7.8	N/A	Anc
Baker Fentress	N	24.71	19 1/2	– 21.1	34.7	Ar
Bergstrom Cap	A	137.09	117 1/8	– 14.6	37.5	
Blue Chip Value	N	9.41	8 3/8	– 11.0	37.5	
Central Secs	A	23.17	24 1/2	+ 5.7	34.7	

Performance records and expenses, in the form of annual fees, are factors investors have to consider in choosing closed-end funds. But many investors world-wide can also shop for bargains.

Because a closed-end fund has a fixed number of shares, investor sentiment can move the price higher, to a premium, or lower, to a discount, compared with its net asset value (NAV). For example, Adams Express is selling at a discount of 16.9%. A discounted price can make a fund more attractive to investors who expect the price to rise or the fund to be liquidated.

COUNTRY FUNDS allow investors to concentrate their investments in a single overseas country, even countries whose markets are closed to individual investors who aren't citizens. When a fund does well, other funds are set up for the same country, so that there are currently several Japan funds and several India funds. Many single-country funds are closed-end funds that are traded through a broker once they have been established.

By buying stocks and bonds in a single country, investors can profit from the strength of an established economy or from rapid economic growth as developing countries start to industrialize or expand their export markets. This has been the case in the Asian-Pacific region in recent years, which is one reason those funds have been so popular. The risk of investing in emerging-country funds, however, is that their value can be eroded in the event of political turmoil.

THE RISK OVERSEAS

Investors who put money into overseas funds don't have to deal directly with currency fluctuations or calculating foreign taxes—they're handled by the fund. But the value of any fund that invests in other countries is directly affected not only by market conditions but by exchange rates.

Overseas bond funds are often volatile because changes in a currency's value directly affect the fund's earnings. For example, if a bond fund is earning high interest, but the investor's domestic currency is weak, the yield is less.

Equity funds are somewhat less vulnerable to currency fluctuation because they profit from capital gains. So if international markets are paying high dividends, a Japanese investor, for example, can make money, especially if the yen is weak. However, if the yen strengthens by 10% during a year in which an overseas stock fund gains 10%, there would be no profit. And if the yen strengthens by 20%—which happens as part of the regular ebb and flow of international markets—there could actually be a loss of 10%.

The Mutual-Fund Market

Mutual funds never invest at random. Funds buy in specific markets, looking for particular products.

Most funds diversify their holdings by buying a wide variety of investments that correspond to the type of fund they are. The charm of diversity is that losses from some investments will almost always be offset—or overshadowed—by gains in others.

FUND TYPES

Mutual funds fall into three main categories:

- **Stock, or equity, funds**
- **Bond funds**
- **Money-market funds**

A typical stock fund may own shares in 100 or more companies that provide a range of different products and services. A government-bond fund may own issues of different terms, paying varied rates. And a money-market fund stays liquid, or cash rich, by owning very short-term debt.

On the other hand, some funds are extremely focused. For example:

- **Precious-metal funds trade chiefly in mining stocks**
- **Sector funds buy shares in a particular industry such as electronics**
- **High-yield bond funds buy risky bonds to produce high income**

The appeal of focused funds is that when they're doing well, the return can be outstanding. The risk is that a change in the economy or in the sector can wipe out the gains.

THE FOUNDING FUND

The first investment trust, the forerunner of modern unit trusts or mutual funds, was put together by Robert Fleming in the 1800s. He collected money from some fellow Scots and traveled to the U.S., where he invested—with notable success—in growing industries and enterprises.

Fleming set a precedent, and founded a firm that's still doing business. So are the first mutual funds in the U.S., the Massachusetts Investment Trust and the State Street Research Investment Trust, both established in 1924.

STOCK FUNDS

The name says it all: stock funds invest primarily in stocks. But stock fund portfolios vary, depending on the fund's investment objectives. For example, some stock funds invest in well-established companies that pay regular dividends. Others invest in young, high-technology firms or companies that have been operating below expectation for several years.

Like individual investors, funds may buy **blue-chip stocks** for income and safety, **growth stocks** for future gains, **value stocks** for stability and growth, and **cyclical stocks** to take advantage of economic booms. For investors, the major difference in buying a fund rather than individual stocks is the diversity they can achieve for the same amount of money.

There are several types of stock, or equity, funds. A key distinction among them is that some stress growth, some stress income, and some, a combination of the two. Some funds involve more risk to capital than others because they buy stock in new companies or emerging markets. Others try to moderate risk by buying stock in well-established companies or by including some bonds in their portfolio.

BOND FUNDS

Like bonds, open-end bond funds produce regular income. Unlike bonds, however, these funds have no maturity date and no guaranteed repayment of the amount invested. On the plus side, though, the earnings can be reinvested in the fund to increase the principal. And buyers can invest a much smaller amount of money than they would need to buy a bond on their own—and get a diversified portfolio to boot. For example, some bonds may require an investment of $100,000, but you can often invest in a fund for $1,000 and make additional purchases for even smaller amounts.

Bond funds come in many varieties, with different investment goals and strategies. There are investment-grade corporate-bond funds and riskier funds, often sold under the promising label of high-yield funds. You can choose long- or short-term government-issue funds, funds that combine issues with different maturities and a variety of global bonds.

IT'S ALL IN THE FAMILY

Mutual-fund companies usually offer a variety of funds—referred to as a family of funds—to their investors. Keeping your money in the family can make it easier to transfer money between funds, but like most families, some members do better than others.

MONEY-MARKET FUNDS

Money-market funds resemble savings accounts. For every dollar you put in, you get a dollar back, plus the interest your money earns from the investments the fund makes. Since these funds are usually price-stable, some investors prefer them to stock or bond funds. But the interest the funds pay is low when interest rates are low. In some cases, money-market funds let investors write checks against their accounts. There's usually no charge for check-writing—although there may be a per-check minimum.

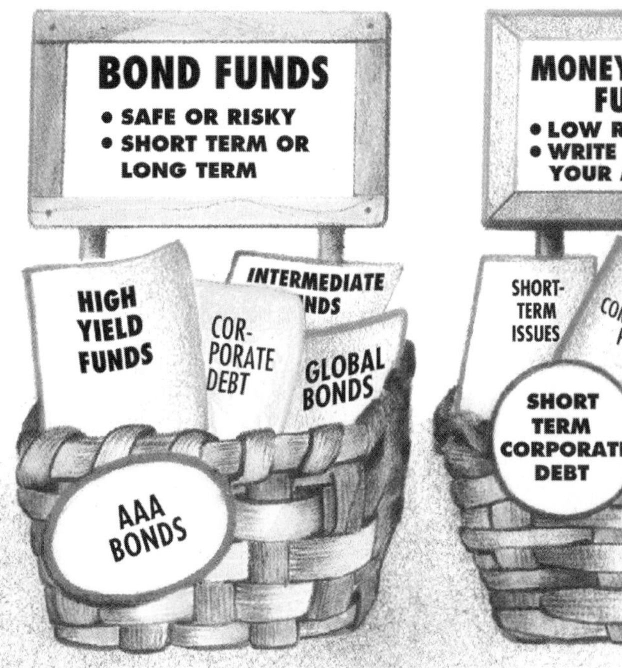

The two main categories of bond funds are those that buy government bonds and those that buy corporate debt. Funds of both types may specialize in issues from one country, or buy regionally or globally. Frequently, buying a bond fund is the only way that individual investors can participate in large-scale supranational bond issues (see pages 80–82).

Money-market funds buy the best-yielding short-term corporate or government issues available in the currency in which the fund is sold. Frequently, a sponsoring company offers a number of money-market funds, each available in a different currency.

Targeted Investments

Mutual funds aim at particular targets. To hit them, the funds make certain types of investments.

INVESTMENT OBJECTIVE

Every mutual fund—stock, bond or money-market—is established with a specific investment objective that fits into one of three basic goals:

- **Current income**
- **Some income and growth**
- **Future growth**

To achieve its objective, the fund invests in securities it believes will produce the results it wants. To identify the securities, a fund often does a vast amount of research, including what's known as a bottom-up style, which involves analyzing individual companies. When the objective is small-company growth or the focus is on emerging markets, for example, the process can be more difficult due to a lack of readily available information.

In addition, each fund manager has a buying style, seeking a particular type of investments from the pool that may be appropriate for the objective. Some equity-fund managers, for example, stress **value**, which means buying stocks whose price is lower than might be expected. Other managers may be **contrarians**, buying investments that others are shunning.

THE RISK FACTOR

There is always the **risk** that a fund won't hit its target. Some funds are, by definition, riskier than others. For example, a fund that invests in small new companies takes the chance that some of their investments will do poorly because they believe some, at least, will do very well.

FUNDS TAKE AIM

These charts group funds in three categories, by investment objective. They also report the correlations between a fund's objective and the risks it may face.

INCOME FUNDS

Investment objective	Kind of fund	Potential risks	What the fund buys
Safety and some income	Money-market	Nearly total safety of capital; income based on current interest rates	Very short-term government and corporate debt
Steady income	Government-bond	Interest-rate changes and inflation	Highly rated government bonds
Steady income	Corporate-bond	Interest-rate changes and inflation	Highly rated corporate bonds, with various maturities
Income	Short/intermediate-term debt	Small risk of loss; less influenced by changes in interest rate	Different types of debt issues in 1–10 year maturities, depending on type of fund
Income and currency gains	International money-market	Changes in currency values and interest rates	CDs and short-term securities
High income	International and global bond	Yield dependent on interest rate and currency values	Bonds in overseas markets
Highest current income	High-yield bond	High-risk bonds in danger of default	Low-rated and unrated corporate and government bonds

GROWTH AND INCOME

Investment objective	Kind of fund	Potential risks	What the fund buys
Primarily income	Income	Limited risk of loss to principal, but less growth in strong market	Primarily bonds, but some dividend-paying stocks
Income and growth	Balanced	Limited risk to principal; some long-term growth	Part stocks and preferred stocks (usually 60%) and part bonds (40%)
Income and growth	Equity income	Limited risk to principal; moderate long-term growth	Blue-chip stocks and utilities that pay high income
Growth plus some current income	Growth and income	Limited risk to principal; moderate long-term growth	Stocks that pay high dividends and show good growth

GROWTH FUNDS

Investment objective	Kind of fund	Potential risks	What the fund buys
Imitate the stock market	Index	Average gains and losses for the market the index tracks	Stocks represented in the index the fund tracks
Above-average growth	Growth	Can be volatile; some risk of loss to principal to get higher gains	Stocks in mid-sized or large companies whose earnings are expected to rise quickly
Long-term growth	Small company growth	Volatile and speculative; risk of above-average losses to get higher gains	Stocks in small companies traded on the exchanges or over the counter
Long-term growth	Aggressive growth funds, also called capital appreciation funds	Very volatile and speculative; risk of above-average losses to get above-average gains	Stocks of new or undervalued companies expected to increase in value
Growth	Sector	Volatile funds, dependent on right market timing to produce results	Stocks in one particular industry, such as energy or transportation
Global growth	Global equity	Gains and losses depend on stock prices and forex fluctuation; some risk to principal	Stocks in various markets

PAYING OUT THE PROFITS

A mutual fund makes money in two ways: by earning dividends or interest on its investments and by selling investments that have increased in price. The fund pays out, or distributes, its profits (minus fees and expenses) to its own investors.

Income distributions are from the money the fund earns on its investments. **Capital-gain distributions** are the profits from selling investments. Different funds pay their distributions on different schedules—ranging from once a day to once a year. Many funds offer investors the option of reinvesting all or part of their distributions in the fund.

Many international funds are based in places that don't tax capital gains or which offer other tax advantages. If a fund's earnings are reinvested tax-free, the long-term gains on the investment are higher.

Special-Purpose Funds

Mutual-fund companies have expanded their horizons—and the opportunities they offer to investors—by developing specialty funds.

Stock and bond funds are the oldest and most enduring mutual funds. But as mutual funds have grown in popularity, a greater variety of funds has become available. Most of these newer, specialized funds have been developed to appeal to people who are looking for very specific investments, such as tracking a market index, putting money into a specific sector or into ethically sound businesses.

SPECIAL INVESTMENT OBJECTIVES

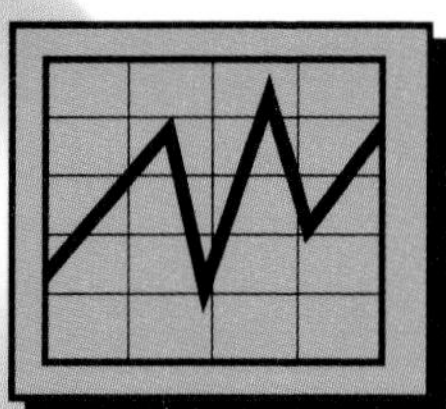

HEDGING
International fund managers often use a practice called hedging. If a currency gains relative to others, investments denominated in other currencies have less value when converted into it. To protect against that, funds often hedge, or buy futures contracts or a currency at a preset exchange rate.

Some funds don't hedge at all, figuring that exposure to other currencies is part of the reason for investing overseas. Others, however, hedge 50% or more of their bets, meaning half of an equity fund's assets would be in currency contracts, not stocks.

INDEX FUNDS
Index funds are designed to produce the return that investors would get if they owned all the stocks in a particular index—such as the Hang Seng Index. While this diversity would be overwhelming for an individual portfolio, it's all in a day's work for an index fund.

Funds can track gauges of entire equity markets, indexes for large, midsize or small companies, or bond-market indicators. An advantage of index funds is that they have lower expenses than actively managed funds. An active-fund manager buys and sells investments to try to beat the market, but an index-fund manager simply makes sure that the basket of stocks in the fund reflects the performance of the index it's supposed to follow. Since there's no need for extensive research or frequent trading, index funds cost less to run.

Lower fees are a particular concern with international funds, which can be more expensive for investors than domestic funds. International stock funds on average have an **expense ratio**, or total annual fees, of 1.8% of an investor's assets. U.S. diversified stock funds on average have an expense ratio of 1.42%, according to recent data from Morningstar Inc, the mutual-fund researcher.

In addition, index funds are popular because the performances of the major stock and bond indexes often surpass the returns that professional mutual-fund money managers achieve by following a particular investment theory.

But there are some limitations. In certain economic cycles, individual fund performance can outpace index funds. And as a rule, index funds that track small companies as a group produce spottier results than targeted growth funds that invest directly in specific small companies.

APPEALING TO INVESTORS

Mutual funds provide a variety of investment opportunities designed to make investing easier.

Advantages of mutual funds:

- Allow purchase of fractional shares
- Provide liquidity, or easy access to money
- Are explicit about investment goals
- Offer simple reinvestment options
- Many sell directly to customers

What mutual funds allow you to do:

- Avoid loads and other fees
- Invest even smaller amounts
- Get money easily in an emergency, though perhaps with some loss of capital
- Choose a fund to meet a specific goal
- Build investment on a regular basis

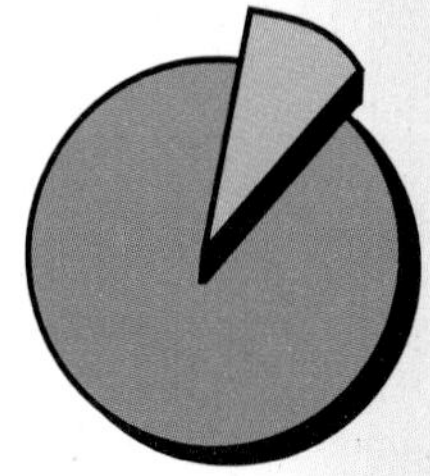

QUANT FUNDS

Quant funds are named for their quantitative investment style. They aim to achieve a stronger performance than the index funds they imitate by relying on statistical analysis to decide which securities will top the benchmarks. Instead of buying all the stocks in the Hang Seng Index, for example, a quant fund would buy comparable stocks that their analysis tells them will turn a higher profit.

Among the mathematically measurable factors that would be considered quantitative are the value of a company's assets, historical and projected sales patterns, costs and profitability, plus what's happening in the money market and the securities market.

SEEKING EFFICIENCY

An **efficient market** isn't one that works quicker or smarter. Rather, it's the object of constant, intensive analysis—and the information is available to everyone, almost immediately.

GREEN AND OTHER CONSCIENCE FUNDS

Some mutual-fund companies have created funds to attract investors whose strong political or social commitments make them unwilling to invest in companies whose business practices are at odds with their beliefs. A green fund might avoid tobacco companies, companies with poor environmental records, or those that sell certain products in developing countries. While green funds in the U.S. rarely make it to the top of performance charts because of the restrictions on what they can buy, many have posted at least average growth.

Unlike other specialty funds, green funds aren't analyzed as a special category. Investors who feel strongly about where their money goes may have to do extra research to find a fund they're comfortable with. Some special-interest groups sponsor their own funds or recommend particular funds.

SECTOR FUNDS

Sector funds focus on the stocks of a particular industry or segment of the economy, such as technology, natural resources, or financial services. In that sense, they are out of step with the underlying principle behind mutual funds—diversity. While a sector fund is more diversified than a single stock, there is nothing in the fund portfolio to offset a downturn in the sector.

Since sectors are highly volatile, they offer an opportunity for big profits to investors who ride the right wave. Generally, though, one year's hot sector is dead the next, and has to wait until a new spurt of interest gives it life.

Precious-metal funds resemble sector funds since all their money is invested in mining stocks and bullion, but they're more predictable. When inflation is high or there's political turmoil, precious-metal funds tend to do well because they are a hedge against instability.

Inside a Mutual Fund

Operating a fund means tracking markets, making investments and serving the investor.

A mutual fund has two distinct yet intertwined businesses: making a profit and providing services to its clients. Each fund, or closely related group of funds, is run by a professional manager responsible for both its day-to-day operations and for its successful performance. In fact, the skill of the manager is so closely linked to the success of a fund that many experts advise investors to pick a fund based on the manager—and even to drop a fund if a star manager leaves.

A typical fund depends on a battalion of employees, including financial analysts, accountants, traders and salespeople, plus support staff. Equally crucial are the programs, computers and other electronic equipment—and the people who keep them running—that make this kind of operation work.

Operating the Fund

A mutual-fund or unit-trust company buys and sells securities in a specific financial market or markets through brokers. Because it trades in large volumes, the company is known as an **institutional investor** (see page 46).

At the beginning of the business day, investors can find information on a mutual fund's performance in the press and other media. Closing prices, changes in price from the previous period and year-to-date percentage return are usually available.

Every day the fund's manager and analysts digest how the markets did the day before, where the fund stands in relation to other funds and the benchmark indexes, and what economic news is affecting the fund's value.

Servicing the Investor

Funds are never static. Money moves in and out constantly—in staggering amounts. Investors' purchases and redemption orders are handled immediately.

Typically, mail pours into mutual fund offices by the ton, and each piece must be opened, coded with an account number, and put in the right in-basket. Checks are credited to the right client accounts at the day's closing price. Then they're shipped off to the bank.

Checks and confirmations from the previous day's transactions are mailed out to clients, making good on the claim that mutual funds are among the most liquid investments.

More and more Asian-Pacific investment companies allow investors to place orders by telephone. But some companies still require orders to be made in person or by mail.

OTHER WAYS TO BUY FUNDS

One big question investors face when buying mutual funds is whether to buy directly from the fund—the process that's described here—or through a broker, bank, or other financial agent. They may wonder, for example, whether professionals can identify better performing funds than they can pick on their own.

In fact, the evidence shows that there's very little difference in performance. Some experts say the strongest argument for using an adviser instead of buying directly from the investment company is not finding better-performing funds, but getting the encouragement to invest actively.

Investment capital generated by mutual funds increasingly provides the resources to create new businesses and technologies.

Fund managers and analysts are always in the market for new securities that meet their investment objectives. Their research staff provides up-to-the-minute price information and analysis.

Trading managers authorize the buy and sell orders. Traders, looking for the best price, keep their eyes on the computer screen and their hands on the telephone. Other employees keep a running count of the fund's balance sheet.

In time to meet daily or weekly press deadlines, staff calculate details of the fund's current value and the change from the prior period.

Investors open accounts, send checks, or have money transferred into their accounts throughout the day. As the orders are processed, the money is invested in shares of the fund. Follow-up documentation can include written confirmation after telephone or electronic transactions.

More and more, companies have telephone representatives available to answer client questions and act on orders. There are very few transactions that can't in theory be done by phone—as long as the client signs up for the services when the account is opened.

In some instances, customers can talk to a service representative after the exchanges close, placing orders that will be acted on the next day. Some companies are starting to offer automated phone and online systems that provide details about earnings, balances and recent trades, as well as other account and performance information.

Mutual-Fund Quotations

As the popularity of mutual funds has grown, so has the information about them.

Every business day, The Asian Wall Street Journal publishes a listing of mutual funds offered by international investment companies that wish to advertise their products. The listing provides investors with current information on price and performance of the funds. The data is provided by Lipper Analytical Services International, Inc., a primary source of information and analysis on investment companies world-wide.

There are also quarterly surveys of funds available through several hundred international investment companies. Each survey provides detailed comparative information on equity, bond and derivative or leveraged funds, based on returns for the quarter, 12 months, and five years.

INTERNATIONAL

Fund Name	GF	AT	LB	NAV Date	CR	NAV	— % Return — YTD	12-Mo.	2-Yr
AIG INTERNATIONAL ASSET MNGT. INC.									
AIG Intl Int Arb Glb	GL	LM	BD	04/15	US	1021.18	1.8	NS	NS
AIG Intl Curr I Glbl	GL	MM	BD	04/15	US	1059.63	7.1	NS	NS
AIG Intl Rel Value	GL	MF	BD			0.00	NA	NA	NA
AIG Intl W Broadway	GL	LM	CY	04/12	US	895.78	−10.4	NS	NS
SoundShore Inv Glbl	US	LM	BD	04/15	US	1091.49	4.5	NS	NS
BANQUE INTERNATIONALE A LUXEMBOURG (ASIA) LTD.									
105 Cecil Street +10-01/04, Singapore 0106 Tel. 65-2227622									
BIL-Keystone Asia Pr	SE	EQ	LX	04/17	US	10.15	NS	NS	NS
CHASE MANHATTAN VISTA FUNDS									
5 Rue Plaetis, L2338 Luxembourg Tel. 352-462-6851									
U.S. Dollar Income	US	MM	LX	04/16	US	1.00	0.9	NS	NS
U.S. Government Sec.	US	BD	LX	04/16	US	102.66	−2.2	6.5	5.9
Global Bond	GL	BD	LX	04/16	US	110.60	−1.4	2.1	5.[illegible]
U.S. Large Cap Eq.	US	EQ	LX	04/16	US	217.36	6.2	25.0	17.[illegible]
U.S. Mid-Cap Eq.	US	EQ	LX	04/16	US	136.90	10.0	28.9	17.[illegible]
International Yield	GL	BD	LX	04/16	US	103.16	4.1	NS	N[illegible]
Europe Equities	EU	EQ	LX	04/16	US	128.91	7.3	19.7	9.[illegible]
Japan Equities	YE	EQ	LX	04/16	US	115.81	4.7	4.0	[illegible]

Fund Name	GF	AT	LB
GLOBAL ASSET MANAGEMENT,			
OFFSHORE FUNDS, Isle of Man			
Tel 44-1624-632632 Fax 44-1624-625956 Intern[illegible]			
http://www.ukinfo.gam.com			
GAM Arbitrage	US	LM	BV
GAM ASEAN	SE	EQ	BV
GAM Asian Devel Mkts	SE	EQ	BV
GAM Australia	AD	EQ	BV
GAM Bond STG	UK	BD	BV
GAM Bond DEM	DM	BD	BV
GAM Bond SFR	SF	BD	BV
GAM Bond YEN	YE	BD	BV
GAM Bond USD Ord	US	BD	BV
GAM Bond USD Special	US	CV	BV
GAM Brasilia	BZ	BL	BV
GAM Cross Market	GL	FO	BV
GAM Diversity	[illegible]	[illegible]	BV

The **investment or management company's name**, and in some cases address, appears first. Then its different funds are listed, in alphabetical order.

Some companies offer a limited number of funds, while others have dozens.

NAV is the fund's **net asset value**. A fund's NAV is the dollar value of one share of stock in the fund, the price the fund pays you per share when you sell. It's figured by totaling the value of all the fund's holdings and dividing by the number of shares. For example, the NAV of the Banque Internationale A Luxembourg (Asia)'s Keystone Fund is $10.15.

If dual pricing is used, however, the figure in the NAV column is the bid price prepared by the fund as of the NAV date.

GF is the **geographic focus**, or the area of the world emphasized in the fund's portfolio. Some of the funds invest in only one market, some in one region and others globally. The GAM Cross Market fund, for example, buys globally, while GAM ASEAN invests in Asia.

AT stands for **asset type**. Funds are divided into 12 categories, based on their principal investment objective, or focus. The information is supplied by the investment company and from the funds' descriptions of their objectives (see box at right).

LB is the **legal base** of the fund, or the country in which it's registered. The fund's base doesn't determine the geographic focus or the currency in which the fund is denominated. A country's economic climate or its tax structure may make it particularly appealing to investment companies.

The performance of each fund, calculated as **percentage total return (% return)**, is reported in three time frames: YTD, or year-to-date, 12-month, and two-year periods. The return is figured assuming reinvestment of all distributions on the day they are credited.

In this example, more funds have shown gains than losses in value in the year to date, and most have posted gains over 12 months and two years.

The two-year return is an annualized number, which means the total return for the period was added and divided by two.

When NS appears in any of the return columns, it means that the fund didn't exist at the start of the period. NA means the data is incomplete. Long-term performance data can indicate how well (or poorly) a fund has fared in different economic climates.

FUNDS IN CYBERSPACE

Investors can find mutual fund information, including details of fund performance, on the Internet's World Wide Web. They may also be able to buy directly, either through discount brokers or a fund company itself.

INVESTMENT FUNDS

NAV Date	CR	NAV	— % Return — YTD	12-Mo.	2-Yr
04/09	US	488.68	3.0	11.7	11.6
04/04	US	438.88	NA	NA	NA
04/10	US	111.20	11.2	NS	NS
04/10	US	254.86	14.8	22.4	8.4
04/09	UK	177.55	−1.7	8.1	5.0
04/09	DM	133.21	−0.4	7.8	4.7
04/02	SF	111.53	NA	NA	NA
04/09	YE	15292.00	−0.5	3.1	2.4
04/09	US	153.07	−3.7	3.3	3.2
04/09	US	200.33	4.4	22.6	3.4
04/10	US	80.07	5.7	24.6	NS
04/10	US	130.49	−0.9	12.4	10.4
04/08	US	214.15	6.7	26.8	9.8
04/10	US	654.65	1.9	−1.7	−3.0
[illegible]	SF	266.73	[illegible]	[illegible]	−1.4

Fund Name	GF	AT	LB	NAV Date	CR	NAV	— % Return — YTD	12-Mo.	2-Yr
LLOYD (MANAGEMENT (HK) LTD									
Suite 380change Square, HK Tel. 852 2845 4433 Fax. 852 2845 3911									
LG Antenna Fund Ltd	DV	EQ	BD	04/12	US	17.64	8.6	16.1	1.4
LG AsianSmallerCo's	SE	EQ	BD	04/11	US	19.40	8.7	18.9	0.7
LG India	IN	EQ	MR	04/11	US	10.99	13.2	−19.2	−13.6
LG Korea	KW	EQ	DB	04/12	US	9.06	1.3	0.1	NS
LG Japan	YE	EQ	DB	04/11	US	8.14	−1.0	4.8	NS
LG StrategicGold	GL	MR	BD	04/12	US	10.64	21.3	6.8	NS
LG-SC China	CN	EQ	BD	04/12	HK	6.80	7.3	14.8	−12.1
MALABAR CAPITAL MANAGEMENT (BERMUDA) LTD									
Sterling House,Wesley Street,Hamilton,Bermuda T(441)295 0653 F(441)2923677									
Malabar Internatl Fd	GL	EQ	BD	04/01	US	24.62	NA	NA	NA
SOCIE[illegible]									
1-13 A[illegible]									
Asia[illegible]									
Bond[illegible]									
Bond[illegible]									
SOGE[illegible]									
Soge[illegible]									
Soge[illegible]									

FUND CATEGORIES

The Asian Wall Street Journal uses categories developed by Lipper Analytical Services Inc. to classify funds by the principal focus of their investments. The asset categories and their abbreviations are:

- **BL** **Balanced/multi-asset**
- **CV** **Convertible bonds**
- **EQ** **Equities**
- **FI** **Fixed income**
- **FO** **Futures/options**
- **GU** **Guaranteed/capital protected/fixed term**
- **LM** **Leveraged/hedge**
- **MM** **Money market and managed currency**
- **MF** **Multifund**
- **MR** **Minerals and natural resources**
- **RE** **Real estate**
- **WT** **Warrants**

NAV date is the date of record of the NAV published in the column. It's the information currently available for each specific fund, though some may be more recent than others. For example, information in this chart is based on numbers that were reported between Dec. 31 and April 16.

CR is the **currency of record**, or the currency in which the fund's shares, or units, are denominated. It's also the currency of the NAV, but not necessarily the currency of the fund's legal base. In fact, different funds sponsored by the same company may be sold in a variety of currencies. For example, the Lloyd George Management (HK) Ltd.'s Antenna fund is denominated in U.S. dollars, while its China fund is denominated in Hong Kong dollars.

Many of the funds are traded in U.S. dollars despite the fact that most of them aren't available to U.S. citizens or residents.

Tracking Fund Performance

There are several formulas for measuring mutual-fund performance. The bottom line is whether the fund is making money now—and how it has done in the past.

Whether a mutual fund aims for current income, long-term growth, or a combination of the two, there are three ways to track its performance, and judge whether or not it is profitable. Investors can evaluate a fund by:

- Following changes in share price, or **net asset value (NAV)**
- Figuring **yield**
- Calculating **total return**

They can compare a fund's performance to similar funds offered by different companies, or they can evaluate the fund in relation to other ways the money could have been invested—stocks or bonds, for example.

Because return is figured differently for each type of investment, there isn't a simple formula for comparing funds to individual securities.

NAV CHANGE

$$\frac{\text{Value of fund}}{\text{Number of shares}} = \text{NAV}$$

for example

$$\frac{\$52{,}500{,}000}{3{,}500{,}000} = \$15$$

A fund's **share price**, or **NAV**, is the value of one share of the fund's stock. You figure the NAV by dividing the current value of the fund by the number of shares. The NAV increases when the value of the holdings increase. For example, if a share of a U.S. stock fund costs $15 today and $9 a year ago, there's been a **capital gain**, or profit, of $6 a share (or about 66%) before expenses.

YIELD

$$\frac{\text{Distribution per share}}{\text{Price per share}} = \text{Yield (\%)}$$

for example

$$\frac{\$.58}{\$10.00} = 5.8\ \%$$

Yield measures the amount of income a fund provides as a percentage of its current price, or NAV. A long-term bond fund with a NAV of $10 paying a 58¢ dividend per share provides a 5.8% yield. Investors can compare the yield on a mutual fund with the current yield on comparable investments to decide which is performing better. Bond fund performance, for example, is often tracked in relation to individual bonds (see pages 88–89).

RETURN

$$\frac{\text{Current value}}{\text{Cost of initial investment}} = \text{Return (\%)}$$

for example

$$\frac{\$8{,}500}{\$5{,}000} = 170\%$$

Total return tells investors how much—as a percentage—they've made or lost on an investment over time. It's figured by dividing the current value of an investment, plus distributions, by the cost of the initial investment. (The current value is the number of shares times the NAV.) If the distributions have all been reinvested, they are already included in the current value and don't have to be added as a separate item. For example, an investment valued at $8,500 that cost $5,000 has a return of 170%.

FOCUS ON FUNDS

FUND SCORECARD / Japanese Bonds Funds

FUND SCORECARD / Chinese Equity Funds

FUND SCORECARD / Global Equity Funds

FUND SCORECARD / Asia-Pacific Equity Funds

nvestment funds which are marketed across national borders and invest in equity securities f the Asian-Pacific region (including Japan and Australia/New Zealand), excluding funds pecializing in single countries.

Ranked on % total return (dividends reinvested) in U.S. dollars for one year ending June 21, 1996.

Fund Size*	Fund Name	Fund Mgt. Co.	% Return in US$** YTD	1 YR	2 YR	5 YR
LEADING 10 PERFORMERS						
42.7	JF Pacific Income	JARDINE FLEMING UNIT TRUSTS	11.44	22.45	7.29	13.79
41.6	Perpet Off-Far East	PERPETUAL UT MGMT (JERSEY) LTD	8.89	18.63	2.86	16.23
76.4	Baring IUF-Pacific	BARING INTL FD MGRS (IRELAND)	7.99	17.99	3.66	14.49
229.3	RG Pacific	ROBECO GROUP	5.66	16.96	5.61	12.75
57.9	GAM Orient Acc	GLOBAL ASSET MANAGEMENT	5.66	16.60	5.51	N/A
53.6	Alld Dun IF-Far East	ALLIED DUNBAR INTL FUND MGRS	10.17	16.16	7.05	17.78
340.6	GAM Pacific	GLOBAL ASSET MANAGEMENT	5.38	15.30	4.52	13.70
2.2	GAM Select-Pacific A	GLOBAL ASSET MANAGEMENT	5.29	15.28	N/A	N/A
15.4	CL EUF-Pacific Grth	CREDIT LYONNAIS INTL AM (HK)	10.04	14.72	1.90	23.52
5.4	FiveAr Asian Opps	ROTHSCHILD AUSTRALIA ASSET MGT	10.13	14.49	8.58	N/A
LAGGING 5 PERFORMERS						
7.2	Keystone Asia SmCp A	KEYSTONE MANAGEMENT SA	– 1.66	– 20.92	N/A	N/A
5.9	Ermitage Asian	ERMITAGE MGT (BERMUDA) LTD	– 4.00	– 7.57	– 16.13	N/A
2.9	Asia Eq Dynamic 90's	WORLD ASSET MANAGEMENT CO SA	3.46	– 6.63	– 10.83	0.55
15.0	Mega Pacific	MEGA STRATEGIC INVESTMENT LTD	10.30	– 4.97	– 4.04	8.05
11.8	ManuReg Gl-Pacif Gr	MANULIFE REGENT GLOBAL FDS LTD	– 1.91	– 2.94	– 11.78	13.33

KEY: * millions of US$ at latest available quarter end
** 2 YR and 5 YR performance is annualized
N/A fund not in existence for entire period or incomplete data

Source: Lipper Analytical Services International
47 Maple Street, Summit NJ 07901 USA
FAX: 1-908-273-6184

MAKING COMPARISONS

A mutual fund's performance is measured in relation to other funds. For example, comparing one fund's results with others that have the same objective shows how successful that fund has been. In every issue, The Asian Wall Street Journal highlights a particular type of fund—giving performance details for the top ten funds in the category and for the bottom five. This example, however, has been edited and omits standard information on the legal base and the currency of each fund due to space constraints.

The funds analyzed here invest in equity securities of the Asian-Pacific region, but not single-country funds. The top-ranking fund, JF Pacific Income, has performed significantly better in the past year than the other funds, though CL EUF-Pacific Growth has the best five-year record. N/A means the fund wasn't operating during the entire period, or the information is incomplete.

FINDING RETURN

The most accurate measure of a mutual fund's performance is its **total return**, defined in the box to the left. Among the things that influence return are the performance of the overall market or markets in which the fund is invested, the effectiveness of the fund manager in creating a strong portfolio, and to a lesser degree, the performance of individual securities within the fund. In the case of international funds, such as the ones under scrutiny here, currency fluctuations add another factor.

Since the majority of high-performing funds here have significantly better returns for the current year and for the past year than they do over two years, it's fair to conclude that the markets in the region faltered or lost ground for a period but have boomed in the last year.

The more fund investors are aware of comparative performance, and the more attuned they are to the probable reasons, the more accurately they'll be able to evaluate their own portfolios.

The Prospectus

The prospectus provides a detailed road map of a fund—covering everything from its objective and fees to its portfolio holdings and manager.

Mutual funds are regulated, but standards vary. A common practice is for potential investors to get a **prospectus** before they can buy into a fund. The comparable document for a unit trust is called a **summary of explanatory memorandum**.

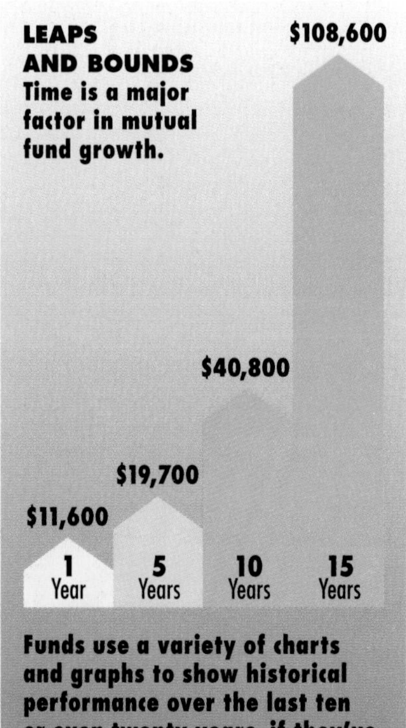

LEAPS AND BOUNDS
Time is a major factor in mutual fund growth.

Funds use a variety of charts and graphs to show historical performance over the last ten or even twenty years, if they've been in existence that long.

THE FUND'S OPERATION

The prospectus explains the fund's objectives and the policies its management uses to achieve the investment goals.

In the U.S., investors have the right to vote on changes a fund proposes in its underlying financial policies, including the amount of money it can **leverage**, or borrow to make additional investments. Since mutual-fund investors are actually shareholders of the fund, they vote in the same way U.S. corporate shareholders do, either in person at the annual meeting or by proxy. Like corporate shareholders, too, their votes affect only major issues; they don't vote on day-to-day matters such as the fee structure.

FEES

The prospectus usually includes a summary of fees and expenses. Asian-Pacific companies tend to offer **load**, or commission-generating, funds. But in the U.S., companies offer both load and **no-load** funds. The latter charge few fees beyond basic management costs.

There are several ways in which load-fund investors can be charged:

- **Management fees** are annual charges to administer the fund. All funds charge this fee, though the amount can vary.
- **Distribution fees** cover marketing and advertising expenses, and sometimes are used to pay bonuses to employees.
- **Redemption fees** are assessed when shares are sold to discourage frequent in-and-out trading. In contrast, a **deferred sales load**, a kind of exit fee, often applies only during a specific period—say the first five years—and then disappears.
- **Switching fees** can apply when money is shifted from one fund to another within the same investment company.

PORTFOLIO TURNOVER RATE

All open-end funds trade securities regularly—some more regularly than others. A fund's **portfolio turnover rate** reveals how much buying and selling is going on. The range is enormous, sometimes reaching as high as 100% annually. In general, high turnovers mean higher stockbroker expenses. That means the fund needs higher returns to offset the cost. There's no rule that says which approach works better, since both styles produce high-performance funds.

While a prospectus provides all the details of a fund's operation, it also tries to portray the fund in the best possible terms. Smart investors carefully sift through all the information.

THE EFFECT OF FEES

The range of load fees varies by country. There is no legal cap on these fees in Asia. But in the U.S., there's a cap of 8.5% on all fees a fund can charge.

Most U.S. funds charge less than that as a commission, often between 3% and 5%, but they increase other fees. One technique has been to introduce different classes of shares, with different fee structures. Or instead of charging a sales commission, a fund might impose asset-based fees. That means charging a percentage of the total value of the investor's shares in the fund every year. The more the value of the fund increases, the more the investor pays.

A load lowers return because it reduces the amount of money that is actually invested. A $1,000 investment in a fund charging a 4.5% front-end load, for example, means that $955 goes to buy shares and the other $45 pays the commission.

LONG-TERM PERFORMANCE

Since mutual funds are usually considered long-term investments, performance over time is given added weight in part because the fund has been through several economic cycles that are likely to occur again. A fund's past performance doesn't guarantee what it will do in the future. On the other hand, funds that have been profitable over ten or even twenty years are often given high ratings by independent analysts.

Futures and Options

Futures and options are complex investments that pose risks but provide protection against changing prices.

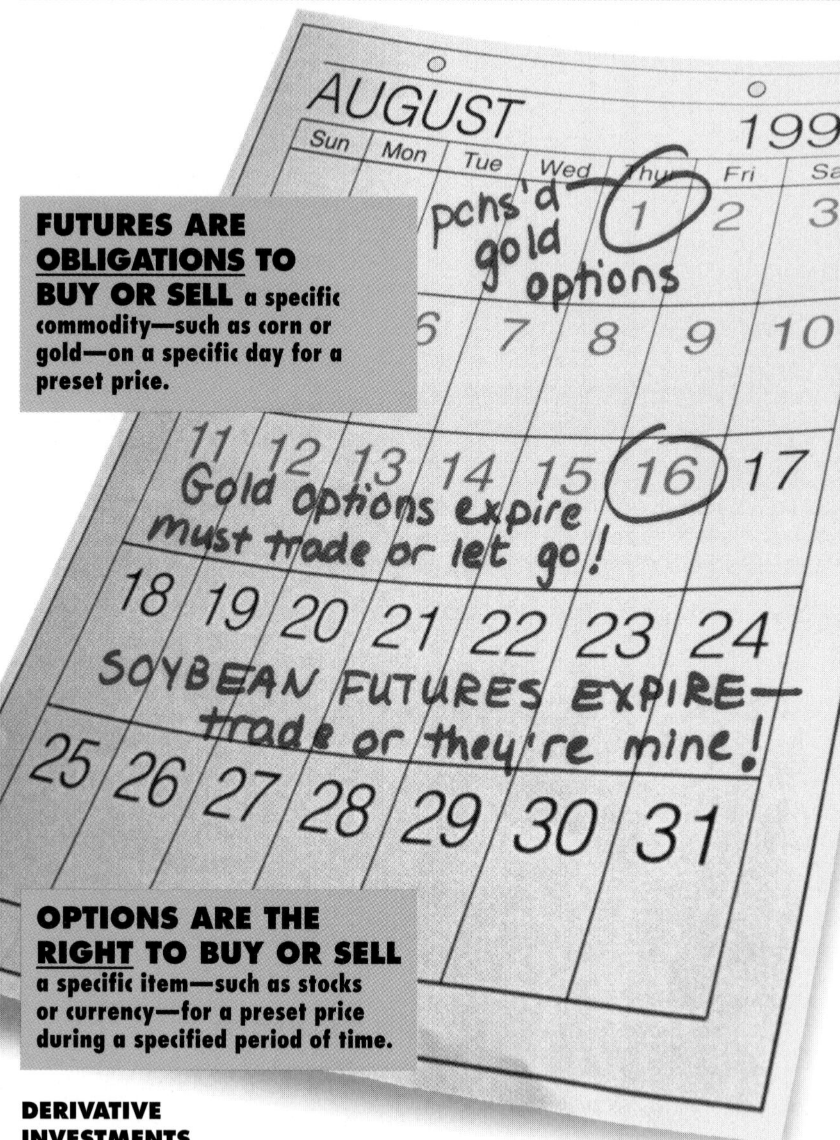

FUTURES ARE OBLIGATIONS TO BUY OR SELL a specific commodity—such as corn or gold—on a specific day for a preset price.

OPTIONS ARE THE RIGHT TO BUY OR SELL a specific item—such as stocks or currency—for a preset price during a specified period of time.

DERIVATIVE INVESTMENTS

One reason futures and options are complex is that they're **derivative**, or hybrid, investments. Instead of representing shares of ownership—such as stocks—or the promise of loan repayment—as with bonds—each futures contract or option is once or twice removed from a real product. A crude-oil futures contract, for instance, is a bet on which way oil prices will move. What happens to the oil itself is of little interest to the investor. And products such as the Nikkei Stock Average futures contract don't represent ownership of stocks in a gauge. They function as a bet on how the index will perform over a given time.

LOOKING AT RISK

For some people, futures and options are a way to reduce risk. Farmers who commit themselves to sell grain at a set price are protected if prices drop. Investors who sell options on stock they own can offset some of their losses if the market collapses.

But other investors trade futures and options to take risk, because the possibility of a big loss is balanced by the opportunity for a huge gain. Individual investors are increasingly small players in the futures and options markets because the stakes are so high and the returns are so unpredictable.

LEVERAGE ENHANCES RISK

Leverage, in financial terms, means using a small amount of money to make an investment of much greater value. That means you can buy a **futures contract** worth thousands of dollars with an initial investment of about 10% of the total value. For example, if you buy a gold contract worth $35,000 (when gold is $350 an ounce) your cost would be about $3,500 and your leverage would be $31,500.

Every time the price of the contract gains 10¢, the value of your investment increases by $10, as shown below. In a commodity as potentially volatile as gold, price swings of $100 within the lifespan of the contract are possible. If the price went up $100, to $450 an ounce, the value of your investment would jump $10,000—almost a 300% gain from the original cost.

A $3,500 INVESTMENT

BUYS A $35,000 CONTRACT

100oz. GOLD

|← LEVERAGE OF →|
$31,500

But the opposite can happen. If the price falls and the value of your investment drops 300%, it could cost you more than $10,000—sometimes a lot more—to make good on the loss. So while leverage makes the initial commitment easy, the nature of derivative investing means you could have major losses.

When Leverage Works

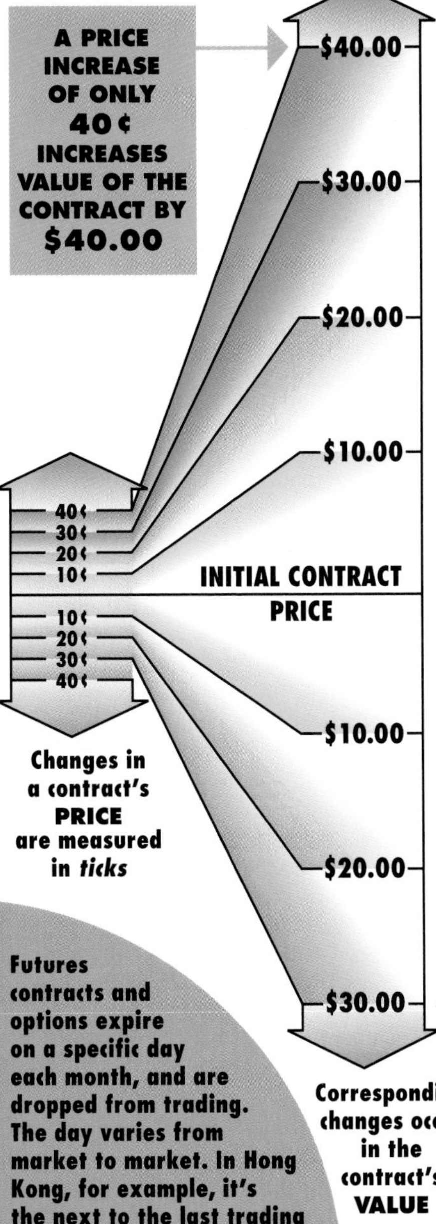

Futures contracts and options expire on a specific day each month, and are dropped from trading. The day varies from market to market. In Hong Kong, for example, it's the next to the last trading day of the month.

When Leverage Hurts

A PRICE DECREASE OF ONLY 30¢ DECREASES VALUE OF THE CONTRACT BY $30.00

TRADING DERIVATIVES

Investors can trade futures and options on certain stock exchanges, on commodities exchanges, on futures and options exchanges and over the counter. Exchange trading is regulated either by the exchange itself or a regulatory authority within the country where the exchange is located, or sometimes by both.

Over-the-counter (OTC) derivatives, on the other hand, are customized and privately traded between two institutions. Usually, one of them is a bank. The appeal of OTC products is that they can be tailored to a client's needs. However, they're considered riskier than exchange-traded products, in part because there's no guarantee that the two parties will live up to the terms of the contract (see pages 142–143).

Commodities

Modern life depends on raw materials—the products that keep people and businesses going. Anticipating what they'll cost fuels the futures market.

Commodities are raw materials: the wheat in bread, the silver in earrings, the oil in gasoline and a thousand other products. Most producers and users buy and sell commodities in the **cash market**, commonly known as the **spot market**, since the full cash price is paid on the spot.

DETERMINING CASH PRICES

Commodity prices are based on **supply and demand**. If a commodity is plentiful, its price will be low. If it's hard to come by, the price will be high.

Supply and demand for many commodities move in fairly predictable seasonal cycles. Grains are cheapest in the summer when they're harvested, and most expensive in the spring before the new crop matures.

But it doesn't always work that way. If a drought in the U.S. wipes out a key part of the U.S. wheat crop, cash prices for wheat surge because bakers buy up what's available to avoid a short-term crunch. Or if political turmoil in the Middle East threatens the oil supply, prices at the gas pumps jump in anticipation of supply problems.

MINIMIZING FUTURE RISK

Since people don't know when natural disasters will occur, they can't plan for them. That's why **futures contracts** were invented—to help businesses minimize risk. Bakers with a futures contract to buy wheat for $3.20 a bushel are protected if the spot price jumps to $3.80—at least for that purchase.

Farmers, loggers and other commodity producers can only estimate the demand for their products and try to plan accordingly. But they can get stung by too much supply and too little demand—or the reverse. Similarly, manufacturers have to take orders for future delivery without knowing the cost of the raw materials they need to make their products. So they buy futures contracts in the products they make or use in order to smooth out the unexpected price bumps.

CASH PRICES ARE CLUES

The derivatives markets watch cash prices closely. The price of a futures contract for next month, or five months from now, is based on today's prices, seasonal expectations, anticipated changes in the weather, the political scene and dozens of other factors, including what investors are willing to pay.

The fluctuation in cash prices also provides clues to what consumers can expect to pay in the marketplace for products made from the raw materials.

FINANCIAL COMMODITIES

Though we don't think of dollars or yen or bonds as commodities, they are. Money is the raw material of trade, both domestic and international. What the interest rate will be next year, or what the dollar will be worth against the yen, concerns people whose businesses depend on the money supply and the value of currencies. They use futures to hedge against sudden changes.

One consequence of the growing emphasis on financial futures trading is that institutional traders now dominate the markets, and the numbers of individual hedgers and speculators have dwindled.

While the same forces of supply and demand affect the shopper in the supermarket or the driver at the gas pumps, the futures market doesn't deal in five pounds of sugar or ten gallons of gas. Efficiency demands that commodities be sold in large quantities.

Middle East turmoil causes oil shortage

ONE GASOLINE CONTRACT IS 42,000 GALLONS

If gasoline is 54.93¢ a gallon, one contract is worth
$23,071

Oil producers increase output

Insects ravage cane crops

ONE SUGAR CONTRACT IS 112,000 POUNDS

If sugar is 21.33¢ per pound, one contract is worth
$23,890

Health fad causes drop in sugar consumption

Pound is devalued by Bank of England

ONE STERLING CONTRACT IS 62,500 POUNDS

If a pound is selling at $1.5050, one contract is worth
$94,062.50

Dropping interest rates in U.K. lower pound's appeal

Cash Prices

Tuesday, July 16, 1996
(Closing Market Quotations)
GRAINS AND FEEDS

	Tues	Mon	Yr.Ago
Barley, top-quality Mpls., bu........	[illegible]	z	3.75
Bran, wheat middlings, KC ton	107-110	108-11	57.00
Corn, No. 2 yel. Cent. Ill. bu	bpu4.81	5.12½	2.85
Corn Gluten Feed, Midwest, ton....	102-115	102-115	74.00
Cottonseed Meal, Clksdle, Miss. ton	200.00	200.00	116.25
Hominy Feed, Cent. Ill. ton...........	140.00	143.00	84.5[illegible]
Meat-Bonemeal, 50% pro. Ill. ton. .	245-50	245-50	170[illegible]
Oats, No. 2 milling, Mpls., bu	u2.68½	z	[illegible]
Sorghum, (Milo) No. 2 Gulf cwt	u771-772	79[illegible]	[illegible]
Soybean Meal, Cent. Ill., 44% protein-ton	u247-52	251½	[illegible]
Soybean Meal, Cent. Ill., 48% protein-ton	u257-62	261[illegible]	[illegible]
Soybeans, No. 1 yel Cent.-Ill. bu	bpu8.13½	8[illegible]	[illegible]
Wheat, Spring 14%-pro Mpls. bu	u576½-86½	[illegible]	[illegible]
Wheat, No. 2 sft red, St.Lou. bu.....	bpu4.[illegible]	[illegible]	[illegible]
Wheat, hard KC [illegible]	[illegible]	[illegible]	[illegible]

As the chart shows, the price range for bran declined Tuesday from the level it was at Monday. But the prices surpassed the $57 fetched a year ago. So consumers might reasonably expect to pay more for bran products next autumn. But the other prices illustrate that the cash market in each product operates independently of the others. Most are up, but at different rates.

The Futures Exchanges

Futures are traded on exchanges that offer markets in everything from pork bellies to stock indexes.

Futures contracts are listed and traded on exchanges. Trading is handled either on the floor of the exchange, using an open outcry system, or electronically, using a computerized system. Some exchanges, including the one in Hong Kong, use both systems. Either way, the exchange has the responsibility to guarantee that an agreement between a buyer and a seller is fulfilled.

When orders are traded on the floor of the exchange they are filled by **open outcry**. That means an order to buy or sell is called out publicly, in a type of auction process called **price discovery**. It also means that those who scream the loudest often make the most deals. It's probably a major factor in creating the wild image that the exchanges have in the public mind—along with the occasional broken arm suffered as a result of pushing and shoving.

Since electronic systems are less expensive to operate, some experts predict that an increasing percentage of exchange-traded derivatives will move from open outcry to computer-based trading.

LINKED EXCHANGES

Exchanges have been forming one-on-one links that allow members of one exchange to trade another's best-selling options and futures. Alliances have been cropping up as exchanges try to attract new business and retain customers in an increasingly global derivatives business.

The Philadelphia Stock Exchange, for instance, struck an accord allowing its popular currency options to be traded in the pits of the Hong Kong Futures Exchange. The Sydney Futures Exchange and the New York Mercantile Exchange linked their proprietary electronic systems, permitting members of the Australian exchange to trade Nymex energy and metals products. And the Singapore International Monetary Exchange and the Chicago Mercantile Exchange have a longstanding pact involving Eurodollar contracts.

Where the Exchanges Are

The Asian Wall Street Journal reports on activity at a number of exchanges around the world. Each exchange specializes in specific products, and the name of the exchange is often denoted by an acronym or code. For instance, the New York Mercantile Exchange is often referred to as Nymex, but its code in daily lists is NMER. And the London International Financial Futures Exchange is generally referred to as Liffe, but its code is LIFE. Some of the exchanges and their acronyms or codes are listed below:

ASIAN-PACIFIC REGION

Australia
Sydney Futures Exchange: **SFE**

Hong Kong
Hong Kong Futures Exchange: **HK FE**

Japan
Osaka Securities Exchange: **OSE**
Tokyo Commodity Exchange: **TCE**
Tokyo Stock Exchange: **TSE**

Malaysia
Kuala Lumpur Commodity Exchange: **KLCE**
Kuala Lumpur Options and Financial Futures Exchange: **Kloffe**

New Zealand
New Zealand Futures Exchange: **NZFE**

Philippines
Manila International Futures Exchange: **MIFE**

Singapore
Singapore International Monetary Exchange: **SIMEX**

NORTH AMERICA

U.S.
Chicago Board of Trade: **CBOT**
Chicago Mercantile Exchange: **CMER**
Mid-America Commodity Exchange, Chicago: **MACE**
Kansas City Board of Trade: **KBOT**
Minneapolis Grain Exchange: **MGRX**
New York Cotton Exchange: **NCTN**
Coffee, Sugar and Cocoa Exchange, New York: **NCSE**
New York Mercantile Exchange, **NMER**
Comex division, New York Mercantile Exchange: **NCMX**
New York Futures Exchange: **NYFE**
Philadelphia Board of Trade: **PBOT**

Canada
Winnipeg Commodities Exchange: **WCMX**

EUROPE

Britain
London International Financial Futures Exchange: **LIFE**
London Metal Exchange: **LME**

How Open Outcry Works

Most exchange floors are divided into pits where the actual trading occurs. To impose some order, each commodity is usually traded in one specific area on the floor. **Options** on the futures contracts, when they're available (see page 135), are traded in an area next to the corresponding futures area.

A **trading pit** is usually tiered into three or four levels. During heavy activity, traders jockey for position to see over the heads of the traders in front of them. Some pits are divided into sections so that several different commodities can be traded at the same time.

The trading area has **pit recorders**, whose job is to pick up the trading cards thrown to them, time-stamp them and key the information into a computer. Trades are recorded on **trading cards**, the only written record of the details of a transaction. Some exchanges have begun the move to hand-held computers to create an instant electronic record.

Brokerage-firm traders and some individual members, called **locals**, can trade on the trading floor.

BUCKET SHOPS

Not all futures trading takes place on exchanges. Dealing also takes place in illegal operations called bucket shops.

Hong Kong, Taiwan and China have all had problems with such illicit trading. Bucket shops use real-time information from legitimate exchanges, often obtained through commercial quotation systems. Using the information, the operator creates a local futures market—but the money never leaves the room. Participants think they're investing in some legitimate futures market, and track prices shown on computer screens. But what they're purchasing is the right to participate in a shadow market.

The illicit brokerage house takes a commission, and matches up the offsetting trades in a back room. The shadow market can operate smoothly as long as the real markets don't move sharply in either direction. When a sharp change occurs, the operator can't balance out the trades and simply closes shop.

Trading Futures Contracts

You don't need to invest much to enter a futures contract, but you need nerve—and luck—to ride this financial rollercoaster.

To trade futures, an investor gives an order to buy or sell a commodity on a particular date in the future—such as wheat for October delivery, or December pork bellies, or June '99 Eurodollars. The price is determined in trading.

The cost of the contract is what the commodity will be worth if it is delivered. But the price of buying the contract is only a fraction (2% to 10%, depending on who the client is) of that total. It's paid as a good faith deposit, called the **initial margin**. For example, a contract for 5,000 bushels of wheat is $17,500 if wheat is $3.50 a bushel. The margin required would be about $1,750.

AFTER THE ORDER

When an order is filled, the contract typically goes into a pool on the exchange floor with all the other filled orders, with buyers and sellers anonymously paired. Since contracts are traded aggressively, the pairing process is always in motion.

Since the price of a contract changes daily—usually many times over—the value of an investor's account changes too. At the end of each trading day, the exchange moves money either in or out of all the accounts on record, depending on the shifting worth of the contracts. The process is called **marking to the market**. The financial effect on a portfolio is often dramatic, as shown below.

Winning and Losing with a Futures Contract

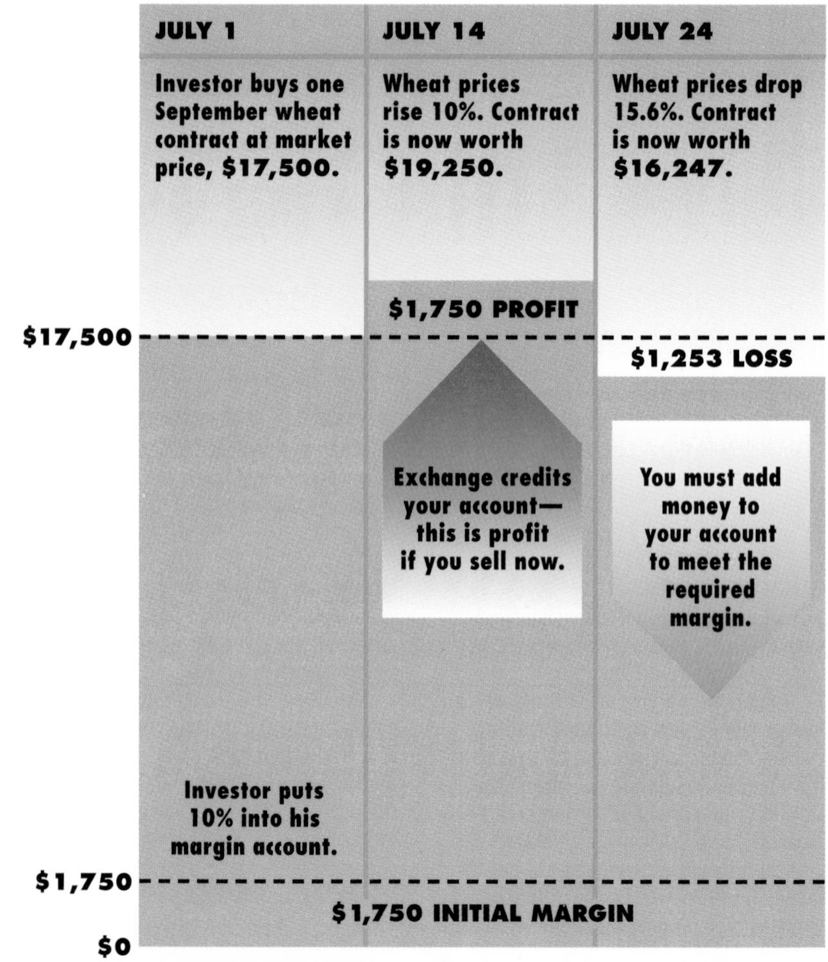

JULY 1	JULY 14	JULY 24
Investor buys one September wheat contract at market price, $17,500.	Wheat prices rise 10%. Contract is now worth $19,250.	Wheat prices drop 15.6%. Contract is now worth $16,247.

$1,750 PROFIT

$17,500

$1,253 LOSS

Exchange credits your account—this is profit if you sell now.

You must add money to your account to meet the required margin.

Investor puts 10% into his margin account.

$1,750

$1,750 INITIAL MARGIN

$0

THE LANGUAGE OF FUTURES

Futures trading involves contracts that cancel, or offset, each other: for every buy there's a sell and vice versa. The language of futures trading reflects this phenomenon.

To enter the market	Which means	To leave the market	Which means
GO LONG	**ENTER A FUTURES CONTRACT TO BUY**	**GO SHORT**	**ENTER A FUTURES CONTRACT TO SELL**
GO SHORT	**ENTER A FUTURES CONTRACT TO SELL**	**GO LONG**	**ENTER A FUTURES CONTRACT TO BUY**

MEETING THE MARGIN

In the U.S., an investor's margin level must be kept constant, in part to reassure the exchange that the terms of the contract will be met. If an account is down at the end of the day, it has to be brought up to the required margin level. For example, if wheat slipped to $3.25 a bushel from $3.50—a little more than a 7% drop—the margin account would be down $1,250 (a loss of 25¢ a bushel times 5,000 bushels). When that happens, the investor must add money to the account to bring it up to the required minimum.

Similarly, if the price of wheat dropped again the next day—perhaps on news of a bumper crop in Russia—the same thing would happen again. The original margin required could grow quickly to many thousands of dollars while the underlying value of the commodity continued to fall.

LOCK-LIMIT PROTECTION

Some exchanges have a mechanism, called the **lock-limit**, to protect investors in a fast-moving market. If a contract price moves up or down to the pre-established price limit, the market locks up or locks down, and doesn't open for trading again until the price gets to an acceptable level.

In reality, the lock-limit system often means that investors sustain huge losses or benefit from comparable gains because they are unable to sell a contract until the price has stabilized at the underlying commodity's new real price. A suddenly devalued currency, for example, could send futures contracts on that currency into a tailspin. And when the dust cleared, the value of the contract would probably be significantly less than it was when trading began.

In the U.S., the average individual investor keeps an account open for about 11 months before closing it and taking what's left somewhere else to invest.

LEAVING THE MARKET

Fewer than 2% of all U.S. futures contracts actually result in the transfer of goods. The remaining contracts have been **offset**, or neutralized, with a contract that carries the opposite obligation.

For example, if you buy a September wheat contract at $3.50 per bushel with a $1,750 margin payment, you expect the price to go up.

If the price of the contract climbs to $3.80 after a storm-plagued July week devastates the wheat crop, your account is credited with $1,500, so you're ahead of the game.

You then sell a September wheat contract, which cancels your obligation to buy, take your profit and your margin amount (minus commissions and other expenses) and invest in a different futures contract.

But it can work the other way, too.

If prices drop and you're losing money, you may sell an offsetting contract at the best price you can get to cancel your obligation and get out of the market before your losses become any greater. Statistics suggest that somewhere between 75% and 90% of traders in some futures markets lose money every year.

REDUCING TRADING RISKS

The strategy called **spread trading** is one of the techniques used by futures traders to reduce the risk of losing large sums of money from a sudden shudder in the market, though it also limits rewards.

Basically, it means buying one contract and selling another for the same commodity at the same time. One contract will always make money and the other one will always lose. The key to ending up with a profit is getting the **spread**, or the difference between the two contracts' prices, to work in your favor. For example, if you lose money on a sell contract but make money on a buy contract, the difference between those prices is the spread. If it's 5¢ in your favor, you'd make $250 on a wheat contract. If it's 5¢ against you, the $250 would be your loss.

Hedgers and Speculators

Futures have the reputation of being a game for high-risk speculators. But they perform the important function of stabilizing prices.

There are two distinct types of participants in commodities futures markets.

Hedgers are interested in the commodities. They can be producers, such as farmers, mining companies, foresters and oil drillers. Or they can be users, such as bakers, paper mills, jewelers and oil distributors. In general, producers sell futures contracts while users buy them.

Speculators, on the other hand, trade futures strictly to make money. If you trade futures but never use the commodity itself, you are a speculator. Speculators may either buy or sell contracts, depending on which way they think the market is going in a particular commodity.

HOW HEDGERS USE THE MARKET

Hedgers are mainly interested in protecting themselves against price changes that will undercut their profit. For example, a textile company may want to hedge against rising cotton prices as a result of boll weevil infestation. In August, the company buys 100 December cotton futures, representing five million pounds of cotton, at 58¢ a pound, for a total cost of $2.9 million.

During the autumn, the cotton crop is infested and the prices shoot up. The contract now trades at 68¢. But the textile maker has hedged against exactly this situation. In December it can take delivery of cotton at 58¢ a pound, 10¢ less than the prevailing market price, and save $500,000 (10¢ times five million pounds).

Or the company can sell the futures contracts for 10¢ a pound more than it paid for them, and use the profit to offset the higher price it will have to pay for cotton in the cash market. In either case, there's no nasty surprise in added commodity costs because the cash price and the futures price cancel each other out.

HOW SPECULATORS USE THE MARKET

Speculators hope to make money in the futures market by betting on price moves. A speculator may load up on orange-juice futures in November, for instance, betting that if a freeze sets in and damages the orange crop, prices of orange juice and the futures contract based on them will soar.

If the speculators are right, and the winter is tough, the contracts on orange juice will be worth more than they paid. The speculators can sell their contracts at a profit. If they're wrong, and there's a bumper crop, the bottom will fall out of the market and the speculators will be squeezed dry.

in the event of a freeze, and orange farmers couldn't earn enough money in a good year to pay their production costs.

Speculators also keep the market active. If those who produced or used the commodities were the only ones trading, there would not be enough activity to keep trading going. Buy and sell orders would be paired slowly, erasing the protection that hedgers receive when the market responds quickly to changes in the cash market.

SPECULATORS ARE INDISPENSABLE

Speculators may be the highest-flying gamblers in the investment game. But they are crucial to the success of the futures market because they complete a symbiotic relationship between those wishing to avoid risk and those willing to take it.

Since hedgers, in planning ahead, want to avoid risk in what is undeniably a risky business, others have to be willing to accept it. Unless some speculators were willing to bet that orange-juice prices will rise while others bet that prices will fall, an orange-juice producer could not protect against dramatically increased costs

INFLUENCES ON CONTRACT PRICE

While the price of a futures contract is often influenced by the weather, it's also affected by the economic news that the government releases, the length of time the contract has to run and what speculators are doing and saying.

Virtually every day, governments release economic data, sell bonds or create new policies that influence the price of commodity contracts and financial futures. News on new home sales, for example, directly influences the price of lumber futures, as hedgers and speculators try to anticipate the amount of lumber the construction industry will be ordering.

If a producer agrees to hold a commodity for future delivery, the contract will reflect storage, insurance and other carrying costs to cover daily expenses until delivery. Generally, the further away the delivery date, the greater the carrying costs. Even so, prices rarely go up regularly in consecutive months. When the prices do increase this way, the situation is called a **contango**. The reverse condition, an inverted market, is called **backwardation**.

Speculation also influences a commodity's price. Sudden demand for a contract—sparked by rumor, inside information or other factors—can drive its price sky high. Or the reverse can happen when rumors or events make investors scramble to sell.

Futures and options are different from stocks, bonds and mutual funds because they are **zero sum markets.** That means for every dollar somebody makes (before commissions), somebody else loses a dollar. Put bluntly, that means that any gain is at somebody else's expense.

How Futures Work

Though they have different goals, hedgers and speculators are in the market together. What happens to the price of a contract affects them all.

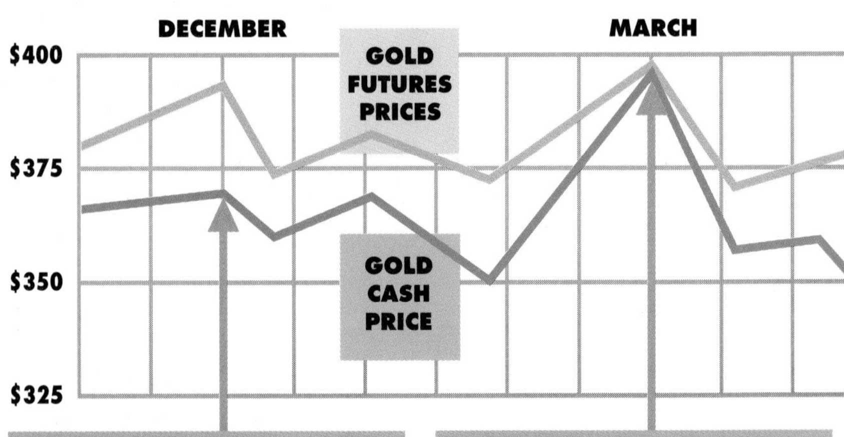

DECEMBER

GOLD IS $370 AN OUNCE IN THE CASH MARKET AND $385 FOR THE JUNE CONTRACT

In December, the price of gold in the cash market—what a buyer would pay for immediate delivery—is $15 less than the price of the June contract.

PRODUCERS (HEDGERS)

Gold producers hedge by selling futures contracts.

The gold producers sell June futures contracts because they won't have gold ready for delivery until then.

Earned in December sale **$385**

USERS (HEDGERS)

Gold users hedge by buying futures contracts.

The gold users buy June futures contracts because that's when they need the gold.

Cost of December buy **- $385**

SPECULATORS

Speculators buy gold futures contracts if they think the price is going up.

Cost of December buy **- $385**

MARCH

GOLD IS $395 AN OUNCE IN THE CASH MARKET. THE JUNE CONTRACT IS SELLING FOR $398

In March, the price of gold has gone up to $395 in the cash market. The June futures contract is selling for $398. The hedgers wait for the expiration date. Speculators sell offsetting contracts, thinking price has hit the top.

PRODUCERS (HEDGERS)

The producers can't sell their gold because it isn't ready yet.

USERS (HEDGERS)

This upswing in the cash price is exactly what the users were trying to protect themselves against.

SPECULATORS

The speculators sell, thinking gold has reached its peak. One clue is that the contract price is so close to the cash price. If speculators thought higher prices in the cash market were likely in the near future, they would be willing to pay higher prices for futures contracts.

This time the speculators made money in the market if they sold in March when the contract price reached its peak.

Price from March sell	**$398**
Cost of December buy	**- $385**
Profit on trade	**$ 13**

Note that this example doesn't include commissions or other costs that would result from trading futures contracts, and it assumes that everyone bought one option at the same price.

The oldest futures contracts date back to 17th century Japan when **rice tickets** provided landlords who collected rents in rice with a steady secondary income. They sold warehouse receipts for their stored rice, giving the holder the right to a specific quantity of rice, of a specific quality, on a specific date in the future.

The merchants who paid for the tickets could cash them in at the appointed time, or sell them, at a profit, to someone else. Like futures contracts today, the tickets themselves had no real worth, but they represented a way to make money on the underlying commodity—the rice.

JUNE

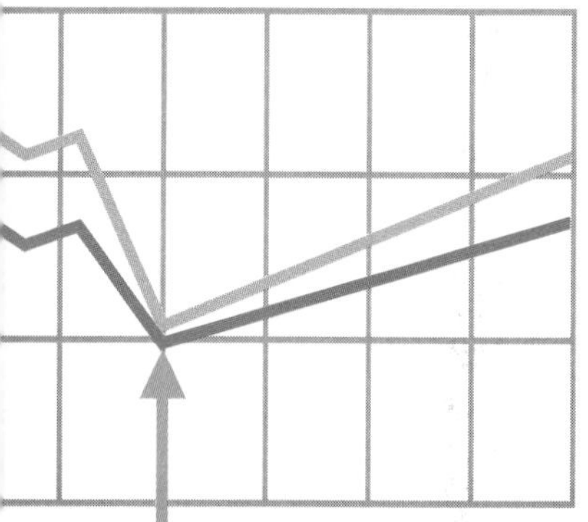

JUNE

CONTRACTS EXPIRE WHEN GOLD IS $350 AN OUNCE IN THE CASH MARKET AND $352 IN THE FUTURES MARKET

In June, when the contract expires, both the producers and the users equalize their profit or loss in the futures market through offsetting trades in the cash market.

PRODUCERS (HEDGERS)

Because the price of the gold futures contract had dropped, the producers made money on the offsetting trade:

Earned in December sale	**$385**
Cost of June buy	**– $352**
Result of trade (profit)	**$ 33**

Even though producers had to sell their gold in the cash market for less than the anticipated price, the profit from their futures trades gave them the expected level of profit.

Earned in cash market	**$350**
Futures profit	**+ $ 33**
Gross profit	**$383**

USERS (HEDGERS)

THE GOLD USERS

The users lost money on the futures contracts because it cost more to sell the offsetting contacts than they had paid to buy.

Earned in June sell	**$352**
Cost of December buy	**– $385**
Result of trade (loss)	**– $ 33**

Since it cost the users less to buy gold in the cash market than they had expected, the total cost was what they anticipated.

Cost in cash market	**$350**
Cost of futures trade	**+ $ 33**
Actual cost of gold	**$383**

In any given futures contract, the profit or loss of the hedgers could be reversed, depending on the rise or fall of the futures price. In the end, however, their profit or loss in the futures trade would be offset by profit or loss in the cash market. The speculators could lose as frequently—maybe more frequently—than they gained, depending on changing prices and the timing of entering or leaving the market.

THE COST OF TRADING

In the U.S., traders charge their clients hefty commissions to execute their orders to trade futures contracts. Unlike the commissions on stock transactions, one for buying and another for selling, futures brokers charge only once, called a **round-turn commission**, to open and close a position. Commissions are higher though, often 18% or more of the cost of the transaction, instead of 2% or less.

Reading Futures Tables

For futures traders, daily price reports chronicle the changing value of their accounts. For others, they're a glimpse at future prices.

The tables in The Asian Wall Street Journal reporting on activity in futures markets show opening and closing prices, price history and volume of sales every day. Because the futures markets reflect current political and economic conditions, the charts also provide interesting commentary on the state of the economy and where people feel it's headed.

The **product** is listed alphabetically within its particular grouping. Cotton, for example, is listed under the heading Fibers. Generally, detailed information is given in these charts for the most actively traded futures contracts. Activity for additional contracts is summarized at the end of the column under the heading **Other Futures**.

The list shows the **exchange** on which a particular contract is traded. For instance, NCSE stands for the Coffee, Sugar and Cocoa Exchange in New York. Some commodities, such as wheat and corn, trade on more than one exchange. The exchange whose activity is watched most closely is the one that is shown in the tables.

Open is the opening price on the previous trading day. Depending on what's happened in the world overnight, the opening price may not be the same as the closing price the day before. Since cotton prices on this exchange are listed in cents per pound, the 78.60 means cotton opened for sale at 78.60¢ per pound. Multiplying this amount by 50,000 pounds (the contract size) equals $39,300 per contract.

High, low and **settle** report the contract's highest, lowest and closing prices for the previous trading day. Taken together, they're a good indication of the commodity's market

COMMODITY

Open interest reflects previous trading day.

North America and London

Futures Prices

	Open	High	Low	Settle	Change	Lifetime High	Lifetime Low	Open Interest
FIBERS								
COTTON 2 (NCTN) 50,000 lbs.- cents per lb.								
Jul 96	73.40	74.10	73.20	73.25	+ 0.30	96.00	72.68	2,778
Oct 96	75.55	76.05	75.35	75.70	+ 0.15	86.50	72.75	8,194
Dec 96	76.10	76.45	75.80	76.18	+ 0.30	84.40	71.80	23,976
Mar 97	77.37	77.40	77.30	77.30	+ 0.20	85.15	73.10	6,033
May 97	78.15	78.15	78.00	78.08	+ 0.23	85.40	73.50	3,141
Jul 97	78.60	78.60	78.45	78.50	– 0.10	85.40	73.75	1,883
Oct 97	...	...	...	77.55	...	81.30	75.50	518
Dec 97	...	...	...	76.75	+ 0.10	80.10	75.00	2,408
Mar 98	...	...	...	77.75	+ 0.10	81.00	78.50	84
May 98	...	...	...	78.20	+ 0.02	81.00	80.25	20
		vol Fri 15,374				Open int 59,035.		
FOOD								
SUGAR 14 (NCSE) 112,000 lbs.- cents per lb.								
Sep 96	22.25	22.28	22.18	22.18	– 0.09	23.33	21.90	4,228
Nov 96	22.56	22.62	22.56	22.62	– 0.04	22.98	21.25	3,904
Jan 97	22.48	22.50	22.47	22.47	– 0.02	22.62	22.05	1,904
Mar 97	22.34	22.37	22.34	22.37	...	22.50	21.90	2,477
May 97	22.56	22.56	22.56	22.57	+ 0.01	22.78	21.95	1,909
Jul 97	...	...	...	22.63	+ 0.03	22.80	22.00	1,910
Sep 97	...	...	...	22.62	+ 0.04	22.79	22.21	1,178
Nov 97	...	...	...	21.88	...	...	...	...
Est vol 755		vol Fri 550				Open int 17,510.		
SUGAR-WORLD 11 (NCSE) 112,000 lbs.- cents per lb.								
Jul 96	12.12	12.13	11.70	11.84	– 0.19	12.91	9.62	21,606
Oct 96	11.40	11.42	11.09	11.23	– 0.16	12.50	9.62	66,258
Mar 97	10.98	11.00	10.74	10.86	– 0.17	11.05	9.48	36,779
May 97	10.77	10.78	10.56	10.63	[illegible]	[illegible]		

The **size of each contract** reflects the bulk trading unit used during the normal course of commercial business. One sugar contract covers the rights to 112,000 pounds of sugar. The **price per unit** is expressed in either dollars or cents per unit, depending on the commodity. Here, it's cents per pound. To find the total cost of the contract, multiply the settle price per unit by the number of units. The March '97 sugar contract settled at $25,054 (112,000 x 22.37¢).

volatility during the trading day. Here, the opening price of a cotton contract was more than the settle price of 78.50¢.

Change compares the closing price given here with the previous closing price. A plus (+) indicates prices ended higher and a minus (–) means prices ended lower. In this case, cotton for July '97 delivery settled at .10 less than the previous day.

The **month of the contract** indicates when it expires. **Jul 97** indicates this contract expires on the third Friday of July 1997. On the expiration date, the contract is dropped from the table.

The expiration cycles for each commodity usually correspond with activity in that commodity. For example, trading in grains follows the cycle of planting, harvesting and exporting.

Lifetime highs and **lows** show volatility over the lifetime of a particular contract. Prices for heating oil, for example, have been more volatile than sugar prices—meaning the investment risks are higher but the chances of making money are also higher.

Open interest reports the total number of outstanding contracts—that is, those that have not been cancelled by offsetting trades. Generally, the further away the expiration date, the smaller the open interest because there's not much trading activity. In the case of grains and oilseed, however, there is increased activity in the months the new crop will be harvested.

MARKETS

	Open	High	Low	Settle	Change	Lifetime High	Lifetime Low	Open Interest
FUELS								
HEATING OIL (NMER) 42,000 gal- cents per gal								
Jul 96	51.00	51.70	50.80	51.30	– 0.06	55.90	45.90	15,450
Aug 96	51.35	52.15	51.25	51.73	– 0.03	55.60	42.70	20,053
Sep 96	51.90	52.60	51.80	52.23	– 0.03	54.70	47.25	9,534
Oct 96	52.55	53.10	52.40	52.78	– 0.03	55.10	47.95	5,479
Nov 96	53.00	53.60	53.00	53.33	– 0.03	55.55	48.70	6,754
Dec 96	53.60	54.20	53.50	53.88	– 0.03	55.95	49.45	18,175
Jan 97	54.35	54.45	54.35	54.18	– 0.03	56.20	49.75	7,936
Feb 97	53.60	54.05	53.60	53.73	– 0.03	55.50	49.60	5,329
Mar 97	52.60	52.60	52.60	52.33	– 0.03	54.10	48.50	2,087
Apr 97	50.90	50.90	50.90	50.73	– 0.03	52.50	47.45	1,444
May 97	49.60	49.60	49.60	49.38	– 0.03	50.90	46.60	1,289
Jun 97	49.15	49.15	49.15	48.93	– 0.03	50.15	46.20	2,132
Jul 97	...	...	...	48.83	– 0.03	50.00	45.95	941
Aug 97	...	...	...	49.28	...	52.65	47.30	256
Sep 97	...	...	...	49.88	...	51.00	49.40	149
Oct 97	...	...	...	50.48	...	50.80	50.50	58
Nov 97	...	...	...	51.08	– 0.08	51.50	50.75	81
Dec 97	...	...	...	51.68	– 0.08	51.90	51.20	11
vol Fri 17,488							Open int 97,158.	
NATURAL GAS (NMER) 10,000 mm btu's, $ per mm btu								
Jun 96	2.630	2.675	2.620	2.620	– 20	2.700	1.675	17,335
Aug 96	2.700	2.725	2.660	2.660	– 43	2.745	1.695	38,862
Sep 96	2.715	2.730	2.675	[illegible]	41	2.730	1.710	20,816
Oct 96	2.720	2.730	2.685	2				
Nov 96	2.735	2.745	2.700	2				
Dec 96	2.765	2.775	2.740	2				
Jan 97	2.765	2.765	2.730	2				
Feb 97	2.650	2.650	2.615	2				
Mar 97	2.450	2.450	2.425	2				
Apr 97	2.250	2.260	2.240	2				
May 97	2.160	2.170	2.145	[illegible]				

	Open	High	Low
Apr 97	401.50	401.50	401.50
Jul 97	...	...	...
		vol Fri	
SILVER(1000) (CBOT) 1,00			
Jun 96	495.0	497.0	494.0
Jul 96	...	...	...
Aug 96	500.0	504.0	499.0
Oct 96	512.0	512.0	512.0
Dec 96	515.0	523.0	513.0
Feb 97	...	...	...
Apr 97	...	...	...
Jun 97	...	...	...
Oct 97	...	...	...
Est vol 100		vol Fri	
SILVER(5000) (CBOT) 5,00			
Jun 96	...	...	...
Jul 96	...	...	...
Dec 96	...	...	...
SILVER (NCMX) 5,000 troy			
Jun 96	...	...	...
Jul 96	512.0	515.5	507.5
Aug 96	...	...	...
Sep 96	517.0	521.0	513.0
Dec 96	525.0	529.0	522.0

Vol. Fri. and **Open int.** are cumulative daily figures for all the contracts in each commodity combined. The volume Friday for heating oil was 17,488 trades. The open interest, or number of outstanding contracts, was 97,158. Estimated volume is also included for some contracts.

ASIAN FUTURES MARKETS
Trading in Asian futures markets is reported regularly in The Asian Wall Street Journal. In this example, the focus is on rubber trading in Kuala Lumpur and Singapore.

Asian Markets

Kuala Lumpur Rubber

(in Malaysian cents per kilo)

Closing prices quoted on Kuala Lumpur Commodity Exchange.

	Buyers	Sellers		Buyers	Sellers
				(Noon prices)	
RSS No 1 Aug	328.50	330.50	SMR 20 Aug	302.50	304.50
RSS No 1 Sept	328.50	330.50	SMR 20 Sept	304.50	306.50

Singapore Rubber

(in Singapore cents per kilo)

	Buyers	Sellers		Buyers	Sellers
ADS	206.50	208.50			
RSS No 2 Aug	186.50	187.50	RSS No 4 Aug	181.25	182.25
RSS No 3 Aug	186.50	187.50	RSS No 5 Aug	177.50	178.50

Financial Futures

Stocks, bonds and currencies are the commodities of the investment business.

Just as dramatic changes in the price of wheat affect farmers, bakers and ultimately the consumer, so changes in interest rates, the future value of currencies and the direction of the stock market send ripples—and sometimes waves—through the financial community.

With the creation of a market in financial futures, traders—such as pension-fund and mutual-fund investment managers—can protect themselves against the unexpected. They're the **hedgers** of the financial-futures market.

Financial Futures in Action

THE HEDGERS

Mutual fund that owns Nikkei Stock Average stocks	**Hedges by taking a sell position** to protect against losses	**If stock stays strong**, gets out of market by buying offsetting contract **If stock prices drop**, offsets losses by selling contract at profit
Mutual fund that plans future purchase of U.S. Treasurys	**Hedges by taking a buy position** to protect price	**If rates stay high**, sells offsetting contract to neutralize position **If rates drop,** and prices increase, fund's price is protected by being locked in

THE SPECULATORS

Speculators gamble on price changes	**Buy when they think prices are lowest**	**Sell when they think prices are highest**

WHAT'S DELIVERED

Like other derivatives, financial futures are based on an underlying commodity. But in the case of index and interest-rate futures, delivering those commodities—in the unusual case that a contract wasn't offset—would be difficult since they're really only numbers in a computer.

Instead, traders would take delivery of the cash value of the contract. Index futures settle at a specific currency value times the point level of the index. If the Nikkei Stock Average settles at 21460 in Tokyo trading, the price of the average-linked futures contract listed on Simex would be 10,730,000 yen at contract expiration, or the index level times 500 yen. Similarly, the price of the All Ordinaries Index contract on the Sydney Futures Exchange would total A$59,750 if the Australian stock-market gauge was at 2390, because the price equals the point level times A$25.

SPECULATION RUNS RAMPANT

As in other futures markets, **speculators** keep the markets active by constant trading. Speculators buy or sell futures contracts depending on which way they think the market is going. World politics, trading patterns and the economy are the unpredictable factors in these markets. Rumor, too, plays a major role.

Financial speculators are no more interested in taking delivery of Australian bonds than grain speculators are in 5,000 bushels of wheat. What they're interested in is making money on their gamble. So the offsetting technique works here as well. If they are betting the market will go down, speculators will try to get out of a contract at what they think is its highest point.

Equity Index

	High	Low	Last	Prev.	Vol.	Open Int.
Nikkei (Simex)						
Sep 96	21,510	21,290	21,455	21,695	15,600	—
Dec 96	—	—	21,485	21,725	20	—
All Ordinaries (SFE)						
Sep 96	2,105.0	2,090.0	2,100.0	2,148.0	12,630	—
Dec [illegible]						
Hang S[illegible]						
July						
Aug						

Bonds and Bills

	Last	Prev.	Vol.	Open Int.
3-year A$ bonds (SFE)				
Sep 96	91.67	91.66	22,989	—
Dec 96	91.58	91.57	—	—
A$ Bank Bills (SFE)				
Sep 96	92.37	92.37	2,705	—
Dec				
NZ$ B[illegible]				
Sep				

Currencies and Interest Rates

	Last	Prev.	Vol.	Open Int.
Eurodollar (Simex)				
July 96	942.20	942.30	620	—
Aug 96	939.90	—	294	—
Euroyen (TIFFE)				
Sep 96	990[illegible]	9901	1,725	473,660
Dec 96		[illegible]65	5,784	807,666

Source: Dow Jones Tele[illegible]

WHAT'S BEING TRADED

The large variety of financial futures contracts available on the exchanges is always in flux, in response to changing economic conditions and the efforts of various exchanges to attract new business. The contracts divide, roughly, into three general categories:

- **Currencies and interest rates**
- **Stock and bond indexes**
- **Bonds and bills**

Currency trading has the longest history in the U.S. financial futures market, dating back to the 1970s. Stock-index futures trading was added in 1982, and interest-rate futures were broken out as a separate category in 1988.

The international scope of financial-futures activity means that contracts on a stock index such as the Nikkei Stock Average, for example, are traded both in its domestic market and in multiple overseas markets.

CURRENCY TRADING

When foreign-exchange transactions aren't handled on the spot (see page 28), they're forward transactions. Outright forward deals, which allow commercial customers to hedge their financial and trade risks by predetermining a rate of exchange, are settled more than two business days after the deal is made.

About half of outright forwards settle in less than a week and about half in more than a week, though rarely as long as a year. The longer the forward period, the greater the credit risk.

More complicated currency swaps involve exchanging income streams in different currencies on one date and re-exchanging them at a later date (see pages 142–143).

ARBITRAGE: MANEUVERING THE MARKETS

Stock index futures and the underlying stocks don't move in lock step. When the two markets are momentarily out of sync, the index futures contract price moves either higher or lower than the stocks the index tracks. Traders can make a lot of money by simultaneously buying the one that's less expensive and selling the more expensive. The technique is known as **index arbitrage**, and the chief tool is a very sophisticated computer program that follows shifts in prices.

Often, the price difference is only a fraction of a dollar. But arbitragers trade huge numbers of contracts at the same time, so the results are significant—if the timing is right. And since many arbitragers are making the same decisions at the same time, their buying and selling can produce changes in the markets they are trying to manipulate.

UP AND OUT

The more expensive a commodity is, the more its derivative product costs. Rising stock-index prices, for example, can drive investors out of the market.

A World of Options

Options are opportunities to make decisions to buy or sell at a later date—if the market takes the right direction.

Holding an option gives you the right to buy or sell a specific investment at a set price within a preset time period. The particular item that an option deals with—stock, index, government bond, currency or futures contract—is called the **underlying investment**. If the stock or futures markets move in the direction an investor thinks they will, exercising the option can mean a healthy profit.

Options are traded on stock or commodity exchanges at a specific **strike (or exercise) price**, which is the amount you'll pay or receive if the trade takes place. The strike price is set by the exchange. The market price rises or falls depending on the performance of the underlying investment on which the option is based.

BUYING OPTIONS

Buying options is a way to capitalize on changes in the market price. People who buy **call** options are betting that the price of the underlying investment is going up. Conversely, people who buy **put** options think the price is going down.

With either type of buy option, the potential loss is limited to the **premium**, or amount, paid to buy the option. That's known in the securities industry as a limited, predetermined risk.

SELLING OPTIONS

The biggest difference between buying options and selling them is the nature of the commitment. Buyers have no obligation to do anything. They can simply let the option expire. Sellers, on the other hand, are required to go through with a trade if the party they sold the option to (by **writing a put** or **writing a call**) wants to exercise the option.

WRITING COVERED CALLS

The most basic form of option trading is **writing covered stock calls**, and it's the first type of option trading most investors do. It means selling the right to some other party to buy from you stocks that you already own for a specific price. The key is that you own them—that's what makes the call **covered**.

NAKED—BEARING IT ALL

The greatest risk in options trading is **writing naked calls**. That means selling an option that allows someone to buy something from you that you don't already own. In a typical worst-case example, you would write a naked stock call. If the price of the underlying stock hit the strike price, the option would be exercised, and you would have to buy the shares at the market price in order to sell them at the agreed-on price. Your cost—and loss—could be substantial.

THREE WAYS TO BUY OPTIONS

Investor buys ten CALL OPTIONS (1,000 shares) on Stock X

Price: $55/share

Strike price: $60

Premium: $750

1. **HOLD TO MATURITY AND TRADE AT THE STRIKE PRICE**
2. **TRADE FOR PROFIT BEFORE OPTION EXPIRES**
3. **LET THE OPTION EXPIRE**

TWO WAYS TO SELL OPTIONS

Investor owns 1,000 shares of Stock X

Price: $55/share

1. **WRITE TEN COVERED CALLS**
   Strike price: 60
   Collect premium: $750

Investor owns no shares of Stock X

2. **WRITE TEN NAKED CALLS**
   Strike price: 60
   Collect premium: $750

THE LANGUAGE OF OPTIONS

In the specialized language of options, all transactions are either puts or calls. A put is the right to sell and a call is the right to buy.

	CALL	PUT
BUY	The right to buy the underlying item at the strike price until the expiration date.	The right to sell the underlying item at the strike price until the expiration date.
SELL	Selling the right to buy the underlying item from you at the strike price until the expiration date. Known as **writing a call**.	Selling the right to sell the underlying item to you until the expiration date. Known as **writing a put**.

TRADE OR EXERCISE

Like futures contracts, options can be sold for a profit before the expiration date or neutralized with an offsetting order. Unlike most futures contracts, though, options are frequently exercised when the underlying item reaches the strike price. That's because part of the appeal of options, and stock options in particular, is that they can be converted into real investments even though the options themselves are intangible.

THE OPTIONS KEEP CHANGING

The underlying investments on which options are available keep growing. At the time of publication, five types of exchange-listed options are generally traded:

- **Individual stocks**
- **Stock indexes and bond indexes**
- **Currencies**
- **Government bills and bonds**
- **Futures contracts**

IF STOCK PRICE RISES TO 65
Trade option at strike price of 60

$5,000 from trade
– $750 premium
$4,250 PROFIT

IF STOCK PRICE RISES TO 60
Trade option at strike price of 60

Less your premium only
$750 LOSS

IF STOCK RISES TO 62
Trade option before expiration at strike price of 60

$2,000 from trade
– $750 premium
$1,250 PROFIT

IF STOCK PRICE RISES TO 60½
Trade option before expiration at strike price of 60

$500 from trade
– $750 premium
$250 LOSS

IF STOCK PRICE DROPS TO 45
There are no takers for an option with a 60 strike price

Less your premium only
$750 LOSS

IF STOCK PRICE RISES TO 57
No takers—options expire

Keep the premium
$750 PROFIT

IF STOCK PRICE RISES TO 60
Buy 10 calls to cancel obligation and prevent losing stocks

$750 premium collected
– $750 premium on offsetting calls
BREAK EVEN

IF STOCK PRICE RISES TO 57
No takers—options expire

Keep the premium
$750 PROFIT

IF STOCK PRICE RISES TO 65
Option is exercised. You must buy 1,000 shares to sell to meet call

$750 premium
– $65,000 to buy
$4,250 LOSS

Option Types and Warrants

Options and warrants are a growth industry: new ways to speculate on what the future holds crop up regularly.

Options are attractive to those who want to protect investments against major swings in market prices or to speculate on market movements. Investors who anticipate a bull market are also drawn to warrants, which entitle the holder to buy shares at a set price—which is usually higher than the current market price—when the contract expires (see page 53).

TRADING WARRANTS

Warrants usually come to market attached to a bond or preferred stock. They are generally issued to help reduce the cost of financing. For instance, a company that wants to pare its interest costs could sell bonds with a low rate of interest and attach warrants as a sweetener. If the market appears to be on the rise, investors would figure the warrants' prospective value far outweighs the small return on the bonds.

Once issued, the warrants are stripped from the bonds and are traded separately. Similar to options, they start to change hands at prices reflecting the movement of the market. But in percentage terms, the moves are usually much bigger than in the underlying market—and changes can occur with lightning speed. So warrants are riskier investments than stocks, especially for individual investors who can't build a diversified portfolio of warrants or closely track every twist and turn of the market.

OPTIONS ON STOCK INDEXES

Speculators also use index options to gamble on shifts in stock-market direction. Similar to other methods of high-risk investing, this one offers the chance of making a big killing if you get it right. Otherwise there wouldn't be any takers. But the risks of getting the price and the timing right are magnified by the short life span of index options.

On the other hand, buying put options on stock indexes is a way for investors to hedge their portfolios against sharp drops in the market. It gives them the right to sell their options at a profit if the market falls. The money realized on the sale will—hopefully—cover the losses in their portfolios resulting from the falling market.

For this technique to work, though, the options have to be on the index that most closely tracks the kind of stocks they own. And they have to own enough options to offset the total value of their portfolio. Since options cost money and expire quickly, regular use of this kind of insurance can take a big bite out of any profit the portfolio produces.

A complicating factor is that indexes don't always move in the same direction as the markets they track. When indexes are out of kilter, there are big profits to be made too—by the arbitrage traders with computer programs fine-tuned enough to take advantage of the movements.

In the U.S., the value of an index option is usually calculated by multiplying the index level by a fixed dollar value from $5 to $500.

TO MARKET, TO MARKET, TO BUY...
The hogs that end up as pork in the supermarkets also supply the futures and options markets—at 40,000 pounds per contract. The hogs get sold, the futures contracts are traded and the options on those contracts are exercised—or expire. The farmer makes money if the hogs are sold for more than it cost to raise them. Futures contract traders make money if the cash price for the hogs means they can trade their contracts at a profit. But option buyers make money only if they guess right on what price a futures contract will be on a specific date. That's what a derivative market is all about.

OPTIONS ON INTEREST RATES

Options on interest rates are actually options on bonds issued by governments. As always with bonds, a change in interest rates produces a change in price.

Bondholders can hedge their investments by using interest-rate options, just as stockholders can hedge by using index options. Interest-rate options are intended to offset any loss in value between the purchase date of the option and the date the bond matures. If the money from the maturing bond has to be reinvested at a lower rate, the profit from trading the option can make up for some of the loss—if the cost of the option doesn't eat it up.

A put option on bonds, with the right to sell at a certain price, is worth more as the strike price gets higher and the exercise date is further away. Call options, with the right to buy, are more valuable the lower the strike price. When interest rates increase—and bond prices go lower—call options increase in value as the exercise date gets further away.

OPTIONS ON CURRENCY

People with large overseas investments sometimes hedge their portfolios by buying options on the currencies of countries where their money is invested. Since the investment's value depends on the relationship between the investor's currency and the other currency, using options can equalize sudden shifts in value.

For example, if the value of the yen lost ground against the Australian dollar, Australian investments in Japanese companies would be worth less than they were when the Australian dollar was weaker. But an option to buy yen at the lower price could be sold at a profit, making up for some of the loss in investment value.

Speculators also buy currency options, sometimes making incredible profits—sometimes so incredible in fact that they trigger a government investigation. But it's generally accepted that currency speculation, such as interest-rate speculation, is not the right market for individual investors.

OPTIONS ON FUTURES CONTRACTS

Options on futures contracts, or the right to buy or sell an obligation to buy or sell, seem to be—whether or not they actually are—the furthest removed from reality and the most difficult to use. An option on a futures contract on feeder cattle, for example, is a long way from the actual cattle prices. And since the hedgers in the futures business buy contracts, not options on contracts, these vehicles belong almost exclusively to the speculators.

There is money to be made in the futures markets, so options on futures are traded regularly, though generally in smaller numbers than options in government bonds, indexes and the most active individual stocks.

Reading Options Tables

Successful stock-option trading requires lots of attention to detail—including information on what's happening in the marketplace.

The price and trading volume of stock options are closely tied to the way the underlying stocks themselves are doing. The most actively traded options have **strike prices** that are usually quite close to actual stock prices except when there's been a dramatic gain or drop in price. That's because the exchanges establish the strike prices with the benefit of lots of analysis, and those options where the price spread is large (called DOOM or **deep out of the money**) don't trade often enough to get reported in the tables.

In fact, the relationship between actual price and strike price is so important to the way options trade that there is a special vocabulary to describe it. **In the money** options are those where the actual price is above the strike price for calls and below it for puts. **At the money** options mean the two prices are the same. **Out of the money** options have a price spread large enough to make them a real gamble. You can make or lose a lot, depending on what you bet.

U.S. LISTED OPTIONS

Option	Strike	Exp.	Call Vol.	Call Last	Put Vol.	Put Last
A S A	45	Jul	562	2 1/16	...	...
Abbt L	45	Aug	475	1	10	2¾
Adaptc	60	Jun	65	2 3/16	501	2
A M D	20	Jun	421	⅛	12	2⅜
AdvTis	17½	Jun	131	1 13/16	210	⅝
Aetna	60	Jun	425	12¾	...	...
AirPd	55	Jun	530	4½	...	...
59½	55	Dec	530	6⅝	...	...
Albtsn	30	Jun	560	10⅛	...	...
39⅞	35	Dec	1120	6	...	...
AlnEnt	5	Jul	210	⅞	...	...
5⅞	7½	Sep	375	7/16	...	...
Alteon	15	Jul	226	2⅛	...	...
Altera	45	Jun	85	4⅜	292	⅞
48⅜	50	Jun	578	1¼	6	2 15/16
AmerOn	50	Jun	592	7¼	341	⅞
56½	55	Jun	746	3⅞	1341	2½
56½	55	Jul	190	6	212	4⅛
56½	60	Jun	536	1⅞	75	5¼
56½	60	Jul	363	4	114	7
56½	70	Jul	228	2 1/16	...	...
56½	85	Jul	2080	¾	...	...
APwrCv	7½	Sep	300	5⅝	...	...
12⅞	12½	Jun	334	¾	96	½
Amgen	55	Jul	...	...	208	1
Anheusr	60	Jun	1265	12⅞	...	...
Anheus o	70	Dec	1265	5⅜	...	...
AppleC	25	Jun	179	2¼	279	⅞
26⅛	27½	Jun	368	1 1/16	...	...
26⅛	30	Jun	1412	⅝	...	...
26⅛	30	Jul	837	1⅛	50	4⅜
[illegible]	17½	Jul	204	[illegible]	90	1¾

Option	Strike	Exp.	Call Vol.	Call Last	Put Vol.	Put Last
48⅝	50	Jun	1022	¾	208	2 1/16
48⅝	50	Jul	490	1 15/16	30	3¼
48⅝	50	Oct	232	3¾	10	4
48⅝	50	Jan	591	5⅝	20	5
48⅝	55	Jun	5	1/16	340	6½
CmpuSrv	25	Oct	245	3¼	...	...
CmpAsc	75	Jun	267	1¾	100	3⅜
Cnseco	35	Jun	275	1¾	...	...
36¼	35	Aug	264	2½	5	1⅛
ConFrt	25	Jul	265	1¼	...	...
23¾	30	Jul	625	¼	...	...
CtrlDt	25	Oct	250	3¾	...	...
24¾	30	Oct	1250	1⅞	...	...
CorctCp	65	Jun	1010	11	5	1⅛
74	70	Jun	9	7	263	2½
74	75	Jul	229	6½	...	...
CypSem	15	Jun	351	¼	80	1¼
CyprMn	30	Oct	835	7/16	...	...
Cytogn	7½	Jun	278	1 11/16	...	...
9	7½	Nov	217	2⅝	40	1⅛
9	10	Jun	495	⅝	...	...
9	10	Jul	407	1	...	...
9	10	Aug	1098	1 3/16	6	1⅞
9	10	Nov	212	1¾	20	2⅛
D S C	35	Jul	1081	13/16	...	...
Deere	30	Jun	950	11⅛	...	...
41⅝	40	Dec	1600	4⅜	...	...
DellCpt	55	Jun	185	2½	339	2⅛
55⅜	55	Jul	51	3¾	206	3⅝
DeltaAr	85	Jul	81	2⅜	600	3⅝
Dig Eq	47½	Jul	...	...	243	[illegible]
52⅛	50	Jun	[illegible]	[illegible]	[illegible]	[illegible]

The **name** of the stock being optioned is often abbreviated and is listed in alphabetical order. Some big names, such as Apple Computer and IBM, are easily recognized. Others, such as DSC, need deciphering. The abbreviations are often, but not always, the same ones that are used in the stock tables.

Information about the most actively traded options and LEAPS, or long-term options, is given separately, at the beginning and the end of the regular listed options columns.

The **number** in the first column—often the same number several times for each option—is the current price of the underlying stock. The relationship between the current price and the strike price is one factor affecting how actively the option is traded. In this example, for instance, America Online sold for 56½ a share at the end of the previous trading day, and the most actively traded option had a strike price of 85.

OPTIONS PRICES

Option prices are quoted in whole numbers and fractions that represent a dollar amount. To convert a whole number and a fraction to an option price, multiply both the whole number and the fraction by 100 and add the results.

for example

2⅝ = (2x100) + (⅝x100)
= (200) + (.625x100)
= 200 + 62.50
2⅝ = $262.50

This chart gives the decimal equivalent of the fractions:

Fraction		Decimal
1/16	=	0.0625
1/8	=	0.125
3/16	=	0.1875
1/4	=	0.25
5/16	=	0.3125
3/8	=	0.375
7/16	=	0.4375
1/2	=	0.50
9/16	=	0.5625
5/8	=	0.625
11/16	=	0.6875
3/4	=	0.75
13/16	=	0.8125
7/8	=	0.875
15/16	=	0.9375

The table includes the **expiration date** and **strike price** of each option on each stock, beginning with the closest month and lowest price.

The date is given as a month, and the option expires on the third Friday of that month. The strike price is the dollar amount a trade would cost if the option were exercised. For example, an IBM June 110 means that any time up to the third Friday in June, an option holder could buy 100 shares of IBM stock for $110 a share.

Often the same month appears several times with different strike prices, with the groupings by price rather than date.

For example, if IBM has options at 100, 105, 110, 115 and 120, all the 110s are together, and so on.

QUOTATIONS

Option	Strike	Exp.	Call Vol.	Call Last	Put Vol.	Put Last
9 7/16	7½	Jun	286	1 15/16	...	...
9 7/16	7½	Jul	1152	2¼	...	...
9 7/16	10	Jun	1083	7/16	...	...
9 7/16	10	Jul	365	11/16	...	...
9 7/16	12½	Sep	365	½	...	...
I B M	100	Jun	189	8¼	282	⅜
106¾	100	Jul	7	9½	507	1⅝
106¾	105	Jun	571	3⅝	726	1 9/16
106¾	105	Oct	25	9⅞	641	5⅝
106¾	105	Jan	4	12⅛	334	7¼
106¾	110	Jun	1841	1 5/16	513	4¼
106¾	110	Jul	508	3½	364	5⅝
106¾	110	Oct	159	7	298	8
106¾	115	Jun	360	[illegible]/16	33	7⅞
106¾	115	Jul	236	1 15/16	20	8⅞
106¾	120	Jun	241	⅛	5	13
IGame	17½	Jun	301	3/16	...	...
Intvce	25	Jun	66	1	370	1⅞
Intuit	40	Jul	250	11¼	...	...
52	55	Jun	320	1¼	...	...
Iomega	25	Aug	256	21⅞	...	...
44⅛	30	Jun	221	14⅞	345	⅝
44⅛	35	Jun	640	10⅜	422	1½
44⅛	37½	Jun	103	9⅛	255	2½
44⅛	40	Jun	895	7⅝	1249	3⅛
44⅛	40	Jul	455	10[illegible]	204	5⅜

Option	Strike	Exp.	Call Vol.	Call Last	Put Vol.	Put Last
Oracle	35	Jun	235	¾	23	2⅝
ParkPar	25	Jul	250	1	...	...
PepsiCo	32½	Jun	268	1⅝	25	⅝
33¼	32½	Jul	64	2	1244	1⅛
33¼	35	Jun	579	5/16	...	...
33¼	35	Jul	433	13/16	40	2½
Pfizer	70	Jun	311	2¼	3	1 9/16
PharUpj	40	Jun	369	1⅝	260	⅜
Ph Mor	95	Jun	92	5½	665	¾
99⅜	100	Jun	184	2	636	2¾
99⅜	105	Jun	220	½	40	6⅝
99⅜	110	Jun	321	⅛	40	11⅜
PhyCor	50	Jun	...	...	1000	⅞
Placer	30	Jul	3074	1 1/16	...	...
29⅝	30	Sep	870	1¾	25	2 1/16
Potash	70	Jun	253	11/16	11	4⅛
Prestek	150	Jun	11	20	285	7⅜
QuakrO	35	Jul	328	1	...	...
Qualcm	50	Jun	1488	5¼	283	1
54 7/16	50	Jul	225	7	168	2½
54 7/16	55	Jun	356	2¼	47	3¼
54 7/16	55	Jul	357	4¼	7	4¾
Reebok	30	Jul	230	2⅝	8	1¼
RepWsfe	30	Jul	211	21	...	...
52	40	Jul	251	12	15	7/16
52	50	Jun	678	3⅜	31	1⅞

Call options—or options to buy—are reported separately from **put options**—or options to sell. Sometimes calls and puts are traded on the same option, and sometimes only one or the other is being traded. When that happens, dashes appear in the nontrading column, as they do in this Intuit example. When volume and price are similar for both calls and puts, they are often offsetting trades.

Volume reports the number of trades during the previous trading day. The number is unofficial, but gives a sense of the activity in each option. Generally, trading increases as the expiration date gets closer if the strike price is in the money. For example, there's much more action in IBM's June 110 option than in the July or October option at the same price.

Last is the closing price for the option on the previous trading day. In this case, the Pepsi June 35 call closed at 5/16, or $31.25, for an option on 100 shares for $3,500. Generally the higher the price, the greater the profit the trader expects to make—like the people buying IBM's June 120 put option for $1,300 or Intuit's July 40 call for $1,125.

Using Options

Options can produce a lot of income quickly, if the price moves the right way and the options are exercised or traded before they expire.

Options are appealing to many traders because they usually don't cost very much to buy—though there are substantial commissions and other charges. By paying only a fraction of the cost of actually buying stocks, government bonds or whatever the underlying investment is, a trader has **leveraged** the purchase, or used a little money with the potential to make a lot within a relatively short time—usually five to seven months or less. If the option is traded or exercised profitably, the yield can be hundreds or even thousands times the original investment amount.

THE COST OF AN OPTION

The **premium**, or nonrefundable price, of an option depends on several factors, including rumor. Officially, the factors are the type of investment the option is on, the investment's underlying price, how volatile the price has been over the last year, the current interest rate and the time remaining until expiration.

The premium fluctuates so you can get back more or less than you paid to buy the option when you decide to sell.

Sellers take their money up front when they write options. It's called a **price premium**, and it's also nonrefundable. In fact, collecting the premium is often the primary reason for writing options.

OPTIONS AS INSURANCE

In addition to the highs that speculating can provide, stock options have practical uses for traders who follow the markets closely and have specific goals, such as providing some insurance for stock-market investments.

One method of reducing risk with options is to buy a **married put**. This means buying a stock and a put (sell option) on the same stock at the same time. If the price of the stock falters or goes down, the put option goes up in value, and part of the loss on the stock can be

The Following Rules of Thumb

The greater the difference between the strike price and the actual current price of the item, the cheaper the premium, because there is less chance the option will be exercised.

When America Online is trading in May at 56½, a **July 55** option costs $600 but a **July 85** is only $75.

Option	Strike	Exp.	Call Vol.	Call Last	Put Vol.	Put Last
AmerOn	50	Jun	592	7¼	341	⅞
56½	55	Jun	746	3⅞	1341	2½
56½	55	Jul	190	6	212	4⅛
56½	60	Jun	536	1⅞	75	5¼
56½	60	Jul	363	4	114	7
56½	70	Jul	228	2 1/16	...	...
56½	85	Jul	2080	¾	...	...
APwrCv	7½	Sep	300	5⅜		
12⅞	12½	Jun	334			
Amgen	55	Jul	...			
Anheusr	60	Jun	1265			
Anheus o	70	Dec	1265			
AppleC	25	Jun	179			
26⅛	27½	Jun	368			
26⅛	30	Jun	1412			
26⅛	30	Jul	837			
[illegible]	17½	Jul				

The closer the expiration date of an out of the money option (where the market price is higher than the strike price), the lower the price.

When IBM is trading at 106¾ in May, an **October 105** option is $987.50 but a **January 105** option is $1,212.50.

Option	Strike	Exp.	Call Vol.	Call Last	Put Vol.	Put Last
I B M	100	Jun	189	8¼	282	⅜
106¾	100	Jul	7	9½	507	1⅝
106¾	105	Jun	571	3⅝	726	1 9/16
106¾	105	Oct	25	9⅞	641	5⅝
106¾	105	Jan	4	12⅛	334	7¼
106¾	110	Jun	1841	1 5/16	513	4¼
106¾	110	Jul	508	[illegible]	[illegible]	[illegible]
[illegible]	110	Oct	[illegible]			

TRIPLE WITCHING
Once every quarter—on the third Friday of March, June, September and December—several options contracts expire at the same time in the U.S. The phenomenon, which can throw the markets into turmoil as traders scramble to offset buy and sell orders, is known as triple witching day.

offset by selling the put. A similar technique, called a **strangle**, involves writing a call (buy option) with a strike price above the current market price and a put (sell option) with a strike price below it. That means that you've collected your premium and neutralized your position at the same time.

Straddle, or **spread**, trading means buying and writing options on the same stock at different strike prices. Then if you are forced to buy or sell because someone exercises the option you've sold them, you can cover the deal by exercising your own option to buy or sell. A **covered straddle** involves buying and selling equal numbers of calls and puts at the same time. Whatever happens, you've collected your premium and have stocks to boot. The premiums can either increase the return you get on your shares or reduce the cost of buying additional shares if the price drops.

LEAPS
Long-term stock options, actually **Long-term Equity Anticipation Securities**, lasting up to three years were introduced to the U.S. options marketplace in 1990. Because they last longer than other options, they are considered less risky. That's true in part because the price of the stock or stock index has much longer to perform as expected. It's also true that the money saved in buying an option instead of the stock itself can be invested elsewhere. On the other hand, options don't pay dividends.

The drawback of LEAPS, as with all options, is that the stock must still perform as expected, and the decision to trade, exercise, or let the option expire still has to be made within the option's life span.

INCENTIVE STOCK OPTIONS
Corporate executives are sometimes given options to buy company stock at below-market price as an incentive to build the business or as a reward for doing it. Then they can sell at a profit.

Usually Apply to Options

The more time there is until expiration, the larger the premium, because the chance of reaching the strike price is greater and the carrying costs are more.

In early May when the price of Cytogn stock is 9, one **June 7½** option on Cytogn stock costs $168.75 but a **November 7½** is $262.50.

Option	Strike	Exp.	Call Vol.	Call Last	Put Vol.	Put Last
Cytogn	7½	Jun	278	1 11/16	...	...
9	7½	Nov	217	2⅝	40	1⅛
9	10	Jun	495	⅝		
9	10	Jul	407	1		
9	10	Aug	1098	1 3/16		
9	10	Nov	212	1¾		
D S C	35	Jul	1081	13/16		
Deere	30	Jun	950	11⅛		
41⅝	40	Dec	1600	4⅜		
DellCpt	55	Jun	185	2½	3	
55⅜	55	Jul	51	3¾	2	
DeltaAr	85	Jul	81	2⅜	6	
Dig Eq	47½	Jul	...	...	2	
52⅛	50	Jun	685	3⅜	7	
52⅛	50	Jul	220	4⅝		
	55	Jun	341	1 3/16		

When call prices are high, puts are low—or the reverse.

The **July 115** option on IBM has a call price of $193.75 and a put price of $887.50.

Option	Strike	Exp.	Call Vol.	Call Last	Put Vol.	Put Last
I B M	100	Jun	189	8¼	282	⅜
106¾	100	Jul	7	9½	507	1⅝
106¾	105	Jun	571	3⅝	726	1 9/16
106¾	105	Oct	25	9⅞	641	5⅝
106¾	105	Jan	4	12⅛	334	7¼
106¾	110	Jun	1841	1 5/16	513	4¼
106¾	110	Jul	508	3½	364	5⅝
106¾	110	Oct	159	7	298	8
106¾	115	Jun	360	7/16	33	7⅞
106¾	115	Jul	236	1 15/16	20	8⅞
106¾	120	Jun	241	⅛	5	13
IGame						

Tracking Options

The most active options trading is reported regularly in several different tables, each keyed to the underlying product.

As the variety of options available in the marketplace has increased, so has the information about current trades reported in The Asian Wall Street Journal. The options tables provide information on the strike price, the expiration date and the current price of the option as well as the volume of trading and the open interest in each option.

But there are some differences among options. The sales unit depends on the item being optioned—100 shares of stock, 37,500 pounds of coffee, 5,000 troy ounces of silver. So do the expiration dates, which in some cases are in a regular pattern and in other cases are random.

INDEX-OPTION TRADING

Like stock options, index options are closely tied to the underlying item—in this case various stock indexes.

Index options have a short time-frame and a broad range of prices. That's because they're so volatile. Trying to predict with any precision where an index will be is even more difficult than with most other options. The farther in the future, the more difficult it becomes.

INDEX OPTIONS

Chicago

Strike		Vol.	Close	Net Chg.	Open Int.
NASDAQ-100(NDX)					
Jun	550p	20	15/16	– 1 15/16	254
Jun	570p	1	1 13/16	– 3/16	43
May	595p	1	1	– 1¼	571
May	600p	1,520	1¼	– ¼	7,908
Jun	600p	2	5	– ¼	136
Jun	600p	12	5	...	278
Jul	600p	5	7⅜	– ⅜	10
May	605p	7	1⅜	– ¼	5,318
May	610p	10	1¾	– ⅜	494
Jun	610p	5			

Strike		Vol.	Close	Net Chg.	Open Int.
Jun	650p	83	16	+ ½	22
May	655c	6	18	+ 2¼	2,313
May	655p	24	10½	– 1	35
Jun	655p	3	15½	– 2¼	5
May	660c	36	15¼	– ½	415
May	660p	32	12	+ ½	90
Jun	660c	20	27¾	+ 2¼	85
Jun	660p	1	21	+ 1	2
Jun	660p	4	21	– ¾	100
May	665c	15	13	+ 1¼	1,425
May	665p	6	12⅝	– 1⅞	55
Jun	665c	1	24	+ 10	12
May	670c	54	12¼	+ 2	11,343
May	670p	6	16⅝	– 2	21
		3	17½	– 2⅛	51
		23	...		2

Strike
Jun
Jun
May
Jun
Jul
Jul
May
Jun
May
Jun
Jun
Jul
May
Ju

The **Index** on which the options are offered is listed. Traders can buy options on a wide variety of indexes, based in countries around the world. There are some indexes that track specific industries or stock markets in other countries.

The **Exchange** on which the index options are traded is shown first. In this case, Chicago trading in the NASDAQ-100 is shown.

Volume reports the number of trades during the previous trading day. In index option trading, the heaviest volume is usually in options closest to expiration.

The **Strike** column shows the expiration date, strike price and whether the option is a put (p) or a call (c). In this example of NASDAQ-100 index option trading, puts predominate at the lower end of the price scale, here at 550 to 600, suggesting that those traders think the market is headed down. But as the strike price increases to 660 and 665, calls and puts are fairly evenly divided, suggesting some traders think the market is going up.

Close is the closing price of the option at the end of the previous day's trading. As with stock options, prices are given in whole numbers and in fractions. For example, the May 660 call is trading at 15¼, or $1,525. (To get the actual price of exercising the option you multiply the strike price by 100, since each option is for 100 shares.)

Net Change is the difference between the price reported here and the closing price two trading days ago. When the two are alike, all the outstanding options have been neutralized by opposing trades.

CHARTING FUTURES OPTIONS

Futures-options trading includes agricultural products, other raw materials and financial commodities such as international currencies and interest rates.

The **futures contract** on which the option is based, the exchange on which it is traded, the number of units in the contract and the price units by which the price of the commodity is figured are shown. In this example, the futures contract is on coffee traded on the Coffee, Sugar and Cocoa Exchange. Each contract is for 37,500 pounds and the price is quoted in cents per pound, so that 115 means $1.15 a pound.

Industry group is a grouping of similar commodities traded on various exchanges. They include options on futures contracts in agricultural products, oil, livestock, currency, interest rates, and stock and bond indexes.

Puts gives the dates of the put options available in each commodity. Prices for puts and calls move in the opposite direction, because they reflect the price movement of the underlying commodity. When calls are selling for more, puts are selling for less, as they are for gold here.

FUTURES OPTIONS

Agricultural

Thursday, April 25, 1996

COFFEE (CSCE)
37,500 lbs.; cents per lb.

Strike Price	Calls-Settle Jun	Jly	Sep	Puts-Settle Jun	Jly	Sep
115	11.10	14.33	16.60	.65	3.20	8.00
120	7.00	10.97	14.60	1.55	5.00	10.40
125	4.00	7.95	12.40	3.55	7.50	13.25
130	2.20	6.10	10.70	6.75	10.65	16.40
135	1.15	4.70	9.30	10.70	14.25	20.00
140	.50	3.50	8.10	15.05	18.05	23.80

Est vol 6,215 Wd 1,766 calls 992 puts
Op int Wed 24,759 calls 13,928 puts

SUGAR-WORLD (CSCE)
12,000 lbs.; cents per lb.

Strike Price	Calls-Settle Jun	Jly	Oct	Puts-Settle Jun	Jly	Oct
1000	.62	.75	.95	.06	.18	.34
1050	.24	.43	.68	.20	.38	.57
1100	.08	.23	.45	.52	.67	.84
1150	.02	.12	.31	.96	1.06	1.20
1200	.01	.06	.20	1.45	1.50	1.59
1250	.01	.03	.15	1.95	1.97	2.04

Est vol 7,111 Wd 1,705 calls 1,557 puts
Op int Wed 39,901 calls 29,563 puts

Oil

Thursday, April 25, 1996

CRUDE OIL (NYM)
1,000 bbls.; $ per bbl.

Strike Price	Calls-Settle Jun	Jly	Aug	Puts-Settle Jun	Jly	Aug
2100	1.46	.85	.54	.26	1.15	1.75
2150	1.10	.65	.41	.40	....	
2200	.81	.52	.30	.61		
2250	.58	.40	.19			
2300						

Gold/Silver

Thursday, April 25, 1996

GOLD (CMX)
100 troy ounces; $ per troy ounce

Strike Price	Calls-Settle Jun	July	Aug	Puts-Settle Jun	July	Aug
380	15.30	18.10	18.30	.10	.50	.90
390	6.00	9.40	10.20	.70	1.70	2.60
400	1.10	3.80	5.00	5.80	6.30	7.40
410	.30	1.40	2.50	15.00	13.60	14.80
420	.10	.60	1.30	24.70	22.80	23.60
430	.10	.40	.80	34.70	32.60	33.10

Est vol 22,000 Wd 5,235 calls 1,201 puts
Op int Wed 234,274 calls 86,935 puts

SILVER (CMX)
5,000 troy ounces; cts per troy ounce

Strike Price	Calls-Settle Jun	Jly	Sep	Puts-Settle Jun	Jly	Sep
500	41.5	43.8	53.0	.4	2.5	7.0
525	19.0	25.2	35.8	2.8	8.8	14.7
550	5.0	12.7	23.0	13.5	21.0	26.5
575	1.6	6.6	14.5	34.5	40.1	
600	.7	4.0	9.5			
625	.2	2.3				

Est vol 4,900 Wd 2...
Op int Wed 43,4...

T-BONDS
$100,000
Strike

Strike
Price
420
430
Est vol 2...
Op int We...
SILVER
5,000 tr...
Strike
Price
500
525
550
575
600
625
Est vol 4,...
Op int We...

Strike price is the price at which the option owner may buy or sell the corresponding futures contract by exercising the option. Each commodity has options covering a range of prices that increase in a regular sequence (120/125/130).

Calls gives the dates of the call options currently available on this commodity. In this example, options on coffee futures contracts are available for June, July and September.

Settle shows that the exchange has adjusted the price to reflect market values at the end of trading. Because futures contracts and the options on those contracts may not trade at the same pace, the exchange will adjust an option's price to coincide with its futures price at the end of the day.

So the settle price for the September 130 coffee option is 10.70, meaning 10.7 cents per pound, or $4,012.50.

Estimated volume reports the number of trades on the previous trading day, separated into puts and calls.

Open interest shows the number of outstanding options contracts, broken out by puts and calls, that have not been offset by an opposite transaction.

Derivatives Over the Counter

Organizations turn to the private market for customized hedging tools.

OTC derivatives, which first appeared in the 1980s, are now widely used by corporations, financial institutions and public agencies as tools to manage risk. The market developed as these organizations found that straightforward contracts traded on futures and options exchanges weren't meeting their more complex hedging needs. They wanted to better hedge their long-term commitments to buy, sell or lend, particularly when foreign-exchange risks were involved.

In this market, institutional investors or borrowers work directly with dealer banks to handle their transactions, typically over the telephone. The dealer bank is generally known as the **counterparty**.

The deals usually don't require collateral to underpin a position, and there is no middleman to guarantee that the parties will make good on their commitments. However, dealer banks are working on developing more uniform standards to overcome problems that have cropped up and made some organizations more hesitant to trade highly sophisticated derivatives.

TYPES OF DERIVATIVES

OTC derivatives, including forwards, swaps and options, are often referred to as either **plain vanilla** or **exotic**. The plain vanilla contracts involve largely standardized products and practices, while the exotic variety introduce numerous elements and are highly tailored. For instance, a deal can be structured so that certain options are activated only under a highly refined set of market circumstances.

DOING A SWAP

A swap is a customized financial tool an investor or borrower uses to exchange one cash flow for another. An interest-rate swap exchanges a fixed interest rate for a floating interest rate.

In a typical currency swap, one party agrees to pay the equivalent of a stream of interest payments and final principal denominated in one currency in exchange for another stream of payments in a different currency at a preset exchange rate.

How a Currency Swap Works

BOND ISSUE

The bond issue raises money in Japanese yen.

Companies often go to a foreign bond market in order to attract investors and get favorable interest rates. Because the issue may be denominated in a currency in which the company doesn't generate revenue, the company will set up a currency swap.

FOREX DEAL

The forex deal converts the yen to Australian dollars so the company can make its investments.

CURRENCY SWAP

The currency swap converts some of the company's earnings in U.S. dollars to yen to pay the interest on the bond.

RISK POTENTIAL

Because of their complexity and the extent to which they may be leveraged, OTC derivatives can pose potentially large risks to the investors who use them.

MARKET BUSINESS
Foreign-exchange contracts and interest-rate contracts account for the bulk of OTC derivatives activity, trailed by equity and commodity contracts. A clear sign of the global nature of the OTC market is that more than half of all OTC derivatives deals are struck by parties from different nations.

Companies doing business in more than one country need to protect against sudden or dramatic changes in the relative value of currencies, so they hedge commitments to invest, sell or borrow with agreements that have predetermined **forex**, or foreign-exchange, **rates**.

For example, a Sydney-based mining company that wants to invest in an Australian gold mine decides to launch a three-year yen-denominated dual-currency issue in Japan, known as a Samurai bond (see page 83). By raising yen in Japan, the company reduces its borrowing costs because Japanese interest rates are lower than Australian rates.

THE INVESTOR'S ROLE
For the investors, the issue is attractive because they will receive higher returns than with Japanese corporate bonds. The returns are higher because one of the currencies involved, the Australian dollar, is linked to higher interest rates than are available in Japan. But the risks are higher, too.

To get the higher interest rate, the investors have to take a greater risk on some part of the dual-currency bond. In this case, they are betting that the yen will at least be stable or perhaps will fall against other currencies over the next few years. The investor gets an instant reward for taking that currency risk, as the annual coupon on a dual-currency bond may be 5% for three years, compared with 0.7% for a three-year deposit in a Japanese bank.

The first thing the mining company wants to do is reduce the risks involved in its exposure to the currency markets. Expecting to have yen from its bond issue on a specific date, the company can plan to sell yen for Australian dollars in the spot market after the bond issuance. Or it can enter a forward contract ahead of the issuance to buy Australian dollars at a certain rate at the time it expects to get the yen.

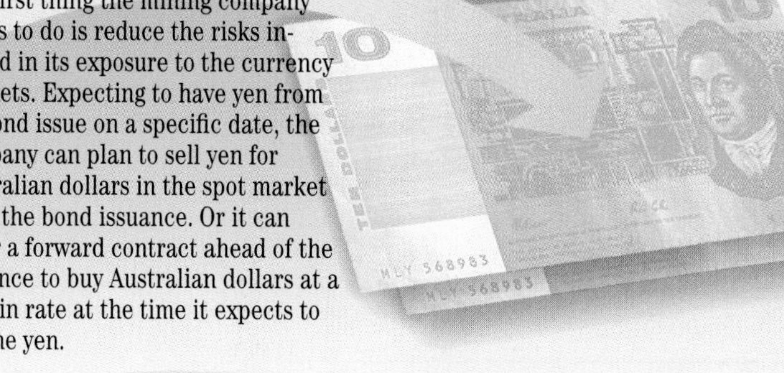

But the company will also pursue a separate agreement for a currency swap. It does this because it needs to make the interest payments on the bond in yen every six months. However, its revenue from the sales of gold produced in its mine is in U.S. dollars. So it sets up the deal, or currency swap, to exchange a portion of that dollar-denominated revenue stream for a stream in yen at a predetermined exchange rate. Then it uses the yen to make the required coupon payments.

Since the bond, or debt, must eventually be repaid in Australian dollars, the company also needs to ensure that it has sufficient capital set aside in that currency to cover the amount owed.

Risk of illiquidity
An investor could face difficulty finding a buyer for a highly tailored product.

Credit risk
The counterparty may prove unable or unwilling to make good on its obligations.

Systemic risk
A collapse at one firm or bank could trigger a chain reaction throughout the global financial network.

A

B

E

F

G

H

I

J

K

L

M

N

O

P

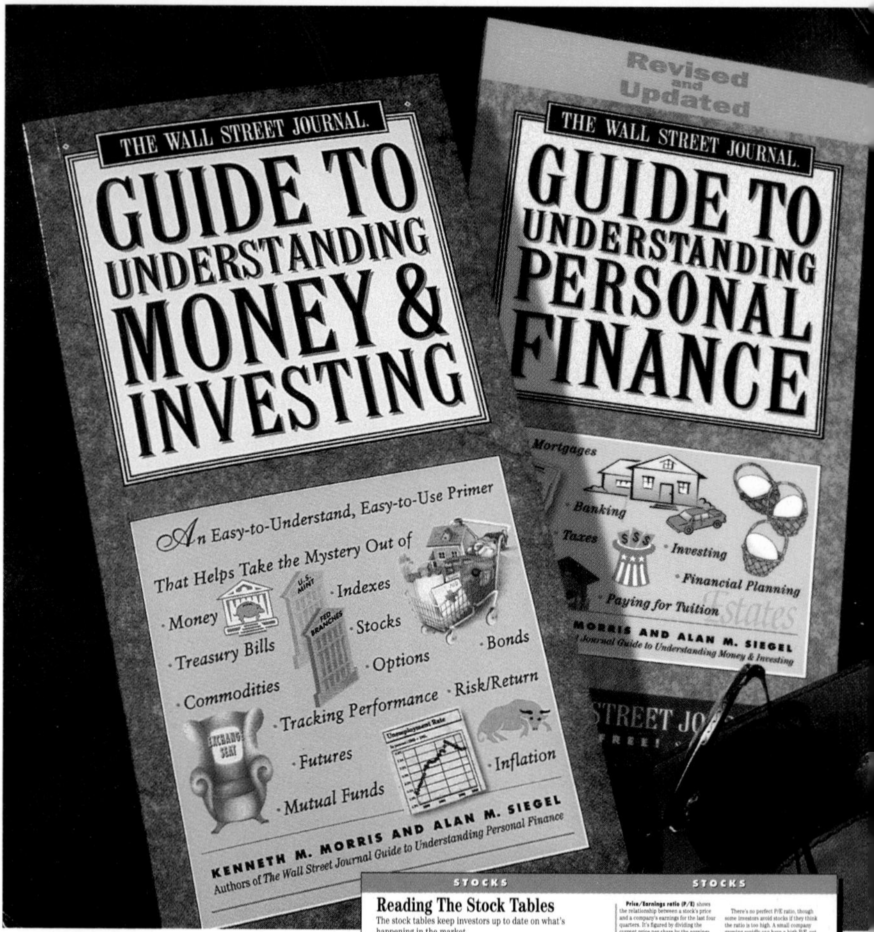

THE WALL STREET JOURNAL.

GUIDE TO UNDERSTANDING MONEY & INVESTING

An Easy-to-Understand, Easy-to-Use Primer That Helps Take the Mystery Out of

Money · Indexes · Stocks · Bonds · Treasury Bills · Options · Commodities · Tracking Performance · Risk/Return · Futures · Inflation · Mutual Funds

KENNETH M. MORRIS AND ALAN M. SIEGEL

Authors of The Wall Street Journal Guide to Understanding Personal Finance

Revised and Updated

THE WALL STREET JOURNAL.

GUIDE TO UNDERSTANDING PERSONAL FINANCE

Mortgages · Banking · Taxes · Investing · Financial Planning · Paying for Tuition · Estates

MORRIS AND ALAN M. SIEGEL

Journal Guide to Understanding Money & Investing

Written by authors with 25 years of experience in the financial and communications fields, these visually appealing, user-friendly guides painlessly initiate you into the mysteries of money and investing. They point out the things you need to know to make smart financial decisions—and to avoid the pitfalls.

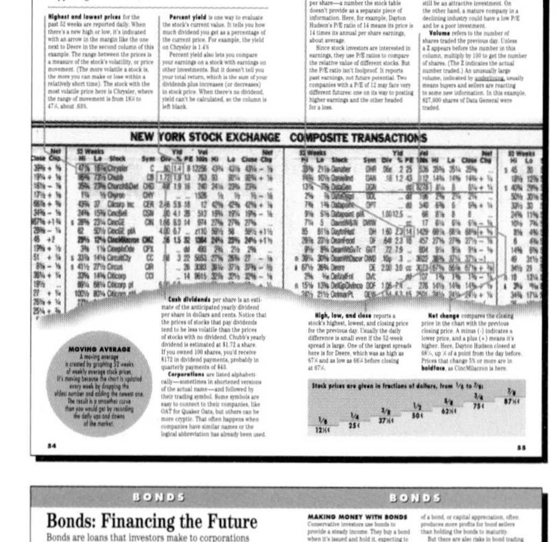

STOCKS

Reading The Stock Tables

The stock tables keep investors up to date on what's happening in the market.

NEW YORK STOCK EXCHANGE COMPOSITE TRANSACTIONS

54 55

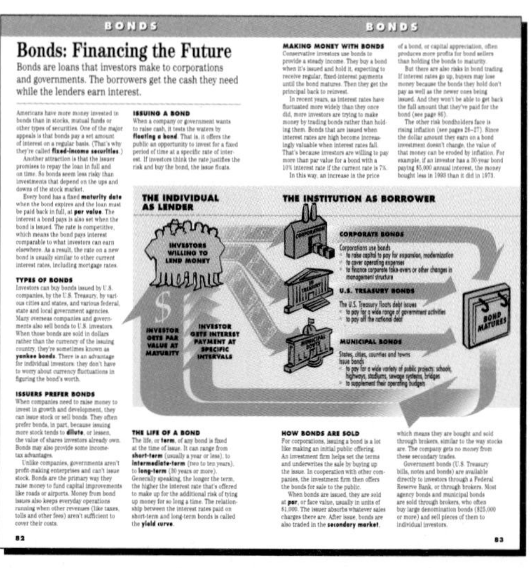

BONDS

Bonds: Financing the Future

Bonds are loans that investors make to corporations and governments. The borrowers get the cash they need while the lenders earn interest.

82 83